Introduction to Hospitality Management

KATHLEEN M. IVERSON

TRITON COLLEGE

River Grove, Illinois

 VAN NOSTRAND REINHOLD
New York

Library of Congress Catalog Card Number 88-20870
ISBN 0-442-23900-9

Printed in the United States of America

Designed by Beth Tondreau Design

Van Nostrand Reinhold
115 Fifth Avenue
New York, New York 10003

Van Nostrand Reinhold International Company Limited
11 New Fetter Lane
London EC4P 4EE, England

Van Nostrand Reinhold
480 La Trobe Street
Melbourne, Victoria 3000, Australia

Nelson Canada
1120 Birchmount Road
Scarborough, Ontario M1K 5G4, Canada

16 15 14 13 12 11 10 9 8 7 6 5 4 3 2

Library of Congress Cataloging in Publication Data

Iverson, Kathleen M., 1955–
    Introduction to hospitality management / Kathleen M. Iverson.
        p.   cm.
    Bibliography: p.
    Includes index.
    ISBN 0-442-23900-9 (pbk.)
    1. Hotel management.   2. Motel management.   3. Food service
management.   4. Tourist trade—Management.   I. Title.   II. Title:
Hospitality management.
TX911.3.M27I95 1989
647'.94'068—dc19   88-20870

To Bruce for his constant support and Eric for his cooperation, and to my students, who made this book possible.

CONTENTS

Preface   ix

PART 1   AN OVERVIEW OF THE HOSPITALITY INDUSTRY   1

1   HOSPITALITY PAST AND PRESENT   3

Origins of the Hospitality Industry   3
The Contributions of Past Leaders   4
The Current Leaders and Their Achievements   12

2   CHOOSING A CAREER PATH   18

Career Directions in the Hospitality Industry   19
Setting Career Goals   22
Choosing a Company   23
Success on the Job   28

3   THE FOODSERVICE INDUSTRY   32

Industry Outlook   32
Commercial Restaurants   36
Catering   40
Retail Foodservice   41
Institutional Foodservice   41

4   THE ENTREPRENEURIAL SPIRIT   47

Starting with an Idea   48
Planning the Restaurant   48
Formula for Success   56

5   FOOD AND BEVERAGE OPERATIONS   60

The Foodservice Staff   60
Cost Control   64
Planning the Menu   70

6   THE LODGING INDUSTRY   79

Classification of Hotels and Motels   81
New Lodging Concepts   86
Ownership of Hotel Properties   90
The Opening of a Hotel   91

7 LODGING OPERATIONS   94

Key Departments and Their Functions   95
Management Training Programs   108

8 TRAVEL AND TOURISM   111

The Hospitality Industry and Travel   111
The Economic Impact of Tourism   112
Travel Segments   114
Marketing Tourism   125

PART 2   SERVICE: THE CORNERSTONE OF THE HOSPITALITY INDUSTRY   129

9 GUEST SERVICE   131

Service versus Hospitality   132
Impact of Poor Service   133
Managing Service   136

10 COMMUNICATION SKILLS   143

Communicating Verbally and Nonverbally   143
Dealing with Guests   149

PART 3   MANAGEMENT SKILLS THAT MOTIVATE   155

11 SUPERVISION   157

Motivating Employees   157
Leadership Style   161
Monitoring Employees' Performance   163
The Manager As Coach   170

12 SELECTING THE RIGHT EMPLOYEE   175

Setting Job Standards   176
Legal Considerations   176
Selecting Service-oriented Employees   181
Recruiting Applicants   182
Prescreening Applicants   183
The Interview Format   184

13 TRAINING AND DEVELOPMENT   192

New Employee Orientation   193
Skills Training   197
Teaching Customer Service   208
Corporate Training Programs   208

14   TRENDS IN THE HOSPITALITY INDUSTRY   213

      Changing Consumer Needs   213
      Food   214
      Legal Issues   216
      Technological Advances   218
      "Hi Tech" versus Hospitality   219

Glossary   222
Index   231

STUDY GUIDE   1

PREFACE

Looking for a promising future? Most of us are. One important aspect of preparing for your future is choosing the right career. Whether you want fame, fortune, or just a respectable position, it is important that your career choice be something that interests you and, yes, even entertains you. The hospitality industry is one of the few fields that offers all of these. Cesar Ritz achieved fame; J. W. Marriott amassed a huge fortune; and few people enjoy their work more than does Richard Melman, a Chicago restauranteur.

This text presents a wide array of career opportunities in the hospitality industry. You will find that the hospitality industry encompasses more than just hotels and restaurants; it also includes catering, in-flight feeding, bed and breakfast operations, and hospital foodservice. In addition to helping you choose the right career, this text provides advice on getting hired and getting ahead. You will learn procedures for starting, staffing, and managing a hospitality-related business. Throughout the book, the focus is on the most important determinant of success in the business: guest service. As all of the great industry leaders have found, pleasing the guest is the main objective. If you achieve this, whatever your position, you will be a winner. The hospitality industry is growing rapidly, and so is the need for formally trained and educated managers. Most hotels and restaurants prefer to hire graduates of hospitality-related programs rather than their noneducated counterparts. In today's competitive environment, there is a fine line between success and failure, and formal training combined with practical experience can help you cross that line.

PART 1

An Overview of the Hospitality Industry

Chapter 1

Hospitality Past and Present

The hospitality industry is currently one of the world's largest employers, and the job outlook for the future is just as favorable. Hospitality is one of the few industries in which it is still possible to begin with a little capital and a lot of hard work and create a thriving business. J. W. Marriott, Ray Kroc, and E. M. Statler did it. In this chapter we shall explore the achievements of these and other entrepreneurs who have shaped the hospitality industry. After examining the lives of both past and present industry greats, we shall discuss their contributions to the field and their particular formulas for success.

ORIGINS OF THE HOSPITALITY INDUSTRY

The foodservice industry has existed for almost as long as mankind. Indeed, ever since Eve marketed the first apple, we have been concerned with the acquisition and distribution of food. Recently, the oldest-known recipe book was discovered in ancient Mesopotamia, now part of Iraq (*NRA News* 1985). Written in the Babylonian language, the recipes were carved in stone in around 1700 B.C. They are surprisingly sophisticated, featuring stag, gazelle, and pigeon cooked in sauces and topped with bread crumbs. In more recent times, inns throughout Europe have provided food to travelers. Some of these are more than four hundred years old and still are operated today, by Trust Houses, Limited. This company, formed in 1903, is dedicated to preserving historic inns.

The oldest-known tavern in America is the Coles Ordinary, opened in 1634 in Boston (Lundberg 1976). Such early taverns featured a simple menu consisting of game served family style, accompanied by ale or wine. Initially, they were under the strict dictates of the Puritans, who fined patrons spending more than a half-hour drinking spirits. Then in 1685, the Huguenots from France took them over and brought music, dance, and entertainment to the early taverns.

The first lodging operations can be traced to ancient Greece and Rome, but the word *hotel* was not applied to them until late in the eighteenth century. *Hotel,* French for a wealthy or prominent person's house, became the generally accepted term when referring to a place of lodging. The early American hotels were some of the most magnificent: In 1850, the Astor House was one of the first to serve French and American cuisine four times each day and to include it in the $2.00 room cost (Lundberg 1976).

THE CONTRIBUTIONS OF PAST LEADERS

The hospitality industry as we know it today owes a great deal to the men and women who pioneered the foodservice and lodging business. Through hard work and foresight, they instilled standards and developed procedures that are still followed. Next we shall examine the lives of a few of these prominent individuals.

Cesar Ritz

By the middle of the nineteenth century, hotels had become a well-established part of American culture, but they were not as popular with prominent Europeans. *Cesar Ritz* was credited with changing this and with making hotels fashionable. The son of a Swiss farmer, Cesar Ritz was apprenticed to a local hotel keeper at the age of fifteen. Later he trained at the most famous French restaurant in Paris during the 1860s, Le Voisin. He was fascinated by the elite and powerful of that era and carefully studied their likes and dislikes. Later, while working at the Imperial Pavilion in Vienna, he secured what was to be the lifelong patronage of the Prince of Wales. Soon Ritz developed a name for himself in the industry through his constant concern for his guests, for whose needs he would go to great lengths to anticipate and satisfy. For example, when he later opened his first hotel, the Paris Ritz, he experimented with the effects of color and lighting to find the most flattering scheme. He supervised all details of the opening himself and even taught the housekeeping staff to make beds. His hotel boasted the finest chef of that era, Escoffier.

Octogenarian Arnold Batliner runs the world's only money laundry, found at the Westin St. Francis in San Francisco. (Photo courtesy of the Westin St. Francis)

Throughout his career, Cesar Ritz demonstrated the importance of service. He was a perfectionist, and his concern for detail in creating stylish hotels made his name synonymous with fashion. He is the only hotelier whose name appears in Webster's Dictionary, in which *ritzy* is defined as "fashionable, posh."

Fine hotels still bear the Ritz name. Pictured is the Ritz-Carlton in Naples, Florida. (Photo courtesy of the Ritz-Carlton, Naples)

Ellsworth Statler

Ellsworth Statler is credited with making luxury hotel accommodations affordable to middle-class America. With little formal education or money, he managed to build the first major hotel chain in America. Statler began his career at the age of thirteen as a bellman at the McClure House in Wheeling, West Virginia. Later, he ran concessions in billiard rooms and bowling alleys, finally opening his own restaurant, The Pie House.

At the age of thirty-one Statler was ready for a new venture and moved to Buffalo, New York, where he operated a cafeteria restaurant in one of the office buildings and served "all you can eat for 25 cents." While operating a 2,100-room temporary hotel at the St. Louis World's Fair, Statler found that his waiters were stealing from him and so replaced them with well-dressed waitresses. A curiosity at that time, the waitresses attracted more customers, providing Statler with enough profit to open his first hotel.

He opened the Buffalo Statler in 1908, which had three hundred rooms, with a bath in each. Indeed, he became famous for the slogan "A room and a bath for a dollar and a half." In addition to being a skilled marketer, Statler was innovative. He offered a telephone in each room, free morning newspapers, and profit sharing for his employees and introduced a cost-accounting method that became a standard in the industry.

Statler was considered a bit eccentric in his personal habits: He was extremely wealthy but wore dime-store eyeglasses and bought cheap, ready-made suits. He was a firm believer in the Protestant work ethic and was known to call in his executives for a conference at 2:00 A.M.

Statler operated under the philosophy that "life is service. The one who progresses is the one who gives his fellow human being a little more, a little better service." He made sure that each employee maintained his high standards, and is credited with saying, "the guest is always right" (Lundberg 1976).

Conrad Hilton

Perhaps one of the best-known hoteliers in the world, *Conrad Hilton* was the first to enter international hotel markets. Born in New Mexico, Hilton began his career in the lodging industry by renting rooms in back of his father's store to traveling salesmen. Later, after having been a banker and a state legislator, Hilton bought his first hotel in 1919, the Mobley in Cisco, Texas. By 1929, he owned seven properties.

It was not until after the great Depression that Hilton was able to expand his small chain. In 1946, he formed the Hilton Hotels Corporation

Conrad Hilton, founder of the Hilton Hotels Corporation. (Photo courtesy of Hilton Hotels Corporation)

Conrad Hilton's first hotel, the Mobley, in Cisco, Texas. (Photo courtesy of Hilton Hotels Corporation)

and a few years later purchased his flagship property, New York City's Waldorf-Astoria, still operated by the chain today. In 1949, Hilton International was formed and eventually grew to include thirty-eight hotels around the world. In 1954, Hilton purchased the Statler chain for $111 million. After deciding to focus on U.S. hotels, the corporation later sold Hilton International to Trans World Airlines, the two groups agreeing not to expand in each other's markets. Later, however, this pact was

The Waldorf-Astoria owned by Hilton Hotels, Inc., in New York City. (Photo courtesy of the Waldorf-Astoria)

relaxed, and Hilton Hotels is once more developing internationally and has recently opened properties in Europe and Australia.

As a businessman, Conrad Hilton was known for his organizational skill. His properties operated in a decentralized fashion, with each retaining its own personality, but with centralized functions in accounting, reservations, and purchasing. Hilton purchased hotels wisely and made large profits from them. The Waldorf-Astoria made $1 million in profits in its first year of operation, and the Palmer House in Chicago even exceeded this amount with first-year profits of $1.45 million. Hilton's keen business sense and economic insight led to the creation of one of the largest hotel empires of all time.

J. Willard Marriott

J. Willard Marriott created the "billion-dollar root beer stand." In 1927, he began his career in the hospitality industry by opening a root beer stand in Washington, D.C. Recently called "a living example of the American dream" by President Ronald Reagan, the husband-and-wife Marriott team saved nickels and dimes until they could expand the Hot Shoppe restaurant chain, still operated today. Marriott worked hard, and only a near-fatal bout with Hodgkin's disease in 1931 forced him to take his first vacation.

Marriott constantly sought for ways to diversify his operation. In 1937, he opened the first airline in-flight kitchen, in which box lunches were

J. Willard Marriott, founder of the Marriott Corporation. (Photo Courtesy of Marriott Corporation)

J. Willard Marriott in the door of the original Hot Shoppe. (Photo courtesy of Marriott Corporation)

prepared for the crew of an Eastern Airlines transport. Today the Marriott Corporation is the world's largest in-flight caterer. During World War II, Marriott operated the first contract feedings at war plants. Later, in 1947, he opened a retail takeout division called Pantry House.

For thirty years, Marriott focused on foodservice, but in 1957, he entered the hotel business, opening the 370-room Twin Bridges Motor Hotel in Washington, D.C. J. W. Marriott was conservative and so was always somewhat uneasy with his company's rapid expansion. His son Bill Marriott is credited with the hotel division's accelerated growth.

Marriott is known for carefully researching consumers' needs and developing innovative ways to meet them. He believed in tight control systems and made a point of frequently visiting and monitoring each of his operations, a practice continued by his son. Although it is a huge conglomerate, the Marriott Corporation has always been centralized. Standards are set by senior management and enforced throughout the corporation.

Marriott's Mormon upbringing in Utah led to the philosophy that guided him during his career. He "had three general ideas in mind, all equally important. One was to render friendly service to our guests, the second was to provide quality food at a fair price. The third was to work as hard as I could, day and night, to make a profit." These ideals still guide the Marriott Corporation.

Ray Kroc

One of America's most renowned entrepreneurs, *Ray Kroc* made building America's fourth largest retailer appear like child's play. After spending nearly twenty-five yaers selling foodservice supplies, he just happened to discover a gold mine in California. When in 1954 he visited his first McDonald's, operated by brothers Dick and Mac, he immediately rec-ognized the void it filled in foodservice and the opportunity it presented for expansion. Although others before him had tried without success, Kroc was able to convince the McDonald brothers to give him the franchise rights to their hamburger stand.

Ray Kroc was a salesman. According to John F. Love's *McDonald's: Behind the Arches* (1986), Kroc was able to put himself in the customer's position, thereby enabling him to forsee market trends. He also applied the same philosophy to his franchises. By making them successful, he became successful. But perhaps his greatest achievement was the part-nership he formed with his franchisees. In return for a reasonable fee, they have access to McDonald's management expertise and excellent training facilities.

Ray Kroc was committed to quality, service, cleanliness, and value and the company's Q S C & V acronym has become a legend in the

Ray Kroc, founder of the McDonald's Corporation. (Photo courtesy of McDonald's Corporation)

fast food industry. Early in the company's development, Kroc realized that if these standards were to become the norm, he had to build a central organization to enforce them. He carefully selected all licensees, gave them extensive training, and monitored them so as to ensure adherence to standards. This process is commonplace today, but back in the 1950s, it was revolutionary.

McDonald's was also the first fast food operation to concentrate on training. In 1961, it opened a full-time training center, *Hamburger University,* located in the basement of the Elk Grove, Illinois, store. Today it is housed in a $40 million facility that can accommodate 750 trainees.

Only Ray Kroc could boast that 96 percent of the American population

First McDonald's Restaurant, in Des Plaines, Illinois. (Photo courtesy of McDonald's Corporation)

had tried his product. With foresight and common sense, he made McDonald's an American institution.

THE CURRENT LEADERS AND THEIR ACHIEVEMENTS

Numerous people are doing great things in the hospitality industry today. Following in the footsteps of their predecessors, they continue to weather bad economic conditions, break ground in new markets, and lead their operations into the future. Bill Marriott expanded Marriott's hotel division and has kept healthy the multimillion-dollar corporation founded by his father. Jeff Campbell's management skill has pushed Burger King closer and closer to McDonald's in sales volume. On a much smaller scale, André Soltner, owner of Lutèce in New York, certainly deserves to be recognized as one of the greatest chefs in this country. Chef Jackie Etcheber, arriving in the United States from her native Hong Kong with only $1,000, managed to carve out her niche in a male-dominated field and to open her own highly regarded restaurant, Jackie's, in Chicago.

J. W. Marriott, Jr. (Bill), chairman of the board and president of the Marriott Corporation. (Photo courtesy of Marriott Corporation)

Finally, there are Tom Monaghan of Domino's Pizza fame and Richard Melman, president of the Lettuce Entertain You enterprise. Let us take a closer look at how these two restauranteurs achieved their success.

Tom Monaghan

Tom Monaghan is the founder of Domino's Pizza, the country's largest privately held restaurant chain. His childhood was difficult, being spent in a Catholic boys' home, foster homes, and work farms near Jackson, Michigan. After serving in the Marines, in 1960 Tom and his brother Jim opened a pizzeria near Eastern Michigan University. Jim sold out soon afterwards, but Tom worked hard at building the business. He learned early that customers did not want to wait longer than thirty minutes for a pizza, and so he guaranteed prompt delivery. He offered pizza in "a half-hour or a half-dollar off," and today if the pizza is late, it will be free or its price will be reduced by $3.00, depending on the location.

Domino's Pizza is booming, and Tom Monaghan has realized many of his dreams. He bought the Detroit Tigers in 1983 and earned a World Series ring in 1984. Long an admirer of architect Frank Lloyd Wright, he built a $300 million tribute to him that houses Domino's world headquarters. It includes a sports medicine center, an employee fitness center, a 150-acre working farm, and a pumpkin patch.

Tom Monaghan's success can be attributed to a few key traits: He is

Tom Monaghan, founder of Domino's Pizza.
(Photo courtesy of Domino's Pizza)

a man who is undaunted by adversity. In 1970, he was $1.5 million in debt but refused to give up. Retaining his sense of humor, Tom wrote checks stamped with the logo of a man wearing only a rain barrel. He also believes in rewarding his employees. Monaghan wears a $12,000 gold watch that he will give to any store manager whose weekly sales top the company record, and he has already given away several. Finally, Monaghan has kept Domino's concept simple. Its limited menu easily lends itself to quick service (Ager 1986, Kahn 1986).

Tom Monaghan's goal for Domino's is to reach ten thousand outlets generating an average of $1 million each. His other aspirations can be found in the "dream file" he keeps in his office, which is filled with clippings of places he would like to see, things he would like to own, and people he would like to meet.

Richard Melman

Chicago restauranteur *Richard Melman* is always branching out. In fact, he is involved in so many ventures that it is difficult to predict where he will turn up next. Currently he owns or manages more than thirty restaurants, most of which are in the Chicago area. His quick rise to fame and his golden touch have earned him the title "boy wonder of the restaurant industry."

Few would have predicted that he would become such an overachiever.

Richard Melman of Lettuce Entertain You Enterprise. (Courtesy of LEY Enterprise)

Melman grew up in the industy. His father owned a delicatessen restaurant where Rich worked during his youth. In high school Melman concentrated on sports and money-making schemes. He once invested in a gold-mining venture and actually earned a modest profit. During his twenties his life appeared to have little direction. He occasionally worked for his father, sold restaurant supplies, hawked Good Humor Bars, and was a kitchen manager but just could not find his niche. He wanted to own a casual restaurant where diners could enjoy healthful food in a relaxed atmosphere, but he could not find financial backing. Later, the opportunity to start such a venture materialized when he met Jerry Orzoff, a successful real estate agent. They formed a partnership, raised capital, and opened R. J. Grunts in 1971. The name reflected the irreverent style for which Melman is known, with R. J. standing for the owners' first initials and Grunts for the noises emitted by a mutual friend when eating. The partners were spurred on by their success and opened several more restaurants before Orzoff's death in 1981.

Since then, Melman has reigned as president of the corporation they formed, the Lettuce Entertain You Enterprise, and the wins just seem to keep piling up. Crowds throng to his restaurants, happily standing in line for tables or waiting weeks for reservations. He is also selling the "Melman touch" to others and was contracted to revamp the old Playboy Clubs and to open Chicago Bear Jim McMahon's establishment.

Although he has a shrewd business sense, the real secret to Melman's success is his creative genius. When working on a new concept, he pages through magazines and free-associates with what he sees. He also develops a "script" for the restaurant. With Scoozi! an Italian cafe located in Chicago's gallery district, he visualized young painters renting a four-hundred-year-old studio in Rome. His ideas for the decor were based on the traces of the past left by previous occupants of the artist's garret. The aged plaster walls and small frescoes in Scoozi! reflect the culture of Italy. Diners at this and other Melman restaurants are not simply entertained but are also transported to a different era or exotic location. Guests at McMahon's feel as though they are dining in the athlete's dorm room. The walls are covered with old uniforms, headbands, and photographs hung at a crooked angle. Melman carefully plans the "set" of each of his restaurants down to the smallest detail.

Rich Melman certainly does not resemble anyone's idea of multi-millionaire. His typical business attire consists of jeans, a windbreaker, and a baseball hat. He has boundless energy and continually spouts new ideas. He claims that success gives him the energy to do more. One of his favorite lines aptly depicts his philosophy: "What the board of directors should never forget is that I started this company to have some fun" (Westerbeck 1987, p. 160).

SUMMARY

These past and present leaders can be credited with much of the progress we have seen in the hospitality industry. In reviewing these leaders' backgrounds, it becomes clear that they possessed some common traits that contributed to their success. All were very hardworking and dedicated and were driven to achieve perfection in all that they did. They were also concerned with service. After carefully assessing their guests' needs, they would devote their energy to fulfilling them. Their ability to innovate was another key characteristic. These entrepreneurs were always searching for new and better ways to do things. Finally, all of them had to overcome some form of adversity, whether physical, emotional, or financial. By trying to acquire the qualities that made these individuals successful, you too can make your mark in the hospitality industry.

KEY TERMS

Cesar Ritz   Ray Kroc
Ellsworth Statler   Hamburger University
Conrard Hilton   Tom Monaghan
J. Willard Marriott   Richard Melman

—————— CASE STUDY ——————

The men and women who have achieved success in the hospitality industry were not afraid to dream. Early in each of their careers they had a goal in mind toward which they worked. Having such a purpose helped them make it through the lean years.

Take a few moments to think about what you want to achieve. Do not be afraid to set your sights high. All of the people described in this chapter did. Tom Monaghan could have easily stopped at one pizza parlor or given up when he was $1.5 million in debt, but he did not. The driving force behind his perseverance was his dream.

If you could have any job that you wanted, what would it be? Would you want to be a great chef, own a hotel or restaurant chain, or perhaps just run a country inn? Formulate your dreams into a description of an ideal job. Explain in detail what your job would entail. Do not be so concerned with what you can do now but, rather, with what you want to do. This exercise will help you get in touch with what you really want from life.

Keep in mind that it is possible to realize such a dream. Who would have thought that J. W. Marriott's root beer stand or Ray Kroc's hamburger joint would have grown into multimillion-dollar corporations?

Discussion Questions

1. What characteristics are needed for success in the hospitality industry?
2. To what do you attribute the success of such companies as Marriott, McDonald's, and Domino's?

REFERENCES

Ager, Susan, 1986. "An Appetite for More Than Pizza." *Nation's Business* 74(2): 81–83.

Hilton, Conrad N. 1957. *Be My Guest.* Englewood Cliffs, N.J.: Prentice-Hall.

Kahn, Joseph P. 1986. "Life After Success." *Inc.* 8(2): 60–65.

Love, John F. 1986. *McDonald's: Behind the Arches.* New York: Bantam Books.

Lundberg, Donald E. 1956. *Inside Innkeeping.* New York: Brown Book Co.

———. 1976. *The Hotel and Restaurant Business.* Boston: CBI.

Miller, Floyd. 1968. *Statler, America's Extraordinary Hotelman.* Statler Foundation.

National Restaurant Association (NRA) News, 1985. "Food for Thought." 5(6): 47.

Neisser, Judith. 1984. "Melman, Service with a Smile." *Chicago Tribune Magazine,* April 1, p. 55.

Ritz, Marie Louise. 1938. *Cesar Ritz, Host to the World.* Philadelphia: Lippincott.

Watts, Stephen. 1963. *The Ritz.* London: The Bodley Head.

Westerbeck, Colin. 1987. "Melmania!" *Chicago* 36(7): 88.

Zuckerman, David. 1985. "J. Willard Marriott: A Retrospective, 1900–1985." *Nation's Restaurant News,* October 7, pp. 17–25.

Chapter 2

Choosing a Career Path

During your lifetime, you will spend roughly eighty thousand hours at your job—that's an average of forty hours per week for forty years. You will decide whether these hours are enjoyable and satisfying or boring and tedious. According to Richard Bolles, author of the well-known job hunters' guide, *What Color Is Your Parachute?* (1972), most Americans are *underemployed;* that is, their jobs do not tap their potential. They do not have the opportunity to create and grow. After years of meaningless activity, American workers are rewarded with retirement and a pension. But if this description of working life in the United States sounds less than heartening, do not despair. Through careful planning and goal setting, it is possible to find a challenging and satisfying career. It is best to begin planning your career at a young age, though many older individuals have given new meaning to their lives by changing career directions. So whatever your age, it is never too late or too soon to start career planning.

This chapter will explore some of the many opportunities for exciting careers in hospitality management. We shall discuss setting realistic short- and long-term career goals to help you get where you want to be in the industry. We also shall examine the job search process, from writing a résumé to choosing the best company.

CAREER DIRECTIONS IN THE HOSPITALITY INDUSTRY

Industry in the United States is changing rapidly. As the "rust belt" industries such as steel and auto production lose ground, the service industry is growing, and the need for employees in the hospitality industry is expected to increase dramatically during the next decade. According to the U.S. Department of Labor, the number of jobs in the foodservice industry will increase 22 percent faster than will that in other fields. Indeed, in fewer than ten years, management jobs are expected to increase by 50 percent (Greenberg 1986).

With such a promising outlook, one of the biggest challenges to incumbent employees will be matching their skills and interests to the right career. As you review the career opportunities discussed in this chapter, begin thinking about which field might interest you. If a particular area arouses your interest, find out more about it. Talk with employees currently holding a job that interests you or do additional reading.

The Lodging Industry

The lodging industry offers a wide range of career choices, including culinary positions, sales management, catering, and personnel management. Hotels offer many opportunities for growth and advancement, and it is relatively easy to transfer from one area to another to gain experience. The more you learn and the broader your area of expertise, the greater will be your chances for moving up to a higher management position. Many of the large chains offer excellent training programs. New managers rotate throughout each department in the hotel and "get their hands dirty" by learning to wash dishes and clean guest rooms before being placed in their departments.

Although large chains like Marriott, Hyatt, and Hilton have more prestige, you should not overlook the advantages of the smaller, moderately priced and budget chains. Many of the moderately priced chains are in the process of revitalizing their image and are upgrading services and opening gourmet restaurants to appeal to upscale travelers. Smaller companies have more opportunities for rapid advancement than do larger ones. Although it might take a promising new employee several years to become a sales manager in a large chain, in a smaller chain the same person might be offered that position immediately.

The Foodservice Industry

Currently, the food industry is the largest employer in the United States, and its fastest-growing segment is foodservice. This field encompasses

The moon rises majestically over The Breakers, a Mobil five-star, AAA five-diamond resort. Built in the spirit of the Italian Renaissance, its 528 rooms include 40 suites overlooking the sights of Palm Beach, The Breakers' golf course, and the Atlantic Ocean. (Photo courtesy of The Breakers)

fine dining restaurants, fast food, catering, and institutional foodservice. The National Restaurant Association reported that nearly 40 percent of all food dollars are spent away from home, a percentage that is expected to increase in the future.

If you enjoy impeccable service and are a connoisseur of fine cuisine, a career in a luxury restaurant might be your best choice. Successful people in this facet of the industry must not only be well versed in food and wine but must also be dedicated to creating a dining experience of the highest quality. The only drawback is that most fine dining restaurants are independently operated, and so opportunities for advancement are limited.

If you prefer rapid advancement and enjoy supervising others, a restaurant chain or fast food operation might be the right choice for you. As in the lodging industry, the training programs are thorough, teaching their participants quality control, marketing, and administrative functions. If you decide to change directions later, these skills can be transferred.

If you want to be your own boss, owning a restaurant might be the right direction for you. It offers independence, recognition, and possibly great financial success. If this is your goal, it will be even more important for you to gain experience in the field: The competition is great, and

The dining room at Gordon Restaurant in Chicago. (Photo courtesy of Jon Miller, Hendrich-Blessing)

roughly half of all restaurants opened fail during their first year. Thus, to ensure your success, you should know exactly where you want to go and obtain the training and expertise needed to get there.

One frequently overlooked sector of the industry is *institutional food-service.* Hospital and prisons quickly come to mind, but this field also includes foodservice in schools, universities, parks, and businesses. In addition to providing excellent training programs and benefits, many institutional feeders offer more regular hours. Many highly regarded chefs have made the switch and for the first time in their careers have a forty-hour, Monday-through-Friday workweek.

Gaining Experience

Perhaps the best way to choose a career is to gain experience in the industry. Although schooling is becoming more important, "hands-on" experience is also helpful. To progress rapidly, you should combine a degree in the field with practical experience. Entry-level positions in a hotel or foodservice operation are readily available. Summer employment or part-time work during school can give you an advantage over other college graduates in both knowledge and experience. The more you learn about the industry now, the better chance you will have of avoiding underemployment during the next eighty thousand hours you spend on the job.

SETTING CAREER GOALS

Career planning and goal setting are important. If you do not take the time now to set your own career goals, other people will do it for you, and you will find yourself living by their standards and not your own. A goal-setting technique that can help you is *Management by Objectives*— MBO for short. It can be effective when used properly and will help you plot your career path.

According to MBO, career goals should have the following characteristics:

Goals must be specific. You should make clear and concise plans for your future. Rather than simply saying that you want to become a hotel manager, be more specific and decide what particular area and position interest you.

Both short-term and long-term goals must be set. If you are a newcomer to the industry, with little work experience, a good long-term goal would be a mid-level management position such as that of sales manager. Once you have identified a long-term goal, next set short-term goals that you must achieve in order to reach it. Do some research and identify the jobs that will act as stepping-stones to the desired position.

Goals must be measurable. To measure goal achievement, establish a timetable indicating when you should reach each short-term goal and when you should reach your long-term goal.

Goals must be achievable. Be realistic when setting your goals: You will not become a general manager of a large hotel overnight. Therefore, if you are not prepared for ten years of hard work, set your goals a little lower, and avoid the frustrations of working toward goals that you cannot reach.

Goals must be challenging. Do your homework and find a career goal that interests and excites you. Although your career goals should be achievable, do not be overly pessimistic and set your sights too low. If a goal is worth achieving, it will require hard work and dedication.

Setting clear, concise career goals will also help you avoid hopping from job to job. Most recruiters for large corporations prefer applicants

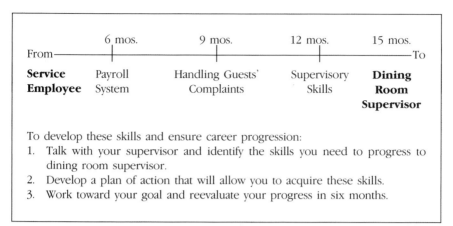

To develop these skills and ensure career progression:
1. Talk with your supervisor and identify the skills you need to progress to dining room supervisor.
2. Develop a plan of action that will allow you to acquire these skills.
3. Work toward your goal and reevaluate your progress in six months.

Figure 2-1 *Skills development by service employee.*

who have a proven track record of promotion in one or two companies rather than those who have worked for five or six companies over the past few years. Find a good company and stay with it for at least three to five years.

After you have found a company that you feel will allow you to grow and develop, work with your supervisor to set career goals. Some operations use a computer to compile a pool of information showing their employees' qualifications and job interests. When positions become available, managers consult the computer and call up the names of those interested in working in their area. But if you choose a company that does not have such a sophisticated system, there still is a great deal that you can do to facilitate your career development.

If, for example, you are a waiter in an outlet of an up-and-coming restaurant chain and your goal is to become a dining room supervisor, you must take steps to ensure your career progression. After you have been with the company for several months and have proved yourself to be a valuable employee, talk with your supervisor about your aspirations. Find out what your weaknesses are. As you overcome them, you will move closer and closer to your goal (see Figure 2-1).

CHOOSING A COMPANY

Most applicants believe that their fate lies in the hands of employers and recruiters, but actually, they themselves control the hiring decision. Just as recruiters screen applicants, you must interview your prospective employers and choose the company that best fits your needs. Begin by listing potential employers and investigating each one. Table 2-1 suggests some sources of information about different businesses. Choose companies

Table 2-1   Assessing potential employers.

What to Look For	Where to Find It
Potential for growth	Trade journals, newspaper articles, company prospectuses
Financial stability	Standard & Poor, annual reports, Value Line
Promotes from within	Personnel office, employees
Training programs	Personnel office, trade journals
Reputation	Industry practitioners, college professors

that offer good training programs, that promote from within, and that have a good reputation in the industry. Pay should not be a priority when choosing your first company. Instead, focus on the job's potential. Be concerned with meeting long-term goals, not short-term ones.

The Résumé

Once you have selected some companies that interest you and you have a clear idea of the department you would like to work in and the position you would like to hold, it is time to create a *résumé.* A good résumé and *cover letter* are crucial, as they are tools that you will use to market yourself. Review the sample résumé in Figure 2-2. Note that it is one page in length, attractively spaced on the page, lists a *career objective,* organizes work experience in chronological order, and is easy to read. This is one format that might be used; your particular experience may require a different one. In any case, because your résumé is a marketing vehicle, it should emphasize your strengths.

Preparing for the Interview

Send your résumé and a cover letter to prospective employers. All material should be typed and addressed to the individual who has the power to hire you. This may not always be a personnel recruiter. For example, in a hotel, a food and beverage director might be your first contact. Although you will eventually be referred to personnel, you will have made yourself known to the person making the final hiring decision, and he or she will be aware of your interest. Wait a week or two, and if there is no response, call the person you contacted. Perhaps your paperwork was lost in the shuffle or there just has not been enough time to contact you. Be polite, and do not harass or pressure the individual. Your call can jog the individual's memory and might result in an interview that otherwise would have been lost.

After the interview has been scheduled, prepare yourself by rehearsing the topics to be covered. Identify your weak areas, such as lack of

Ann Smith
3831 N. Kennicott Ave.
Chicago, IL 60681
(312) 769–2318

CAREER OBJECTIVE: Entry-level position leading to management in the hotel industry.

EDUCATIONAL BACKGROUND

A.A. Hospitality Management, December 1988
Triton College, River Grove, Illinois
Cumulative G.P.A. 4.8/5.0
    Relevant Courses: Front Office Operations
                            Catering Management
                            Hotel Foodservice Management
                            Supervision
                            Menu Planning and Nutrition

BACKGROUND IN THE HOSPITALITY INDUSTRY

The Carriage House Motel   (May 1986 to present)
    Schaumberg, Illinois   255–9600
    Position: Front Desk Clerk
    Responsibilities: Check guests into the hotel
                          Post room charges
                          Act as cashier at checkout
                          Accept reservations

The River's Edge Diner   (June 1985 to May 1986)
    Oak Park, Illinois   381–9231
    Position: Waitress
    Responsibilities: Served breakfast and lunch
                          Acted as cashier when necessary
                          Trained new servers

PROFESSIONAL ORGANIZATIONS

Triton Hospitality Club, president, 1987
National Restaurant Association
Junior Foodservice Executives, college delegate, 1987

REFERENCES

References will be furnished on request.

Figure 2-2   *Résumé.*

experience or breaks in work history, and think about how best to discuss these. Figure 2-3 lists some questions commonly asked during an interview. Review these and plan your answers to each one. By doing this you will avoid becoming tongue-tied or giving an answer that places you in a bad light.

The interviewer will also judge you on your appearance. Be sure to dress professionally. Both men and women should invest in a good, conservative suit in navy, gray, or black. Wear appropriate accessories, and make sure that your hair style is conservative also. A job interview

1. What are your long-term and short-term career goals?

2. What do you see yourself doing in five years?

3. What do you feel are your greatest strengths and weaknesses?

4. Why should I hire you?

5. What qualities does a good manager have?

6. Describe your most rewarding job experience.

7. Do you have a minimum salary requirement?

8. Do you plan to continue studying?

9. In what type of work environment are you most comfortable?

10. What do you know about our company?

11. Are you willing to relocate?

12. In what position are you interested?

13. Describe your ideal supervisor.

14. What problems have you had with supervisors in the past?

15. What do you do in your spare time?

16. In what school or community activities have you participated?

Figure 2-3   *Interview questions.*

is not the time to express individuality in dress. It may sound petty, but we all judge others by appearance, so why not make yours an asset?

The Interview

The job interview will determine whether you are offered an opportunity with the company of your choice. Review the checklist for a successful interview in Figure 2-4. Most interviewers hire people they like. They

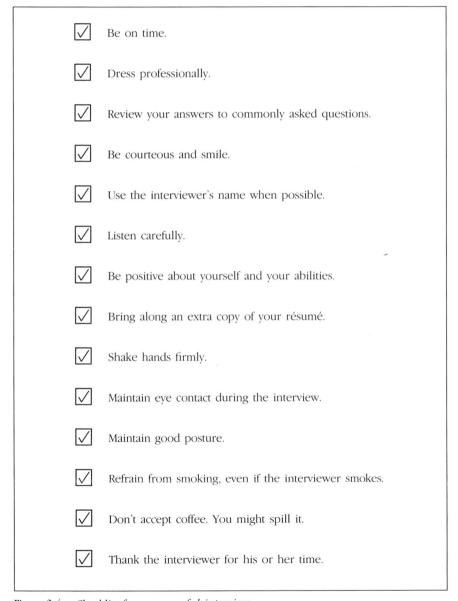

    ☑   Be on time.

    ☑   Dress professionally.

    ☑   Review your answers to commonly asked questions.

    ☑   Be courteous and smile.

    ☑   Use the interviewer's name when possible.

    ☑   Listen carefully.

    ☑   Be positive about yourself and your abilities.

    ☑   Bring along an extra copy of your résumé.

    ☑   Shake hands firmly.

    ☑   Maintain eye contact during the interview.

    ☑   Maintain good posture.

    ☑   Refrain from smoking, even if the interviewer smokes.

    ☑   Don't accept coffee. You might spill it.

    ☑   Thank the interviewer for his or her time.

Figure 2-4   *Checklist for a successful interview.*

also look for individuals who are confident and capable without seeming pompous. If you were unable to list all of your strengths on your résumé, interject into the conversation those that are missing.

Follow-Up

Immediately after the interview, send a brief thank-you letter to the interviewer. This should be typed, using a business format, and should restate your interest in the position and company.

It is acceptable to ask when the hiring decision will be made, which typically is not done for at least two weeks. If you have not heard from the company at the end of the indicated time, contact it.

If the interviewer tells you that a more qualified applicant was hired, ask for some constructive criticism, and use it to increase your chances during the next interview. Avoid dwelling on an unsuccessful interview. Instead, look ahead to your next prospective employer. There are many opportunities out there, and perseverance will pay off.

SUCCESS ON THE JOB

Securing a job is only the first step in ensuring a successful career progression. You may feel that if you do your work, someone will eventually recognize your talent and promote you. But this does not always happen. It is up to you to make yourself visible. You must create your own opportunities on the job: You are responsible for your own success or failure in a company.

The following are some common characteristics of achievers:

Is willing to accept new tasks.
Looks for ways to improve operations.
Avoids gossip sessions.
Is loyal to management and the company.
Dresses professionally.
Has a good working relationship with peers.
Is not overly confident.
Meets all deadlines.
Works beyond the requirements of the job description.

As you work in the field, you will notice that some employees easily gain access to the fast track. They are promoted frequently and, in general, are highly regarded by both their peers and management. These individuals have adopted the characteristics listed earlier and are responsible for their own success. One cannot completely rule out *nepotism,* the special consideration given to family members, but usually people get ahead because of their own drive and good sense.

It is important to begin immediately practicing good work habits when starting a new job. The first impression you make will stay with you during your entire career. For example, one new management trainee did everything wrong during his first month on the job. He was overconfident, did not meet deadlines, alienated his peers, and generally did not do good work. He did improve dramatically during the six-month training program and eventually overcame his initial shortcomings. But the negative first impression he made remained in his supervisor's mind. When he was placed in his permanent position, the supervisor gave him a poor recommendation. Eventually he was fired from the company. Thus the impression you make during your first few weeks on the job can follow you throughout your career.

There are dissenters in every company. These are people who have nothing good to say about the company or management. They love to latch on to the new employee and try to indoctrinate him or her into their negative way of thinking. Avoid these people when possible. Be polite, because a dissenter who is against you will be vocal about it, but do not become that person's best friend. Also, do not fall into the trap of becoming a complainer yourself. Instead of looking for ways to denigrate your company, look for ways to improve it. Dissenters always reach a career plateau. Although they might be knowledgeable and competent, no company will promote employees who are constantly critcizing its methods.

When your supervisor gives you an assignment, make it your first priority. Ask questions so you will understand what is expected, and then take whatever measures are necessary to meet your deadline.

It is important as well to become familiar with your company's *organizational chart*. This will help you avoid an error once made by a new waitress. She mistook the senior vice-president of a large hotel chain for a customer and sternly told him to get his hands out of the olive jar and leave the service area immediately. Fortunately, he saw the humor in the situation, but clearly it is important to be able to recognize key people early in your career.

Keep in mind some elementary marketing concepts when planning your career progression. Package yourself properly. The job is not the place to make a personal statement. Dress professionally, and remember that if you want to be a manager, you first have to look like one. Also, promote yourself on the job. Gain visibility by becoming involved with employee committees and volunteering for projects that will receive the attention of higher management. Look at people in the company who are successful, analyze the reasons for their achievement, and model yourself after them.

There is a certain amount of gamesmanship in company politics. But climbing the corporate ladder does not have to involve insincerity on your part. It is possible to remain true to yourself and your beliefs, to retain a sense of individuality, and yet still to become a valuable company employee. It is up to you to shape your future. How much more satisfying it will be to look back without regret on your life forty years from now, knowing that you have achieved those things that were important to you.

SUMMARY

The hospitality industry offers a wide variety of career options. It is important that newcomers to the industry set goals early in their careers to ensure their achievement. The employment outlook in the hospitality industry is very good, and so you will be limited by only your own foresight and capacity for hard work.

Employers in the hospitality industry look most favorably on job candidates with an educational background in the field, combined with on-the-job experience. The first step in securing a job is seeking out the companies that will best meet your needs. The next step is to write and use a résumé and cover letter to obtain a job interview. During the interview, it is important not only to market yourself as a viable candidate, but also to gain additional information about the company. Each interview should be viewed as a learning experience that will eventually lead to the best job choice.

Securing a job is only the beginning of a career. There is a great deal that you can do to present yourself favorably or unfavorably in the workplace. By developing good work habits, you will become a valuable resource to your company.

KEY TERMS

Underemployed	Cover letter
Institutional foodservice	Career objective
Management by objectives	Nepotism
Résumé	Organizational chart

—————— CASE STUDY ——————

Alice was recently employed as a hostess for the summer at a large theme restaurant. This is her third week on the job, and she is finding that things are not going as well as she expected. She is having problems with the waitresses on her shift. They all have been with the company for several years. Two of the old-timers, Maggie and Joan, are extremely vocal in their negative feelings about management. They are constantly criticizing the three young managers they work for and seem to go out of their way to air their gripes to Alice. They tell her that the stations are assigned unfairly. Rather than rotating them, the managers' favorites always get the best tables. Also, sidework is not assigned fairly. The same people are stuck with the dirty work each day.

Alice feels caught in the middle. On the one hand, she hopes to have a career with the company when she graduates from college, and so she wants to impress management this summer. But she can also see the waitresses' side of the problem and wishes that she could do something to improve working conditions.

Discussion Questions

1. How should Alice deal with the two waitresses when they tell her their problems?
2. What should Alice say to management about the employees' complaints?
3. What can Alice learn from this situation that will make her a better manager in the future?

REFERENCES

Bolles, Richard. 1977. *What Color Is Your Parachute?* Berkeley, Calif.: Ten Speed Press.

Greenberg, Jan. 1986. "A Menu for Success." *Business Week's Careers* 4(3): 96–98.

Chapter 3

The Foodservice Industry

When we think of the foodservice industry, restaurants immediately come to mind. But the industry also includes airline caterers, vending, school-lunch programs, and retail stores. In this chapter we shall examine the many facets of the foodservice industry. Some may be more appealing to you than others. If you want regular hours, there is institutional feeding; for glamour, there is catering; and for high growth, there are convenience stores. Whichever you choose, all offer many opportunities for excitement and challenge.

This chapter will begin by looking at the current status of the foodservice industry and the outlook for future growth. As you read the descriptions of the various foodservice segments, keep in mind that not all operations will fit into a single category. There will be gray areas, and some restaurants may include aspects of more than one segment.

INDUSTRY OUTLOOK

According to Jim Hasslocher, past president of the National Restaurant Association (NRA), "To say that the foodservice industry has grown rapidly is an understatement. In the past 15 years, sales have increased fourfold" (Dee 1987). As outlined in the "1988 National Restaurant Association Foodservice Forecast," sales are expected to reach $213.5 billion (Figure 3-1). Commercial foodservice sales are expected to increase by a hefty 7.5 percent in 1988 and institutional sales to grow by 3.9 percent.

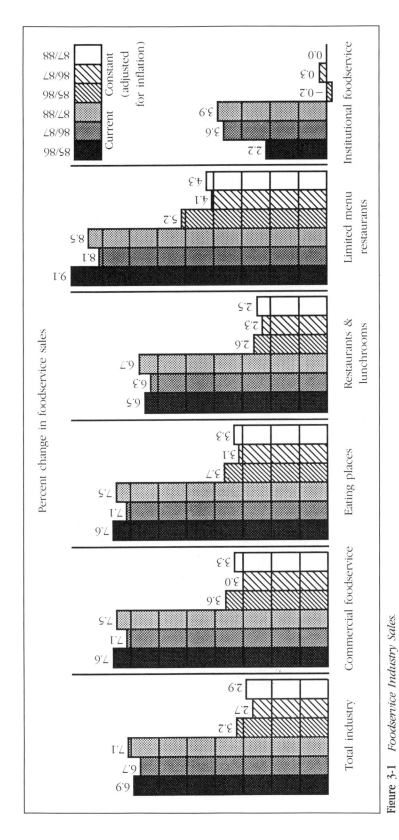

Figure 3-1 *Foodservice Industry Sales.*

NOTE: 1987 and 1988 figures are projected.

SOURCE: Reprinted from "1988 National Restaurant Association Foodservice Forecast."

33

As indicated in Table 3-1, the fast food or limited menu segment is showing the greatest increase in sales, with a gain in 1988 of 8.5 percent, which can be attributed to two-career families' growing need for convenience foods. Restaurant sales in general are expected to climb by 6.7 percent, but after adjustment for inflation, the growth rate will be only 2.5 percent. This segment is expected to be hurt by changes in the allowable tax deduction for business meals.

Market Saturation

The restaurant industry is experiencing *market saturation,* the condition that occurs when new restaurants do not create additional demand, and sales for the new units are gained at the expense of existing restaurants. Today there is one restaurant for every 685 persons, as compared with one outlet for every 845 persons in 1972 (Hale 1987). Restaurant supply is growing at the rate of 6 percent, whereas demand is increasing by only 2 percent. But the entire foodservice market has not yet been saturated. Areas in which growth is still possible are breakfast, takeout and delivery, and off-premise businesses. More mature markets in which growth is less likely are lunch and dinner segments, mid-scale restaurants, and cafeterias. These statistics underscore the need for advanced training and greater expertise before venturing into the restaurant business.

Environmental Factors

Restaurant sales are closely tied to the economic environment; that is, factors that affect the economy can also alter the foodservice industry. Negative influences include double-digit unemployment, high interest rates, and inflation. Positive influences are increased consumer spending and disposable income.

Demographic changes, or changes in the population, also affect the foodservice industry. With more working mothers, single parents, and one-person households, it is easy to see why the fast food and takeout markets are doing so well. Such consumer life-style issues as home-entertainment activities and health consciousness also affect dining choices.

To survive in this volatile environment, the industry practitioner must pay close attention to economic, demographic, and societal changes. The key to success is correctly assessing what consumers want and need and providing it in the most convenient way possible. The restaurants that fail are those that ignore consumer trends.

Table 3-1 Eating place sales: $138.2 billion.

	1985 Estimated F&D Sales ($000)	1987 Projected F&D Sales ($000)	1988 Projected F&D Sales ($000)	1987–1988 Percent Change	1987–1988 Percent Real Growth Change	1985–1988 Compound Annual Growth Rate
Total eating places	$111,598,208	$128,568,470	$138,211,105	7.5%	3.3%	7.4%
Restaurants, lunchrooms	58,444,122	66,142,507	70,574,055	6.7	2.5	6.5
Limited menu restaurants, refreshment places	47,190,521	55,671,888	60,424,713	8.5	4.3	8.6
Commercial cafeterias	3,286,108	3,678,338	3,913,752	6.4	2.2	6.0
Social caterers	1,301,600	1,490,197	1,600,472	7.4	3.2	7.1
Ice cream, frozen custard stands	1,375,857	1,585,540	1,698,113	7.1	2.9	7.3

Source: Reprinted from "1988 National Restaurant Association Foodservice Forecast" published by the National Restaurant Association.

COMMERCIAL RESTAURANTS

Commercial restaurants are the largest and most diverse segment of the foodservice industry. This segment includes everything from the finest dining establishments to greasy spoons. Although the need for good management practices apply to all restaurants, the challenges faced by the various divisions of this segment differ.

Fine Dining Establishments

An exemplary *fine dining restaurant* combines excellent food, impeccable service, and strong management. Although many in the foodservice industry dream of owning a "white tablecloth" restaurant, few possess the knowledge of cuisine, wines, and service needed to be successful.

The owner of a fine dining restaurant cannot settle for mediocrity. With such high charges for both lunch and dinner, these restaurants' clientele expect the atmosphere, food, and service to be extraordinary, which can be achieved only through constant attention to detail in both the kitchen and the front of the house.

Typically, the fine dining establishment is small, seating no more than one hundred people. This allows the chef and manager to exert a great deal more control than is found in larger eateries. The most important

Windows on the World, the spectacular restaurant at the top of the New York World Trade Center. View from the main dining room overlooking Manhattan. (Photo courtesy of Windows on the World)

factor in the fine dining restaurant is food. Some restaurants, such as the world-renowned Lutèce in New York City, are seemingly simply decorated, as their clientele come to experience the cuisine, not to be impressed by the latest decorating fad.

The owner of a fine dining outlet must also be dedicated. John Mariani, author of *Mariani's Coast to Coast Dining Guide* (1986), says that Lutèce, awarded four stars by the *New York Times,* is the best restaurant in the country. He feels that one of the reasons for its success is the chef-owner André Soltner's constant attention. Mariani (1986, p. 600) stated that Chef Soltner "has devoted himself to finding the best way to approach each ingredient, each technique, each preparation."

Mid-Scale Restaurants

Mid-scale restaurants are moderately priced, family-style restaurants that are predominantly independent operations, although there also are many chains, such as Denny's, included in this segment. The increased competition from fast food outlets has resulted in decreased traffic, but many diners are still drawn to mid-scale restaurants offering a quality meal at a reasonable price in a relaxing atmosphere.

Successful mid-scale restaurants today are broadening their appeal. The menus are more varied than ever, often incorporating the latest ethnic foods or more nutritious fare. Many outlets are updating their decor to make the atmosphere more interesting both inside and outside. Another concern is service. Diners today expect quick, courteous service from mid-scale establishments. This personal attention is one of the most important advantages that family-style restaurants have over fast food outlets.

The Denny's chain remains a viable contender in the race for family business, as it reacts quickly to changing customer needs. Its menus have become more regional, featuring such items as Cajun food in the South and New England fare on the Eastern seaboard. Denny's has also added a line of gourmet pies to its menu, in response to consumers' greater interest in dessert. Although mid-scale restaurants have much competition, they can still flourish by paying close attention to current trends and customers' needs.

Private Clubs

Often *private clubs* have several types of eating outlets, including a fine dining restaurant, a mid-scale operation, and a catering business. The private club's main goal is to fulfill the needs of its clientele. Although the dining outlets are not expected to show a profit, the food and service must be of the highest quality at all times. The finest ingredients must be used, and personal service is expected. Foodservice managers must also be flexible and willing to adjust their schedules and practices to meet their club members' whims.

A private club offers many advantages to its employees. As most of its business occurs during the workweek, there is a greater chance of having the weekend free than there is in a typical commercial operation. The pace is slower and business is more predictable. Also, wages are good, often with year-end bonuses and gifts for employees.

Theme Restaurants

Rather than relying on fine food and service to attract customers, the appeal of *theme restaurants* lies in their entertaining atmosphere. The more unusual and creative the theme is, the better it will be for business. This theme must be incorporated into the menu, decor, entertainment, and service.

The greatest challenge is to create a theme that is different, appealing, and long lasting. One very successful theme restaurant, Ed Debevic's, owned by Richard Melman, appeals to current interest in the 1950s. Melman did an excellent job of carrying the theme throughout the restaurant. The outlets contain many artifacts from the 1950s, with a diner menu featuring meat loaf, a blue plate special, and old-fashioned

Ed Debevic's, popular Chicago 50s theme diner owned by Richard Melman of Lettuce Entertain You Enterprise. (Photo courtesy of LEY Enterprise)

malts. The servers exemplify the theme in both their costumes and behavior, being carefully trained to adopt outrageous habits. Customers are greeted with a "Whaddaya want honey?" by a gum-popping waitress who might just plop down next to the customer when taking the order. So far, the public loves Ed's; indeed, the original Ed's in Chicago was so successful that Melman is franchising it.

Ethnic Restaurants

Ethnic restaurants are winning an ever-increasing share of the dining market. In the past, this category included Mexican, Chinese, Japanese, Greek, French, and Italian foods, but more recently, Thai, Indian, Vietnamese, and Caribbean foods have been added.

Ethnic foods appeal to consumers' needs for diversity and adventure. They offer diners a unique cultural experience in their own home town. Although there are some ethnic chains, particularly for Mexican food, most are independent, family-owned and -operated establishments. Most ethnic restaurants strive for authenticity, but in some instances the menu must be adjusted to satisfy American tastes. The most popular ethnic restaurants offer food that is not intimidating to the average customer.

One of the more well known ethnic chains, Benihana of Tokyo, appeals to both the diners' cultural needs and their need for nonthreatening ethnic food. The costumed chefs put on an exciting show while cooking the food; yet the menu includes teriyaki steak, chicken, and seafood, which American consumers like. But Americans are now turning to more adventurous foods such as *sushi.*

Fast Food

Fast food restaurants are expected to continue growing. As consumers' need for convenience continues to increase, fast food will respond. The emphasis today is on service and quality. Consumers are now more discriminating, and the fast food giants must respond quickly, for example, to their desire for lighter, healthier fare.

Although competition has increased among the major chains in the past few years, McDonald's still retains the top position. The key to its success lies in its control systems. Even though the number of franchises has grown rapidly, the company has never allowed its high standards to be compromised.

One feature that has revitalized the fast food industry is the drive-through window, which gives customers even quicker service and more convenience. The interest in meals eaten off the premises has skyrocketed, and in response, the chains have emphasized drive-through service. Indeed, several businesses offer only drive-through service. One of these, Central Park U.S.A., has returned to its original formula for fast food success: limited menus, low prices, and speedy service. It does this by offering only burgers, fries, and soft drinks, avoiding the many menu items featured by the major chains.

Another interesting development in the fast food industry is the revival of turnpike foodservice. Several of the fast food chains have purchased the right to convert Howard Johnson's turnpike operations into franchisees, and consumers have responded favorably to this change.

One major challenge faced by the fast food industry is staffing. As the American population continues to age, the industry will no longer have the large pool of teenagers from which to draw. The major chains are beginning to consider alternative labor sources and currently are trying to attract seniors and mentally handicapped workers. They are also continually automating their equipment and reducing the number of workers needed per outlet. But as the fast food segment continues to grow, still more new labor sources will be needed.

CATERING

What could be more enjoyable than planning a party? Many individuals are drawn to a career in catering because of the excitement and variety it offers. Each day brings a new challenge. If you are an *on-premise caterer,* you may be planning a roaring-twenties theme dinner for a thousand people. Or if you are an *off-premise caterer* who travels to another site, you may be feeding famous stars on location while filming a movie.

Many people enter into the catering business by accident. They begin by helping friends plan parties, then gain more experience by volunteering to plan community events, and eventually, realizing that they have talent in this area, turn to catering as a profession.

Catering is one segment of the foodservice industry that does not require a large initial investment. It is possible to work at home, adding additional equipment as needed. For example, Helen Benton began her catering business in this manner (Baker 1982), eventually employing 352 people and catering parties for such Hollywood stars as Marlo Thomas, Merv Griffin, and Shirley MacLaine.

An off-premise catering operation is sometimes also part of a larger business. Restaurants, gourmet carryout shops, and delicatessens may cater social events in the home or office. This segment is growing rapidly, and many restaurants find that adding catering to their existing facility boosts revenues and reputations with a minimal investment.

Caterers must have a wide range of skills in order to be successful. They must be able to market their business and attract clients and so will need a background in personal selling. A knowledge of food and wine is important when planning menus. Caterers must also be excellent cooks and be able to organize and supervise the work of their employees. Service expertise is essential, but perhaps the most necessary prerequisite for today's caterers is creativity.

Catering requires a great deal of resilience, as the possibility of error in this business is tremendous. The floral decorations might wilt; the musicians' union might strike; or worst of all, two different parties might be booked in the same room on the same evening. But there also are advantages. What other job would allow you to attend a Mardi Gras celebration one day and a Hawaiian luau the next? When everything falls together and the guests are pleased, the rewards are many.

RETAIL FOODSERVICE

One fast-growing but often overlooked segment of the industry is *food-service* operations in retail stores. Although foodservice is not the main focus of their business, many retailers find it to be profitable. Retail foodservice can range from the deli counter at a 7-Eleven to the specialty restaurants found in Neiman-Marcus.

Convenience stores are making substantial inroads into the fast food market. Some major contenders are the Convenient Food Marts—offering a sandwich, drink, and chips package that it markets as the "Movable Meal"—and Circle K—featuring an elaborate fountain display. Some fast food chains are jumping on the bandwagon. Winchell's Donuts and Hardee's hamburgers are being offered in covenience stores, but it will be some time before such stores pose any real threat to fast food. In 1985, sales in convenience stores were estimated at $3.2 billion, compared with $47 billion in fast food sales (Raffio 1986).

At the other end of the spectrum are the foodservice operations in large department stores. There may be as many as five or six different restaurant concepts in one store, thereby offering shoppers and local business people a wide selection. One elite chain, Neiman-Marcus, has given retail foodservice new dimensions (Gindin 1985). Each of the restaurants in its stores exemplifies one of four concepts: a sophisticated upscale dining room, a table-service salad-and-sandwich outlet, and two different sandwich-counter concepts. With foodservice sales 3 to 4 percent of the overall revenue per store, Neiman-Marcus's high standards and concern for quality are being rewarded.

INSTITUTIONAL FOODSERVICE

Like retail foodservice, an institutional outlet operates as a small but important part of a large business. One advantage that institutional feeding has over commercial is its captive audience. Diners are offered little opportunity to go off premise, and so it is relatively simple to project the daily sales volume. Nonetheless, to keep these captive customers happy, variety and quality are needed.

Although more than half of the institutional foodservice operations are independently operated, more businesses are turning to *contract management companies* such as Marriott, Service America, and Canteen. For a fee and a portion of the profit, the institution frees itself from the day-to-day concerns of managing a foodservice operation. The contractor staffs and operates the outlet, and the institution simply provides the customers.

The institutional manager has two superiors to answer to: the customers and the business they are housed in. The institution itself pressures management to keep costs low, but at the same time, the customers' expectations must be met. Being caught in the middle is a disadvantage in institutional feeding, but many managers find that the advantages far outweigh the drawbacks. More and more commercial foodservice managers are being drawn to institutional feeding because of the regular hours, excellent benefits, and comparable pay. Although institutional feeding lacks some of the glamour and excitement of commercial establishments, it does have its rewards.

Health Care Foodservice

In the past, health care foodservice was thought to be recession proof. But more recently, owing to stricter insurance guidelines regarding the length of patients' stays, hospitals have been forced to compete with one another for their share of the market. One of the areas on which they are focusing is foodservice. Hospital food has always had a bad reputation. Even though it may be nutritious, many patients find it unappetizing. Many health care operations, therefore, have taken steps to improve their food, by hiring chefs and adopting some of the production techniques found in the commercial sector. For example, St. Vincent Charity Hospital Center in Cleveland has developed a gourmet menu, which is used in its Epicure Program. For an additional $10.00, patients are served a gourmet meal, consisting of appetizer, entrée, and dessert, complete with formal place setting and flowers (Erickson 1987b).

To meet accreditation standards, each health care foodservice operation must be overseen by a registered dietitian, who must ensure that the menu meets the patients' nutritional needs. The actual food production is usually handled by the chef or foodservice manager. Trays must be prepared quickly, and so an assembly line is used. Tray delivery and pickup must be orchestrated efficiently. And while preparing and serving the patients' meals, strict rules of sanitation must be followed, beginning

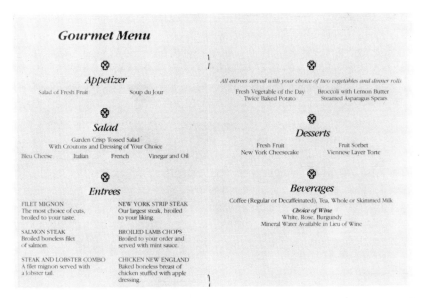

The Epicure menu served to patients at St. Vincent Charity Hospital in Cleveland, Ohio. (Courtesy St. Vincent Charity Hospital)

with the hiring process, during which new employees are carefully screened for communicable diseases.

In many health care organizations, the foodservice manager is also responsible for catering and banquet events in the hospital and cafeteria. Nursing home foodservice directors also have the same responsibilities, but on a smaller scale. They may have only a full-time manager supervised by a regional dietitian.

School Foodservice

Most institutional feeding takes place in an educational setting. The largest feeder in this category is the *National Student Lunch Program* (NSLP) administered by the U.S. Department of Agriculture (Erickson 1987a). This program has been extremely successful and has grown to include nearly ninety thousand schools. Since its development in 1946, the NSLP has served more than 115 billion meals. The program receives 30 percent of its funds from state and local governments, allowing it to offer free and reduced-price lunches to needy children. But like other recipients of federal funding, the NSLP is constantly threatened by budget cutbacks.

At the other end of the educational hierarchy is university feeding. When students live on campus, they sign a board agreement with the college and pay an annual fee for one or more meals to be consumed in the cafeteria. This gives the foodservice operations a predictable income and volume which makes the budgeting process fairly simple. In the past, university cafeterias relied on high volume, but now with declining enrollment and new voluntary participation options for students, they must work to attract customers. Public relations plays an important role, and the foodservice manager must be prepared to market the operation. For example, the University of Pennsylvania has developed an aggressive marketing program (Ryan 1986). Although the cafeteria program is completely voluntary, the university has managed to attract 80 percent participation in the contract program. To achieve this, Donald Jacobs, the dining service director, regularly surveys the students for their food preferences and adjusts the menu to meet their requests. For example, the cafeteria features "wellness bars" consisting of soups, sandwiches, and meatless entrées, and it also posts "Bitch Boards" on which students can register their complaints.

Employee Feeding

Foodservice in business and industry is expected to remain healthy as the labor force continues its moderate growth. Employee feeding includes foodservice outlets in manufacturing and industrial plants and commercial and office buildings. As with hospital and university cafeterias, the operator must please both the company and the employees, with an emphasis on variety and quality.

Employee foodservice often competes directly with commercial operations for its share of the market. If employees feel that the quality of the food is poor or the prices are too high, they will either bring food from home or go outside the workplace for lunch. This has forced employee cafeterias to remain abreast of current trends and to introduce such items as lighter meals and ethnic foods. In addition, the interior of many employee cafeterias has been refurbished. The customary drab, dark decor and conventional food lines are history. For example, Allstate Insurance Company recently revitalized its foodservice facilities to give them a light, contemporary style (Riggs 1986), by using light-colored carpeting, wall coverings, natural oak furniture, and recessed lighting. The new dining room gives employees a more pleasant place to dine and keeps them from leaving the premises for lunch.

SUMMARY

In the future, competition among foodservice establishments will be intense. As new units continue to be built and demand levels off, some segments of the industry will find it harder and harder to maintain their market share. But there should be continued growth in convenience and take-home items and a decline in the traditional or mid-scale restaurant segment. The ability to respond quickly to new trends, especially those appealing to the aging baby boomers, will become increasingly important.

The need for well-trained managers and employees in all phases of the foodservice industry will continue to escalate, and fast food and convenience segments will need to develop more creative recruiting techniques.

As always, those foodservice operators who practice sound management principles, are creative and flexible, and are able to respond quickly to environmental changes will flourish.

KEY TERMS

Market saturation
Fine dining restaurants
Mid-scale restaurants
Private clubs
Theme restaurants
Ethnic restaurants

Fast food restaurants
On-premise catering
Off-premise catering
Retail foodservice
Contract management companies
National Student Lunch Program

———————— CASE STUDY ————————

The following is a fictional account of the United States' economic, demographic, and societal environment in the year 2000. After reviewing this information, decide which restaurant concept would be most successful, and answer the discussion questions.

Economic Environment

The economy as a whole is doing poorly, as the gross national product decreased by 2.5 percent. The unemployment rate is high, at 11 percent, and consumer spending has dropped, with inflation on the rise. Last year, sales in limited-menu or fast food restaurants rose by 3 percent; sales in restaurants grew by 1 percent; and sales in cafeterias increased by 2 percent.

Demography

There are more people than ever over the age of fifty-five; this age category has increased by 20 percent since 1985. There also are fewer family units, more singles, and fewer children than ever before.

Societal Trends

Because of the high unemployment rate, more adults are turning to college for retraining. Consumers are extremely value conscious and concerned with quality and freshness when dining out. The aging population is very health conscious, and many are restricting salt and fat intake. Beef and red meat consumption is at an all-time low, with consumers' preferred foods being chicken, seafood, fruits, vegetables, and whole grains.

Discussion Questions

1. Based on this demographic information, what customer group would you try to reach if you were opening a foodservice outlet?
2. What will people's particular concerns be in the year 2000?
3. What restaurant concept do you believe would be most likely to succeed in the year 2000? Why?

REFERENCES

Baker, Nancy C. 1982. *Cashing in on Cooking.* Chicago: Contemporary Books.

Dee, Dorothy. 1987. "Boardroom: Association Officers Unveil Foodservice Forecast to Media." *Restaurants USA* 7(1): 37.

Erickson, Pam. 1987a. "School Lunch: No Small Potatoes." *Restaurants & Institutions* 97(12): 204–205.

———. 1987b. "Sometimes a Get Well Card Just Isn't Enough." *Restaurants & Institutions* 97(12): 206.

Ginden, Rona. 1985. "Neiman-Marcus: A Showcase for Specialty Dining." *Restaurant Business* 84(9): 163–178.

Hale, William C. 1987. "The Saturation Syndrome." *Restaurant Business* 86(7): 189–197.

Mariani, John, ed. 1986. "New York." In *Mariani's Coast to Coast Dining Guide.* New York: Times Books, pp. 568–623.

Raffio, Ralph. 1986. "Convenience Stores: How Big the Threat?" *Restaurant Business* 85(9): 126.

Riggs, Sylvia. 1986. "Allstate's Revamped Facility Ensures a Happy Staff." *Restaurants & Institutions* 96(11): 195.

Ryan, Nancy Ross. 1986. "University of Pennsylvania Dining Services." *Restaurants & Institutions* 96(10): 226–228.

Chapter 4

Entrepreneurial Spirit

The failure rate of new restaurants is amazingly high at 80 percent annually. Considering this, it is surprising to find thousands of new foodservice outlets opening each year. What makes these entrepreneurs risk all to own their own restaurant? Perhaps it is the lure of being in charge. After years of working for others, many restauranteurs want to give orders rather than to receive them. Ownership also gives them an opportunity to put their ideas into action, to take responsibility for new ventures, and to test their mettle. Others might open a restaurant to gain the celebrity that it often brings. Chicago restauranteur Richard Melman's name has become almost a household word in that city. Still others do it for the sense of accomplishment that a successful restaurant brings. Many restauranteurs receive a great deal of satisfaction from having their fine culinary skills or management ability praised. And some would-be restauranteurs believe that ownership is fun. They see life as one long dinner party and themselves as the host. Finally, many enter into the restaurant business hoping to make a great profit, knowing that if their business is successful, they will make much more money than they ever could working for someone else.

Whatever the reasons, the idea of restaurant ownership is appealing. There is no sure formula for success, but proper planning can give entrepeneurs an edge over their competition and place them in that successful 20 percent of new restaurants that survive each year.

STARTING WITH AN IDEA

It has been said that a new business requires 1 percent inspiration and 99 percent perspiration. Even though this may be true, the 1 percent that is most crucial to the future success of a restaurant venture is inspiration. No amount of effort can make a restaurant succeed if it does not attract customers. But what led to Richard Melman's opening Grunts, one of the country's first upscale eateries for singles? Perhaps it was market timing. Melman recognized the maturing baby boomers' need for a casual atmosphere and lighter, more healthful food. He also made dining fun. Melman has been touted as one of today's most creative restauranteurs. He is constantly at the forefront of new trends. Most recently, he opened Cafe Ba-Ba-Reeba! featuring Spanish *tapas,* or small amounts of savory dishes accompanied by wine. Once again, the venture has met with great public favor. But where does he get these great ideas? Melman explains: "Well, I listen to people. Many have said, 'I just love appetizers—I wish I could make a whole meal of them' " (Scarpa 1986, p. 20). Clearly, Melman is able to discern consumers' needs and then design a new restaurant concept that will fulfill them.

Successful restauranteurs today must be flexible and willing to look beyond old standbys. They must be in tune with the current fast-paced life-style and must have a feel for their potential customers, informally survey them, and develop a *restaurant concept* that they will find appealing. Another traditional Italian restaurant or fast food outlet will not receive much attention in an upscale neighborhood, but what about combining the two concepts? Opening a pasta takeout restaurant would respond to consumers' need for quick service and more nutritious Italain fare.

Once you have a concept in mind, write down a description of it, including the restaurant's name, ambience, menu, service style, number of seats, potential customers, type of entertainment, and price range. Answer such questions as: What can your restaurant offer its customers? What is unique about it? Why will it appeal to your customers? What will make them choose your restaurant over the competition?

Once the entrepreneur has an idea, it is time for the other 99 percent of perspiration to come into play. Ideas are relativley easy to think up, but it takes money, guts, and know-how to make them a reality.

PLANNING THE RESTAURANT

The system used to plan a new restaurant depends on the type of restaurant to be opened, the owner's level of expertise, and the available financial resources. If money is not a problem for the would-be restaurant owner, it is best to seek out the advice of professionals in the field.

But often, funds are limited, and so the restauranteur himself or herself must be responsible for much of the planning.

It would be especially foolhardy today to base such decisions as the location, concept, and decor of a new restaurant solely on the owner's intuition. Although instinct is certainly important, these decisions are expensive and should be made only after facts and figures are accumulated. This chapter will present information regarding location, zoning, licensing, and loan acquisition. As you read it, remember that each state sets its own guidelines regarding these factors. Although the information presented is common to most areas, you should check with your city and state governments before planning a new business.

Working with Professionals

If the budget allows, a new restauranteur should hire professionals to help plan the project. At the least, a lawyer and an accountant specializing in small business administration should be consulted. Other additions to the planning team might include an architect to coordinate the restaurant's physical design and a foodservice consultant to develop the concept, conduct market research, assess financial needs, and create menus. Depending on the project's complexity, a lighting consultant, landscape architect, and acoustical engineer might be retained.

Assembling a large planning team can be expensive, and so it is important that the best-qualified individuals be chosen. The new restauranteur would be wise to consult other restauranteurs who have recently completed a new project and to ask professional organizations for a list of their members. Team members should be interviewed before being hired and should provide examples of their work, names of individuals they have worked for in the past and also those they are working for now, and references. The team members that are selected should be qualified, able to communicate with the rest of the team, and have a proven track record (Minno et al. 1985).

Market Research

The first step in determining the feasibility of a particular location and concept is to conduct a *feasibility study,* to determine the characteristics of the target market or potential customers, to evaluate the competition, to identify traffic patterns in the area, and to assess the local businesses. Once again, if the budget permits, it is best to hire a restaurant consultant or marketing consultant to conduct the research. But if funds are limited, much information can be accumulated inexpensively. The following are a few of the agencies that will provide demographic information free of charge or for a small fee.

U.S. Census Bureau
Local libraries
Local utility companies
Banks
Real estate agents
Chambers of commerce
Small Business Administration

Next, the would-be restauranteur should make an informal survey of the area's restaurants, by visting the outlets and noting their menu, prices, service style, number of seats, food quality, and any special features. Using a standard survey form, like that in Figure 4-1, will ensure that the same information is collected on each visit.

Location

Perhaps one of the most important decisions to be made regarding a new restaurant is its location. Occasionally, restaurants may do well in spite of their location. This was the case with Gordon, a fine dining restaurant that opened several years ago in one of the less attractive areas in Chicago. It was an overnight success even before major renovation began in the neighborhood. But even though some restaurants can prosper in an unpromising area, it is certainly not the norm. The restauranteur should thus review the demographic information about the area, making sure that it can support another restaurant and determining where customers would originate, whether it be the local luncheon trade from office complexes or breakfast and dinner business from area residents. The site selection may be less complicated if a new restaurant is to be built, but few people have the financial backing for this sort of venture. Most restauranteurs begin by either purchasing a restaurant or transforming existing space into a foodservice outlet.

When assessing a potential site, would-be restauranteurs should observe transportation patterns in the area. Can the building be seen from the street? Is there adequate parking, and is it easily accessible? Will some of the customers arrive on foot from local businesses or residential areas? What are the physical characteristics of the building, both inside and outside? What remodeling is necessary; is the floor space in both the back and the front of the house adequate; and does the building have "curb appeal"? Restauranteurs should also consider the appropriateness of the structure for a foodservice outlet. Is the electrical supply sufficient? Is the plumbing sound? Can appropriate gas hookups be made? They should check with the local utilities to find out the status of the building. Naturally, it is best to locate a restaurant in an area that is prospering rather than declining. Restauranteurs should thus look at

Restaurant name	
Location	
Owner	
Type of restaurant	
PHYSICAL DESCRIPTION OF RESTAURANT	
Number of seats	
Decor	
Adequacy of parking	
Visibility of sign	
VIABILITY OF BUSINESS	
Peak service times	
No. of peak customers	
No. of off-peak customers	
Target market	
ASSESSMENT OF MENU	
Type of menu used	
Preparation methods	
House specialties	
Price range of entrées	
SERVICE	
Uniforms	
Style of service used	
Service problems	

Figure 4-1 *Competitive survey.*

construction starts in the area and observe the upkeep of nearby businesses.

Once the choices are narrowed to a particular site, it is wise to have a reputable building inspector check it out. This is much less expensive than purchasing a building that needs, for example, thousands of dollars of rewiring to bring it up to code.

Licenses and Permits

Another consideration when selecting a site is obtaining the proper licenses and permits. Each city has different requirements, and so it is a good idea to contact local government offices to verify ordinances

PRETHEATER MENU SERVED 5:30-6:30 p.m.
Sunday through Friday*

"OPENERS"

Artichoke Fritters Bearnaise
Eggplant Duxelle with Maytag Blue Cheese Glaze
Grilled and Marinated Asparagus with Smoked Whitefish Butter
and Grilled French Bread
Todays Soup
Smoked Salmon with House Made Wheat Crackers, Smoked Tomato,
Sweet Onion and Herb Salsa
Medallion of Venison with Red Wine, Apple and Chervil

******
Seasonal Greens with Herb Vinaigrette
******

"MAIN ACT"

Sauteed Whitefish with Ligurian Olives and Basil Oil
Grilled Salmon Steak with Chinese Mustard Glaze
Sauteed Duck Breast and Duck Confit with Caramelized Onions
and Spinach
Grilled Sweetbreads with Fire Roasted Onion Salsa and Fried
Leeks
Grilled Aged Sirloin with Spicy Ratatouille and Roast
Potatoes
(3$ supplement)

"CURTAIN CALL"

Flourless Chocolate Cake with Unsweetened
Whipped Cream
Chilled Lemon Souffle with Warm Caramel Sauce
Coconut Bavarian Cream with Vanilla Sauce and Toasted Coconut
Orange Ice Cream with Candied Orange Slices and Vanilla
Waffers
COFFEE or TEA

$18.00

At left, Gordon Sinclair, owner of Gordon, a fine dining restaurant in Chicago. At right, a pretheater menu served at Gordon. (Courtesy of Gordon Sinclair)

early in the planning process. A restaurant owner may think that he or she has found the perfect building but later find that it will cost thousands of dollars to bring it up to fire code. Or worse yet, the owner might purchase a building hoping to open a restaurant and bar operation, only to find that it is located too close to a school and thus cannot obtain a liquor license. It is best to get legal advice at this stage from someone specializing in small business start-up procedures.

The local government provides specific guidelines that must be met by both new and existing structures. Most have codes or regulations regarding fire, health, sewage, garbage, and parking. Restauranteurs will be required to present a blueprint indicating any structural changes to be made. The blueprint will require the assistance of an architect, and all permits must be acquired before construction is started.

Several licenses are required to operate a new business. If the business's name is anything other than just the name of the owner or owners, a *fictitious name registration* must be made. If liquor is to be served, it is best to look into obtaining a liquor license as soon as possible. Many local agencies limit the number of liquor licenses they issue, thereby making it difficult, and often impossible, to obtain one. There are strict guidelines, in any case, regarding the location of the business, the character of the new owner or owners, and the previous owner's business practices.

The location that is chosen should be properly zoned for the type of business to be opened. There are special requirements for foodservice operations, bars, outdoor cafes, and even the placement of outdoor signs. A building permit will also be required before any construction can begin.

Financial Planning

The financial planning of a new restaurant is what most would-be owners find most discouraging. They may have a great concept, have found the perfect site, but spend months trying to accumulate enough money to start the project. Many restaurants fail because their owners do not correctly assess the amount of money they will need to run the business. A good rule of thumb is to have enough cash on hand to keep the operation going for six months without any income produced on its own. The restaurant should be given an opportunity to establish itself. Many new restauranteurs mistakenly assume that the business will generate profits immediately and thus count on these to see them through. When this does not happen, they are forced either to sell the business at a loss or to declare bankruptcy.

The first step in ensuring a business's financial success is to develop a detailed plan with an accountant and a lawyer. This plan will be a financial outline of the business that can be presented to potential investors and lenders. It indicates that the new owner is serious about the venture and will increase his or her image as being a good risk. The following information should be included in the financial plan.

Business Structure

The financial plan should begin by identifying the legal structure of the business. There are three possibilities. First is the *sole proprietorship,* which has one owner and is simple and inexpensive to start up. If offers some tax advantages, in that profits are taxed only once as personal income, but the disadvantages for the foodservice operator are overwhelming. In a sole proprietorship, the owner is personally liable for any expenses that the business cannot meet. Thus, if the business cannot pay its creditors, the owner can lose personal property such as a house or car in meeting the debt.

A *partnership* has the same advantages and disadvantages of a sole proprietorship, the only difference being that it is a business owned by two or more people.

The *corporation* is a legal entity separate from its owners. The advantage is that its owners cannot be held personally liable for any debts the corporation may incur. But the corporation is more complicated and expensive to form, and any profits are taxed as both corporate income and personal income when the owner makes withdrawals. Yet these disadvantages are outweighed by the advantage of limited liability, thereby making the corporation the best route for the restauranteur.

After deciding on the legal structure, the restaurant owner should develop an organizational chart, identifying who will be in charge of the operation and who will hold the various positions.

Capital Budget

The *capital budget* lists all the funds that will be required during the restaurant's development. It should estimate the money needed for operations, land acquisition, architectural costs, construction fees, furniture, fixtures, equipment, preopening expenses, and loan origination fees. This information should also be itemized.

Operations Funding

After determining the capital expenditures needed for the business start-up, the restauranteur will have a clearer idea of the funding requirements or amount of investment needed to open the restaurant. Again, the cash flow needs of a new business do not end with the opening expenses, and so it is necessary to have enough funds to operate the business for six months. Accordingly, the restauranteur should draw up an *income and expense statement* (see Figure 4-2) detailing anticipated revenue and costs during the first year.

XYZ Restaurant
PROPOSED BUDGET
19XX–19XY

ESTIMATED REVENUE		
Food sales		$130,000
ESTIMATED EXPENDITURES		
Food	$50,000	
Salaries and wages	30,000	
Benefits	5,000	
Depreciation	2,000	
General expenses	1,500	
Insurance	2,500	
Interest on mortgage	1,250	
Office supplies	500	
Linens	1,500	
Uniforms	500	
Utilities	2,000	
Maintenance and repairs	1,000	
Total estimated expense		$97,750
ESTIMATED NET PROFIT		$32,250

Figure 4-2   *Proposed budget.*

Next, the amount of funds needed should be established, including the portion that will be provided by the owner or owners and the amount that must be raised. The proposed owner's credit history and assets must be summarized in preparation for obtaining financial backing.

Obtaining Financial Backing

There are two major sources of funding for a new restaurant, *equity financing,* or money from investors, and *debt financing,* or money from a financial establishment. Most restaurants require a combination of both. Conservative advisers suggest that the debt-to-equity ratio be fifty-fifty, meaning that half of the capital come from equity and half from a loan. The more money that is borrowed, the greater will be the financial burden placed on the new business in the form of monthly payments.

The equity investment in a business can come from several sources. One is the money invested by the owner, which is called *owner equity.* Another possibility is to form a partnership, with either a general partner who would help run the restaurant or a *limited partner* who would not be involved in the day-to-day operation. Still another way to raise equity is through *venture capital,* or money from investors willing to accept a high risk in return for a portion of the business profit. Banks and life insurance companies also sponsor venture capital investment operations that might be willing to invest in a promising new restaurant.

When considering debt financing, the first place that one thinks of is a bank. But banks are cautious and will want to make sure that the risk is not high. They will assess the potential borrower's background in the business, the product itself, and the owner's management skills and business sense. When applying for a bank loan, it is important to have an accurate feasibility study and loan application. Banks will also ask for collateral, in the form of personal holdings such as stock, property, or other assets that can be converted quickly into cash should one be unable to meet the payments. It is difficult for a new restaurant owner to qualify for a bank loan. The restaurant business is risky, and if an operation fails, it will be difficult for the bank to recoup its investment.

Another possible source of funding is a Small Business Administration loan. The Small Business Administration is a government agency that guarantees a percentage of the loan and also will make direct loans if the borrower meets its strict criteria and is patient enough to wait out its lengthy qualifying period. Also, the city and state governments may have information about other funding that may be available. Sometimes local governments offer special low-interest, easy-to-obtain loans to entrepreneurs who cannot find funding elsewhere.

FORMULA FOR SUCCESS

Even with careful planning, many foodservice operations do not survive. But what makes a well-located operation with great food and atmosphere fail, whereas another restaurant with the same qualities succeeds? Although the reasons for success vary from restaurant to restaurant, some common denominators can be found in most long-lived operations.

Product Quality

No business can survive if its product is of poor quality. A restaurant cannot generate repeat business if the food is not fresh and well prepared and presented. Alice Waters, owner of Chez Panisse, a well-known Berkeley, California, restaurant is very particular about the food she serves: It must be at the peak of freshness (Ryan 1986). Waters also avoids tired, listless ingredients, and she feels that customers should be served only great tasting food. Although this may seem obvious, many restaurants fail in this requirement.

Service

Another irritant to customers is poor service. Many factors can contribute to this problem, including a lack of training, unmotivated employees, poor selection techniques, or the failure to develop standard procedures. One California-based chain, Rusty Pelican, developed a new strategy to improve the service in their outlets: It gives its employees training that

Alice Waters, owner of Chez Panisse in Berkeley, California, uses only the freshest ingredients. (Alec Duncan)

allows them to increase their productivity and improve their selling and merchandising skills. Employees set their own targets for improvement. They also become involved in team problem solving and, as a group, identify service bottlenecks and think of solutions (Wyckoff 1984).

Customer Involvement

Successful restaurants make customers feel important. They offer special attention or amenities that tell customers that their business is valued. For example, one Chicago restauranteur, Lou Mitchell, makes each diner feel welcome by greeting them personally at the door, providing a fresh newspaper, and offering them a box of "milk duds" after their meal. Although the food is good and the service is prompt, it is this special attention that makes customers line up around the block to dine there. Michael Hurst, owner of 15th Street Fisheries in Fort Lauderdale, Florida, offers his customers "recognition, recommendations, and reassurance" by remembering their names, ensuring that his servers are familiar with the fish he sells, and responding quickly to any problems (Ryan 1986, p. 194). Restaurants that consistently meet their customers' needs find that they can rely less on advertising and more on word-of-mouth recommendations to bring in business.

Consistency

Another important characteristic of a successful restaurant is consistency. Customers quickly lose interest in a restaurant that offers terrific food one week and terrible food the next. They want to feel that they will receive the same high-quality meal and service each time that they dine there. Consistency in product and service is one major factor responsible for McDonald's success. Each time a customer enters an outlet, the product they receive will be identical to what they had last week. Consistency is a result of a restaurant's attention to detail, proper training procedures, and retaining their employees for a long time. Restaurants that are unable to meet their customers' expectations each time they dine will be unable to generate repeat business.

SUMMARY

Many people dream of owning their own restaurant, but few are able to do so. Owning a restaurant brings such rewards as celebrity, a sense of accomplishment, increased income, and freedom from working for others. Almost 80 percent of all new restaurants fail within their first year. In order to succeed, would-be restauranteurs must plan ahead, and so this chapter examined planning procedures. Demographic information about the area considered must be compiled. Possible locations must be analyzed. A financial plan must be developed and a loan secured. Permits and licenses must be obtained, and finally, the new staff must be hired and trained.

This chapter also discussed factors responsible for restaurants' continued success. To survive in this highly competitive market, owners must be concerned with product quality, service, and customer needs and, perhaps most important, must consistently meet high standards. Attention to these areas fosters repeat business, which is the key to longevity in the foodservice industry.

KEY TERMS

Restaurant concept	Capital budget
Feasibility study	Income and expense statement
Fictitious name registration	Equity financing
Sole proprietorship	Debt financing
Partnership	Limited partner
Corporation	Venture capital

—————— CASE STUDY ——————

Two young entrepreneurs opened an upscale, avant-garde establishment in Cincinnati, Ohio, fashioned after a successful California restaurant. It featured a "hi-tech" design and an extensive art collection. The menu was eclectic, featuring grilled sweatbreads, carpaccio with *shiitake* mushrooms, and *sushi*. The average cost of an entree was $25.00.

These entrepreneurs opened their restaurant in an area that was very active on Friday and Saturday nights but quiet Sunday through Thursday, and it had little lunchtime business.

Initially, there was a great deal of traffic, but business began to slow after the first two months. After six months, the owners began finding it difficult to meet their payroll, and their purveyors began having to extend credit.

Discussion Questions

1. What were some of the reasons for the new restaurant's sales to drop?
2. What did the restaurant owners fail to do before opening their restaurant?

3. What can the owners now do to turn around their business?

REFERENCES

Minno, Maurice P., J. M. Woodburn, and R. Bhayana. 1985. "The Project Planning Team." *NRA News* 5(6): 24–26.

Ryan, Nancy Ross. 1986. "The 1986 Ivy Awards of Distinction." *Restaurants & Institutions* 96(10): 153–248.

Scarpa, Jim. 1986. "Cafe Ba-Ba-Reeba!" *Restaurant Business* 85(9): 258–262.

Wyckoff, D. Daryl. 1984. "New Tools for Achieving Service Quality." *Cornell H.R.A. Quarterly* 25(3): 78–91.

Chapter 5

Food and Beverage Operations

The successful operation of a foodservice establishment requires a great deal of technical expertise. In addition to leading and motivating employees, the operator must plan, organize, and control all aspects of the business. A restaurant may have an ideal location, stunning decor, and the best chef in town but fail to show a profit if it is poorly managed. In this chapter we shall review key positions in foodservice operations and examine two important determinants of profitability: menu planning and cost control.

THE FOODSERVICE STAFF

Figure 5-1 is an organizational chart for the dining room in a large foodservice establishment, and Figure 5-2 indicates the chain of command in the kitchen. This section will describe the various positions. Whether we are discussing a fine dining establishment or a fast food outlet, the staff's basic duties remain the same. Each employee, from dishwasher to chef, is responsible for controlling costs and pleasing the guests. They must work as a team, supporting one another when necessary.

The Restaurant Manager

The restaurant manager oversees the entire foodservice operation and is responsible for staffing, leading, organizing, planning, and controlling all aspects of the business. This position requires a great deal of experience

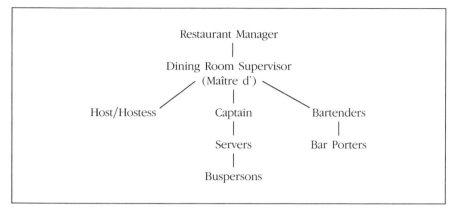

Figure 5-1 *Organizational chart for dining room.*

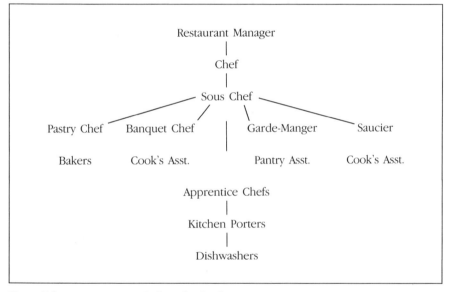

Figure 5-2 *Organizational chart for kitchen.*

and job knowledge, and because of the rapid advances in the industry and computer technology, a college degree is also valuable.

The restaurant manager oversees the dining room supervisor and chef, does all hiring and firing, and is responsible for the financial end of the business. He or she supervises the reservation system, forecasts future revenue, analyzes costs, and maintains company policies and procedures. Many restaurant owners occupy this position, as it allows them to keep a careful watch on all aspects of the business.

In a large operation, the restaurant manager's job is mainly administrative, that is, supervising the work of other managers. But in a smaller outlet, the manager has time for more customer contact and may have responsibility for the daily operation of the dining room. But in either case, it is his or her job to see that the outlet runs smoothly and to analyze revenue and expenses.

The Dining Room Staff

Depending on the style of service and size of the operation, the dining room staff can be either small or large. The following are some dining room positions:

Supervisor: Oversees the entire operation. The supervisor spends most of his or her time in the dining room ensuring smooth service.

Host/Hostess: Takes reservations and greets and seats guests.

Maître d': Supervises the wait staff and also acts as host. This position is found in fine dining establishments.

Captain: Offers service and supervises waiters and waitresses in fine dining restaurants.

Server: Takes customers' orders and serves food and beverages.

Cashier: Takes payment for meals directly from customers or servers.

Busperson: Sets tables, cleans tables after meals, and performs sidework such as folding napkins, filling condiment containers, and stocking supplies.

Beverage Operations

Many restaurants also include a bar operation. The markup (profit) on liquor is quite high, making this a lucrative addition to a foodservice operation. An elaborate lounge may have a separate manager, but usually the restaurant manager and the dining room supervisor oversee the beverage operation. It is staffed by one or more bartenders who dispense drinks and porters who stock the bar and help clean up. If there is seating, the bar staff might include cocktail servers who take orders and bring drinks to the customers.

The key to a successful bar operation is a friendly, efficient staff and good control systems. Liquor must be inventoried daily, and access to the storeroom must be limited so as to prevent theft.

The Chef

Perhaps one of the most important positions in a foodservice establishment is that of *executive chef.* This individual is responsible for managing all aspects of food procurement and preparation. In a small establishment, the chef purchases, receives, stores, and prepares all food. In a larger outlet, the chef supervises the work of others but does little of the actual food preparation. Many owners also act as the executive chef, preferring to keep tight control of the kitchen operation.

Finding a good chef is difficult. The position requires an extensive knowledge of food, excellent administrative abilities, and, today, an understanding of computerized inventory procedures. All of these are acquired only with years of experience. Many young chefs combine formal training with the practical knowledge learned during an *apprenticeship program*. Most cities sponsor an apprentice program in which the trainee works with an experienced chef for several years, learning cooking and administrative skills.

Kitchen Staff

Depending on the operation's size and complexity, the kitchen may be staffed by just a few employees performing general duties or by many workers performing very specialized jobs. The following lists some of the positions found in a kitchen operation:

Sous chef: "Under chef" who is responsible for aiding the chef in administrative functions and supervising the kitchen staff.

Chef de partie: Working cook who is in charge of a section of the kitchen. This might be a *saucier* or sauce cook, *garde-manger* in charge of cold food preparation, or *chef patissier* or pastry chef.

Banquet chef: Chef who is in charge of banquet food production in a large hotel or restaurant that offers in-house catering.

Cook's assistant: Cook who is below a chef. The first cook is the senior assistant.

Pantry assistant: Assistant to the garde-manger who helps with cold preparation in the pantry.

Apprentice: Trainee who is learning while working.

Expediter: Person who receives orders from the servers and transmits them to the cooks.

Purchasing agent: Person who buys food and kitchen supplies and also takes competitive bids from purveyors, places orders, and maintains inventory.

Storeroom clerk: Person who receives goods, keeps records, and stores and distributes food.

Kitchen porter: Person who helps clean up, washes pots, and transports food.

Dishwasher: Person who is responsible for washing all dishes, pots, pans, and silver.

COST CONTROL

The most important aspect of operating a profitable foodservice outlet is cost control. A typical breakdown of costs as a percentage of sales revenue in a full-service restaurant is (1) food, 30 percent; (2) labor, 35 percent; (3) overhead, 20 percent; and (4) profit, 15 percent. Managers in both the kitchen and the dining room must pay close attention to these figures to avoid unnecessary expenditures. Even a restaurant that brings in a great deal of revenue cannot make money if there is waste or theft.

Operating Ratios

Restauranteurs use *operating ratios* to anaylze the success of their business in generating revenues and controlling expenses. These ratios are compared with figures compiled during previous periods by the same operation or by different outlets in a chain. Some commonly used ratios and financial terms used in foodservice are the following:

Average check: Total revenue divided by the number of guest checks. Indicates the average amount spent by each party.

Average cover: Total revenue divided by the number of guests. Indicates the average amount spent by each customer.

Food cost: Food cost divided by total revenue. Shows the percentage of revenue dollars spent on food.

Labor cost: Labor cost divided by total revenue. Shows the percentage of revenue dollars spent on labor.

Sales per employee hour: Total revenue divided by total employee hours. Indicates the amount of sales dollars generated by each employee.

Purchasing Control

Control of the purchasing function ensures that the goods received are of the quality ordered and that the prices are the best available. In most restaurants, the chef is responsible for overseeing the purchasing and the work of the purchasing agent and receiving clerk.

To control purchasing, the chef must draw up a product specification list for each item used. Figure 5-3 is an example of a spec sheet, which

---

SPECIFICATION SHEET

ITEM: Onions, Spanish
U.S. GRADE: #1

UNIT: Bag
WEIGHT OR COUNT: 50 lb

DETAILED REQUIREMENTS: Mature, firm, free from decay, uniform size and shape. Three inches minimum diameter.

_____
_____
_____
_____
_____

Figure 5-3 *Specification sheet.*

is used by the purchasing agent when obtaining product quotes from purveyors. It describes the quality, size, form, and condition of each item.

Before placing an order, the purchasing agent contacts several purveyors to obtain competitive bids. These bids are recorded, and the lowest one is accepted. When the goods are delivered, the chef or receiving clerk inspects each item, verifying its quality, quantity, and price to make sure they are consistent with what was ordered. If the goods are not acceptable, they must be returned to the purveyor, who should issue a *credit memorandum* indicating that the restaurant's account will not be charged for the returned items.

Goods must be stored in a secure, clean environment whose temperature can be controlled. As few people as possible should have access to the storage area, so as to prevent theft. All goods should be requisitioned on paper before they are removed, so that there is a record of distribution at all times. An *inventory* should be taken at least once a month. Ideally, the storeroom clerk, chef, and restaurant manager are present during the inventory. The inventory is then valued, and the cost of sales is determined. The procedure for valuing inventory is as follows:

Opening inventory	$10,000
Purchases	+ 15,000
Food available for sale	$25,000
Ending inventory	− 5,000
Cost of sales	$20,000

In this example, $20,000 is the food cost for the period. This figure should be compared with the sales data and the budgeted cost of sales figures to determine whether there is a discrepancy. If the actual food used is way over budget and not supported by an increase in sales volume, this may indicate theft or waste.

Some operations adopt a perpetual inventory system for more valuable items such as meat, seafood, and liquor. Every item entered is logged in, and when requisitioned, it is logged out. At any given time, the exact amount of the item in stock should be readily available.

When controlling liquor in operations that have more than one place of use, a different colored stamp is used on bottles sent to various locations, thereby allowing management to keep track of the liquor used in each area. Many beverage operations also inventory their liquor at the end of every bartender's shift. Bottles are measured in tenths, with five-tenths indicating half-full. The number of ounces used is then compared with the number sold. If there is consistently a discrepancy, it should be investigated, as the bartender may be overpouring or not ringing drinks on the register.

Controlling Revenue

To avoid theft and ensure maximum profitability, it is important that the restaurant or bar operator keep track of sales revenue. Policies regarding lost checks and proper use of the cash register system must be established and enforced. Guests' checks should be in duplicate form, and the dining room supervisor must keep a record of which checks were issued to which servers. At the end of their shift, the servers should be able to account for all checks issued or pay a penalty. One copy of the check is given to the customer and the other to management at the end of the shift.

The servers' ordering procedure must also be controlled so as to avoid loss. No order should be prepared without a guest check, and all used checks should be marked by the kitchen staff to void them and prevent their being used again. For beverage distribution, the same system should be used by the bartenders or the cocktail servers. Occasionally an employee will steal from the business by not ringing a sale on the register, presenting an old check to the bartender or cook, and pocketing the guest's payment for the meal or drink. One way to avoid this situation is to have a printer connected to the computerized cash register. When the order is entered in the register, the kitchen or bar automatically receives a printout and only then should proceed to prepare the item.

At the end of the day, the manager reconciles the reading from the register with the cash on hand and the guests' checks. This will ensure that all food or beverages sold were entered properly on the register and that payment was received.

Labor Control

Labor costs are controlled by several means. First, employees must be scheduled properly. When making up the weekly schedule, sales data should be reviewed to determine peak business periods, and the bulk of the week's employee hours should be scheduled at these times. Shifts can be overlapped, and part-time employees can be used to cover busy periods.

Next, a strict overtime policy should be established and followed, making sure that all overtime receives prior approval by management and can be justified. For example, one dishonest restaurant bookkeeper arrived two hours early each morning but, instead of working, used this time to nap in the women's locker room. She therefore was paid for ten hours of unproductive overtime each week. Because she arrived before her manager did, she was able to do this for several months before she was caught. Her naps cost thousands of dollars in unnecessary overtime.

Time-card control also affects labor costs. Some unethical employees punch one another's time cards, thereby indicating a longer-than-actual work period. Employees should report to their supervisor at the beginning and end of each shift to punch their time card. An alternative is to purchase a computerized time clock that allows employees to punch in and out only at the beginning and end of their shift. If they work overtime, management must override the system.

Computer Applications

All of these cost control measures can be completed more quickly and accurately with a computer, a valuable tool in both front-of-the-house and back-of-the-house organization. Learning to use new hardware may be time-consuming and frustrating, but once mastered, it can greatly facilitate all administrative functions.

Front-of-the-House Applications

Computers can organize both service and food preparation. Servers enter orders on a POS (point of sale) cash register that produces hard copy or a printout both on the guest check and in the kitchen. The chef reads the printout detailing the food order and special requests and begins production. This system reduces kitchen traffic, speeds service, and allows the wait staff more time with their customers. It also reduces the possibility of the server's selling food not entered in the register.

A computer system also aids the customer by providing a detailed check listing all expense information (Figure 5-4) with an accurate total.

BRANDYWINE
room
IN THE HOTEL DU PONT

```
--LOOKING FORWARD TO SERVING YOU AGAIN--

MARY MAH  CK# 9021
01/21/85 08:50PM 02 TABLE- 45 COVERS-  6

 2 LIQUOR      WHISKY           3.25
 3             SCOTSH PREM      3.50
 4             VODKA            3.00
 5             VODKA            2.75
 6             BOURBON PREM     3.25
   *****TOTAL LIQUOR         15.75
 1 WINE        WINE/GLASS       2.75
20             461 MARTI CABS  16.50
26             461 MARTI CABS  16.50
   *****TOTAL WINE           35.75
 7 FOOD      2 SPINACH SALAD    7.50
 8             SEASONAL SALAD   3.00
 9             SEAFOOD BISQUE   3.00
11             / BISQUE         0.00
12             /SOUP DAY        0.00
13             OYSTERS 1/2      5.25
14             SCALLOPS        15.75
15           2 CHATEAUBRIAND   42.00
16             / PRIME RIB     19.75
17             / DOVER SOLE    19.75
18             SIRLOIN SIZZLER 18.50
19             OYSTERS ROCK     6.50
21             / FRUIT TART     0.00
22             /SUCHARD CAKE    0.00
23           2 ICE CREAM        5.00
24           2 COFFEE           3.00
25             TEA              1.50
   *****TOTAL FOOD          150.50
 202.00 SBTL   0.00 TX   202.00 TTL
```

Gratuity	$
Grand Total	$

Please print name: ____________

Hotel room no: ____________ C/L Account No: ____________

Signature: ____________

Box 991 Rodney Square/Wilmington, Delaware/Phone (302)-656-8121 REV. 5/84

Figure 5-4 *Guest check from point of sale register.*

At the end of the shift, management benefits from the complete sales summary that the system provides for each server (Figure 5-5). Cash is balanced quickly and accurately on the readout.

A computerized cash register system also furnishes valuable data that assist with marketing and menu planning. The system will provide a printout listing the number of each menu item sold, the time that the transaction took place, and the person who sold it. It is simple to gauge the popularity of various menu items and also to track peak sales periods. Advertising campaigns and special offerings can be targeted to boost profitable items that are not selling well and to increase traffic during off-peak hours. And when it is time to revise the menu, this information will help management decide which items to retain and which to eliminate.

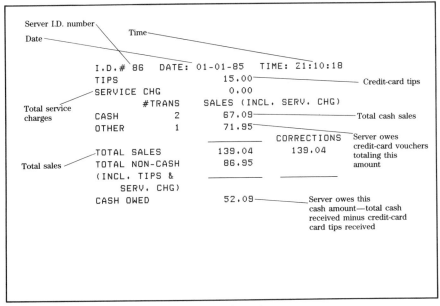

Figure 5-5 *Sales summary from point of sale register.*

Back-of-the-House Applications

The computer can help with numerous back-of-the-house functions such as accounting, payroll, purchasing, and inventory control. Many integrated systems work with the POS register to reduce inventory automatically as sales are made and to analyze food costs. Integrated systems are expensive, however, and basic functions can be performed by most data management software combined with a personal computer with a 640K memory.

A computer can also be used to manage *standard recipes.* Once the data for each menu item are entered, the cost and yield can be adjusted quickly and easily. Other applications analyze the profitability and popularity of each item, making menu planning more accurate.

Purchasing and inventory control can be simplified by using a computer (Scanlon 1985). A central purchasing list is compiled that includes all food items on hand. Each is assigned a code number that also appears in the standard recipe listing of ingredients (Figure 5-6). The recipe index can be programmed to adjust the inventory automatically. For example, if the chef requests a recipe printout for five gallons of cream of mushroom soup, each ingredient in the inventory record will reduce by the appropriate amount. These data can then be compared with the results of the physical inventory taken at the end of each period.

Food cost information can be generated daily by a computer. The

```
ITEM.... SEQ-NO PACK....LABEL DESCRIPTION.......   S PRICE..    PORTION-PRICING
         ******CEREALS                 ******
670195-7 000017 70-IND   KELL  CORN FLAKES          10.26/CS
670205-4 000017 70-IND   KELL  ASSORTED CEREAL      12.54/CS
670375-5 000017 50-IND   QUAKE 100%NATURAL-PLAIN355  8.87/CS
670390-4 000017 50-IND   G-MLS WHEATIES              7.80/CS
670450-6 000017 8-3#     Q-OAT STEAM TABLE OATS 262 15.58/CS
670490-2 000017 8-420Z   QUAKE QUICK OATS #281      13.00/CS    8-UNIT   1.625
670520-6 000017 12-280Z  NBC   REGCREAMOFWHEAT#1378 16.30/CS
670530-5 000017 12-280Z  NBC   QUICKCROFWHEAT#1379  16.30/CS
670535-4 000017 12-220Z  P/L   WHEATENA CEREAL      12.08/CS    12-UNIT  1.007
670560-2 000017 12-180Z  P/L   INST RALSTON         10.15/CS    12-UNIT   .846
670580-6 000017 12-140Z  P/L   INST MAYPO CEREAL    11.07/CS    12-UNIT   .923
670835-8 000017 12-240Z  POST  GRAPE NUTS           21.09/CS
         ******COFFEE WHITENERS       ******
680005-6 000000 12-50    CARN  COFFEE-MATE PACKETS  18.73/CS
680020-5 000027 12-180Z  NESTL EVERYDAY NON DAIRY   16.06/CS
680080-9 000027 8-5#     LOL   NON FAT MILK POWDER  56.75/CS
680085-8 000027 1-50#    LOL   -NON FAT MILK POWDER 67.91/CS
680170-8 000027 6-10     MON B MILK EVAPORATED      22.90/CS    6-UNIT   3.817
         ******SPAGHETTI PROD         ******
690000-5 000021 1-20#    MON   SPAGHETTI             7.42/CS    1-UNIT   7.420
690010-4 000021 1-20#    MON   SPAGHETTI THIN        7.42/CS
690020-3 000021 1-20#    MON   ELBOW MAC             7.42/CS    1-UNIT   7.420
690040-1 000000 1-20#    MON B SHORT ZITI            7.52/CS
690090-6 000021 1-10#    MON   CURLY LASAGNA         6.71/CS    1-UNIT   6.710
690100-3 000021 12-1#    P/L   LASAGNA              10.34/CS
690110-2 000021 1-10#    MON B FINE NOODLES          5.22/CS
690120-1 000021 1-10#    MON   MED NOODLES           5.22/CS    1-UNIT   5.220
690130-0 000021 1-10#    MON B WIDE NOODLES          5.22/CS
         ******DRY BEANS              ******
700070-6 000020 24-1#    WICKS PEAS SPLIT GREEN      8.47/CS    24-UNIT   .353
700125-8 000020 24-1#    WCKS  BEAN PEA NAVY        10.89/CS
700135-7 000000 3-10QT   DURKE POP-ALL POPCORN OIL  39.34/CS
```

Figure 5-6 *Computerized product list.*

cost of all recipes prepared is totaled and compared with the sales summary generated by the cash register. If there is a discrepancy between a recipe yield and the actual number of portions sold, management can immediately investigate the possibility of waste or theft.

PLANNING THE MENU

The menu is an important planning tool. It defines the restaurant's product, revenue, purchasing procedures, and kitchen design. But before you prepare a menu, investigate your target market and find out who your customers are, their likes and dislikes, their income, and their dining habits. Other valuable information can be obtained from analyzing your competition. You will need to know exactly what they are doing in regard to menu offerings, service, and price.

Menu Content

Before planning the menu, you must also decide on the type of service you will offer (Scanlon 1985). In addition to the more familiar service styles such as fast food, buffet, or cafeteria line, other possibilities include

Family style: Bowls and platters of food are placed on the table, from which diners serve themselves.

American: The food is put on a plate and is then served by a waitperson.

Russian: The food is brought out in tureens or platters, and then each diner is served individually by the waitperson.

French: This style is similar to Russian service, but with some tableside preparation of the food.

Your menu offerings must be compatible with your service style. If you choose to offer French service, you must include several items on your menu requiring tableside preparation, such as Steak Diane or Cherries Jubilee. Next, consider the needs of your customers. Review the demographic information you have collected, and try to pinpoint your clientele's dining requirements. Do you expect a heavy luncheon crowd from nearby office buildings? If so, you will need to offer both low-cost, easy-to-prepare items for diners on their lunch hour and more elaborate, expensive fare if you hope to attract diners conducting business at lunch. You must also consider your staff's capabilities. If your menu is elaborate, you will need an experienced chef and several assistants. A simple, fast food restaurant can cut corners on staffing.

Another primary concern is kitchen size and equipment. You must have the right equipment to prepare the items you choose. In addition, you must determine the amount that your equipment can produce during peak hours. If your menu consists mainly of grilled items and your equipment's cooking load is fifty pieces per hour, you will have to stay below this amount.

Selecting Menu Items

Today's customers want a menu offering variety and imagination. To be able to incorporate such items into your menu, you should attend food shows, read trade magazines, and stay abreast of new developments. You should also pay close attention to the nutritional value of your food offerings, including some low-fat, low-cholesterol, low-calorie items.

Select items that offer contrasts in taste, color, texture, and preparation. A good basic menu appropriate to a moderately priced full-service operation might include

Three appetizers
Two soups
Four salads
Six sandwiches
Four beef entrées
Two chicken entrées
Three seafood items
Two veal or pork entrées
Four or more desserts
Side dishes
Beverages

If your operation permits, you can expand this by offering several pasta choices or ethnic dishes to add interest. It is important to appeal to the tastes of as many people as possible but at the same time to limit the number of selections. A menu offering sixty different items will cause production problems in the kitchen. Ideally, your menu should include no more than thirty to thirty-five items.

Standard Recipes

The key to consistent food quality and cost control is to use standardized recipes. By standardizing your recipes, you will ensure that the same high-quality dish will be prepared each time. Figure 5-7 provides an example of a standard recipe card. Notice that it lists all ingredients and their amounts, direction for preparation, the recipe's yield, and the portion size. A separate card should be prepared for each item on your menu, and the cooks should be trained to use them when purchasing and preparing food. Before you can prepare a standard recipe card, you must be familiar with weights and measures. Table 5-1 is a brief review of cooking measurements.

Once a recipe's ingredients have been standardized, the recipe can be analyzed to determine its product cost. A separate cost card then should be made out for each recipe (Figure 5-8). It is best to list the amount of each ingredient in the same unit in which it is purchased. For example, if you buy onions by the pound and your recipe calls for eight onions, the amount should be changed to pounds, to facilitate the costing process. To calculate the cost per portion, the costs of all ingredients are added together and divided by the number of portions. A computer can be used for this process.

Menu Pricing

Once the menu items are chosen and the portion cost is determined, the next step is to price the items. First decide on the pricing format

```
::::::::::::::::::::::::::::::::::::::::::::::::::::::::::::::::::::::
   0615 ESCALLOPED CLAMS                        (ESCALLOPED)

   COST/PORT: $ 0.255   NO. OF PORT:1188    WT OF PORT:  4.00 OZ
   YLD:  36.00 2" PANS  POPULARITY:    0    FIDF NMBR:
   PREP UNIT:
   -----------------------------------------------------------------
   FIDF  NAME OF INGREDIENT          QUANTITY        WT/LBS  COST $
   -----------------------------------------------------------------
   3025  ONIONS,CHOPPED              2.25 GALS        12.50   1.625
   3037  CELERY,CHOPPED              2.25 GALS        11.30   1.841
   2406  MARGARINE                   3.00 LBS          3.00   0.930
   0001
   0001  SAUTE IN KETTLE FOR 5 MINS.
   0001
   1035  MINCED CLAMS DRAINED      240.00 LBS        240.00 235.200
   0001
   0001  ADD TO ABOVE AND DRAIN SOME OF THE LIQUID SO AS TO
   0001  LEAVE CLAMS JUST BARELY COVERED.RESERVE EXCES LIQUID
   0001
   2302  TOBASCO SAUCE               0.50 CUPS         0.25   1.265
   2431  LEMON JUICE                 1.06 GALS         8.48   5.283
   2304  WORCESTERSHIRE SAUCE        1.50 QTS          3.00   0.972
   2183  SALT                        1.50 CUPS         0.94   0.118
   2178  WHITE PEPPER                0.25 CUPS         0.06   0.154
   0001
   0001  ADD TO ABOVE. MIX WELL TO BLEND AND SEASON.
   0001
   5045  BUTTER SOLID                9.00 LBS          9.00  14.895
   2092  SALTINES                   36.00 LBS         36.00  33.192
   0001
   0001  USE 4 OZ BUTTER TO LINE BOTTOM OF PAN AND TO DOT TOP
   0001  MAKE ALTERNATE LAYERS, SALTINES ON BOTTOM FIRST THEN
   0001  CLAM MIXTURE
   0001  USE 1 LBS SALTINES PER EACH 2" PAN
   0001  MAKE AT LEAST 2 LAYERS OF CLAM MIXTURE AND SALTINES
   0001
   5050  MILK                        4.50 GALS        36.00   7.920
   0001
   0001  ADD 1 PT ON TOP OF EACH 2" PAN
   0001  NOTE: IF MIXTURE APPEARS TO BE TOO DRY ADD SOME OF
   0001  THE RESERVED CLAM LIQUID   BAKE  375  20-30 MINUTES
   0001  SPRINKLE A LITTLE PAPRIKA ON TOP  BEFORE BAKING

         TOTAL RECIPE COST                               303.395
```

Figure 5-7 *Computerized standard recipe.*

you will use. The menu might be *table d'hote,* in which an entire meal is purchased for one fixed price, *à la carte,* in which each item is priced separately, or a combination of both formats.

Review the price structure of your competition to determine the ranges being used. For example, you might find that the price of a

Table 5-1   Equivalent weights and measures.

Amount	Equal to
3 teaspoons	1 tablespoon
16 tablespoons	1 cup
2 cups	1 pint
2 pints	1 quart
4 quarts	1 gallon
1 gallon	128 ounces
1 tablespoon	1/2 ounce
1 cup	8 ounces
1 pint	16 ounces
1 quart	32 ounces
1 pound	16 ounces
1 gross	144 items

hamburger with fries and coleslaw is $3.00 at the low end and $4.50 at the high end. Your hamburger platter thus should be priced within this range. Many restaurant operators base their price structure solely on the results of their competitive survey, but to ensure maximum profitability, food costs, labor costs, and overhead must also be considered.

Many formulas can be used to price menu items. One of the more popular ones is the food cost percentage method, which is calculated as follows:

1. Determine the desired food cost percentage and convert it to a decimal.
2. Determine the portion food cost for the item to be priced.
3. Divide the food cost of the item by the desired food cost percentage.

Example:

$$\text{menu price} = \frac{\text{item food cost}}{\text{desired food cost \%}} \qquad \frac{\$3.00}{.30} = \$10.00$$

If an item costing you $3.00 to prepare is sold for $10.00, your food cost will be 30 percent of sales revenue. That is, for each dollar you make in revenue, $.30 will be attributed to food cost.

Designing the Menu

While you are designing the menu, keep in mind its main goal. The menu is a merchandising tool that will allow customers to select your product efficiently and accurately while at the same time reflecting the restaurant's concept. Make sure the print is easy to read, the material

```
ITEM:   Mushroom Omelet      CODE #      205

PORTION:  8 oz.              YIELD:       1
    INGREDIENT     UNIT     PRICE    AMOUNT USED    EXTENSION
    Eggs           Dozen     .60     3 ea.             .15
    Cream          64 oz    1.59     1 oz              .03
    Mushrooms      16 oz     .89     4 oz              .22
    Spices                                             .02

    TOTAL COST:    .42                 SELLING PRICE:  $1.95

    PORTION COST:  .42                 FOOD COST %:     22%
```

EXPLANATION:

ITEM:	Name of food item
CODE:	Assigned by chef to record recipes numerically and to correspond to the code number on the standard recipe card.
PORTION:	Number of ounces served to the guest.
YIELD:	Number of portions that the recipe produces.
INGREDIENTS:	List of recipe ingredients.
UNIT:	Amount purchased.
PRICE:	Purchase cost.
AMOUNT USED:	Amount needed for the recipe.
EXTENSION:	Cost of the amount used in the recipe. (Price: unit) × amount used = extension
TOTAL COST:	Sum of extension column gives the total cost of the entire recipe.
PORTION COST:	The cost of one portion. Total cost: yield = portion cost
SELLING PRICE:	Menu price
FOOD COST %:	The percentage of sales revenue assigned to food cost. Food cost: sales revenue = food cost %

Figure 5-8 *Recipe cost card.*

THE GRILL ROOM AT THE FOUR SEASONS

* available as a Main Course
** available as an Appetizer for two or more

APPETIZERS

* Carpaccio 13.50
* Spinach Pasta with Crabmeat 16.50
Chilled Green Pea Soup with Smoked Salmon 12.50
* Shrimp and Corn Cakes with Ginger and Cilantro 13.50
* Steamed Calf's Brains with Radish Vinaigrette 12.50
SPA CUISINE [R] : An Endive, Beet and Grapefruit Salad 11.50
* SNAILS Baked in Curry Butter 12.50
Blue Point Oysters 11.00
Little Necks or Cherrystones 10.00
* Duck Won Ton in the Oriental Manner 12.50

THE GRILL ROOM CURRIES

** Chicken, Mild Yellow 30.00
** Langoustine, Spicy Red 35.00
** Beef, Extra Spicy Green 32.00

MAIN COURSES

The Grill Room Rijstafel 34.00
Escalope of Venison, Juniper Cream Sauce 36.00
Veal Birds with Goose Liver and Spinach 33.50
Breast of Pheasant, Apple Roesti 33.50
** Filet of Monk Fish with Ginger and Rice Noodles 33.00
Médaillons of Lamb, Eggplant Timbale 33.50
Sautéed Dover Sole with Tomato and Mushrooms 35.00
** Baked Quails Stuffed with Oysters and Sausage 33.00
SPA CUISINE [R] : Baked SWORD FISH with Olives and Scallions 32.00
Fish Grilled on Charcoal 30.00
Sirloin Steak or Filet Mignon 32.50

WINES

Tonight's Wines by the Glass 5.75

Chardonnay, Domaine Michel, Sonoma 1985
Saint Véran, Château de Beauregard 1985
Merlot, Sterling, Napa 1984
Moulin a Vent, G. Duboeuf 1986

*Menu from the Grill Room at the Four Seasons
in New York. (Courtesy of the Four Seasons)*

is durable, the size of the menu is easy to handle, and any art work coincides with the overall concept (Gray 1986).

Some basic considerations when designing a menu are the following:

1. Avoid cute names or descriptions. The menu items should be clearly recognizable and briefly described.
2. Use the menu's focal point, located just above the center of the page, to sell high-profit items.
3. Hire a proofreader to detect misspelled words and grammatical errors.
4. Choose colors that harmonize with your decor. Darker print on a lighter background is easier to read.
5. Make sure that your customers can easily read the small print on your menu.
6. Follow the basic meal sequence of appetizers, soups, salads, entrées, desserts, and beverages.
7. Avoid an overly crowded menu. At least 40 percent of your menu should be blank space.

8. Avoid unusually shaped menus, as they can be clumsy and difficult to store.
9. If you are offering daily specials, leave a blank space on the menu for them, to enable you to list them without covering up other items.

SUMMARY

We often hear that the most common reason for restaurant failure is poor management. Competition is fierce, and so a restaurant's success will depend on proper staffing and control procedures. Many managers do not have enough technical expertise to manage properly the financial end of their business, and their profits may be eaten away by theft and waste. But the control procedures discussed in this chapter can eliminate such problems.

Procedures for purchasing, inventory control, food production, and labor planning must be established and strictly followed. Computer applications can facilitate both back-of-the-house and front-of-the-house control. Integrated systems link these two areas and provide valuable sales data.

The menu is both a control measure and a marketing tool. Standard recipes ensure consistent quality and can be easily analyzed to determine product cost. Design the menu from a marketing standpoint, and use it to promote and sell your food items.

KEY TERMS

Maître d'   Food costs
Captain   Credit memorandum
Executive chef   Inventory
Apprentice program   Standard recipes
Sous chef   American service
Garde-manger   Russian service
Expediter   French service
Operating ratios

——————— CASE STUDY ———————

Evans is a moderately priced steak house located in a suburban area. It has been in business for three years now and has established a loyal following. Although business is brisk, the owner and manager, Mike

Evans, is concerned about his narrow profit margin. Food and labor costs have been steadily escalating and now account for a large portion of the restaurant's revenue: In the past six months, food costs have risen from 30 to 38 percent and labor costs from 25 to 30 percent.

Mike installed a POS register, hoping that this would lead to tighter control, but so far it has not resolved the problem. The system he is using for service is as follows:

1. A stack of guest checks is placed near the register, and servers take them as needed.
2. Servers take the guests' orders and ring them on the register.
3. Checks are brought to the kitchen and placed on the wheel for preparation.
4. Servers are responsible for handling cash and must reconcile their sales recorded on the register with their cash bank at the end of their shift.

In the back of the house, the chef is in charge of purchasing, receiving, and storage. She takes inventory once a month and is assisted by one of the cooks. Standard recipes are available, but their use is not enforced. When the chef notices that supplies are running low, she orders them from her favorite purveyor. The goods usually arrive during the lunch rush, which makes inspection impossible. One of the kitchen porters puts them away in the storeroom.

Discussion Questions

1. Which back-of-the-house procedures may be responsible for the increase in food costs?
2. What changes in production, purchasing, and inventory control should be made?
3. What service controls need to be installed to control revenue better?

REFERENCES

Gray, Norma J. 1986. "17 Steps to Developing a Winning Menu." *NRA News* 6(2): 16–22.

Scanlon, Nancy L. 1985. *Marketing by Menu*. New York: CBI, Van Nostrand Reinhold.

Chapter 6

The Lodging Industry

The lodging industry has had a great impact on our society both economically and socially. According to the American Hotel and Motel Association's 1987 *Lodging Industry Profile,* there are 44,500 properties across America, with 1.47 million employees. In 1986 alone, more than 270 million guests stayed in hotels or motels; that is more than the U.S. population itself.

Visting hotels has become a way of life for many people. The largest number of guests are still vacationers (Table 6-1), although business travelers and conventioneers also are a major source of income.

Lodging facilities range in size from the large convention property with two thousand or more rooms to the modest bed and breakfast inn. Each appeals to a different group and fulfills its particular needs. Table 6-2 provides a breakdown of properties by location, rate, and size. Although urban hotels are the largest in size, the greatest percentage of lodging rooms is found in the 75- to 149-unit highway properties, which charge $30.00 to $50.00 per night.

One of the best predictors of a hotel's success is its location. The large chain operations spend great sums of money studying the feasibility of potential sites. A match must be made between the needs of the community and the type of operation planned. Thus it would be a poor choice to build a resort in an area in which the occupancy rate in similar operations is low. A better decision would be to enter an underdeveloped market that appears to be opening up. For example, several years ago, Marriott decided to build a hotel in Times Square in New York City,

Table 6-1   The typical lodging customer.

Percent	Purpose of Travel
20	Business
19	Conference
29	Vacation
4	Government/military business
8	Weekend trip
17	Personal/family reasons
3	Job/residence move

Source: Lodging Industry Profile, 1987. American Hotel and Motel Association.

Table 6-2   Property/room breakdown (mid-1987).

By Inventory	Property (%) (Total: 44,500)	Rooms (%) (Total: 2.69 million)
Urban	8.5	17.2
Suburban	29.3	31.2
Highway	51.8	32.4
Airport	3.9	7.4
Resort	6.5	11.8

Source: Lodging Industry Profile, 1987. American Hotel and Motel Association.

in the "red light district." Even though the area was not a typical site for a large convention hotel, the Marriott Marquis was built. The company gambled on the hotel's revitalizing the area and eventually becoming a popular convention site.

A second element of success is design. Luxury hotels must offer spacious rooms, fine furnishings, and an impressive lobby. Guests do not expect the same opulence from the roadside inn but still prefer tastefully decorated surroundings and a pleasant atmosphere.

A third factor is pricing. A rate structure is established for each property, based on competition, the target market, and profit goals. The rates must be low enough to attract guests but high enough to ensure a profit.

Finally, and most important, is service. Just as the automobile industry produces cars, the lodging industry produces service. If the product is not good, people will not buy it. Most lodging operations depend heavily on repeat business. To earn it, rooms must be spotless, employees courteous, and dining facilities excellent. Pleasing the guest must be the first priority of all employees.

Restored art deco Park Avenue lobby and the Waldorf cocktail terrace at the Waldorf-Astoria in New York. (Courtesy of the Waldorf-Astoria)

CLASSIFICATION OF HOTELS AND MOTELS

The lodging industry is both varied and fast growing. It is difficult to categorize because of the great amount of overlap; that is, a resort hotel may also handle conventions, or a luxury hotel may also be a resort. Next we shall describe the major lodging sectors.

Convention Hotels

To attract convention business, *convention hotels* must be able to accommodate large groups of people. Typically, a major convention hotel has one thousand to two thousand guest rooms, several restaurants, lounges, shops, and mammoth banquet facilities. Such hotels can be found in major cities such as New York, Chicago, Los Angeles, and San Francisco, although some smaller metropolitan areas are expanding and competing with the giants.

Guests staying at convention hotels want to be entertained. For most of them, their convention is an annual event giving the participants a break from their routine. It is important that the hotel have several impressive hospitality suites and be able to handle elaborate banquet functions. Convention hotels offer their employees perhaps the most

The 1,072-room Century Plaza Hotel, owned by Westin, hosts many Los Angeles convention groups. (Courtesy of Century Plaza Hotel)

challenging opportunity in this industry. Each department within this type of hotel is extremely specialized; yet they all must function together as one unit to service a large group. The pace is fast, hours are long, and emergencies arise by the minute. When you achieve success at a convention hotel, you will feel that you can handle anything the lodging industry might present to you.

Resort Hotels

When thinking of a *resort hotel,* most of us imagine a sprawling, modern structure located on a tropical beach or high on a snow-covered mountain. Although most resort properties are indeed in exotic places, some are near major cities like Chicago or New York. The primary attraction of a resort property is the opportunity it offers to relax, participate in recreational activities, and generally to be entertained. But not everyone who visits a resort is on vacation. Many large corporations view its isolation and pleasant atmosphere as an advantage and hold their meetings, workshops, and even small conventions at a resort property.

Working at a resort can be an enjoyable experience, especially after the hustle and bustle of a convention hotel. The pace is typically a bit slower, except during the tourist season, and the atmosphere is more

The Broadmoor, a 560-room resort in Colorado Springs, appeals to both tourists and convention groups. (Jenny McIntyre)

relaxed. Some operations allow their employees use of the recreational facilities, which is an added benefit.

Resort properties face special challenges. Their business tends to be seasonal, which means that they must employ a large temporary staff during the busy time and cut back to a skeleton crew during the off-season. Comprehensive training programs can do much to make this high turnover rate bearable.

The transportation of materials is another problem. Most resort properties are spread over several acres of land. Thus, food, beverages, and supplies must be moved from one end to another and up and down hills, often by using small trucks and golf carts.

As people continue to become more health conscious and their disposable income increases, the popularity of resorts will continue to grow. For those who do not mind working where others play, resort properties offer many opportunities to service employees.

Suburban Hotels

One market area that has experienced a great deal of growth is *suburban hotels*. As more businesses relocate to less expensive outlying areas, the

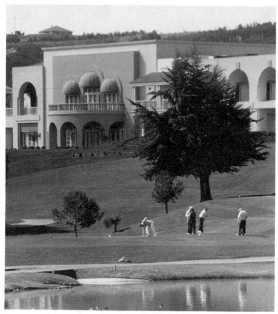

La Costa spa, in Carlsbad, California, recently under-went a $70 million renovation, adding a 50,000-square-foot conference center. (Courtesy of La Costa)

need for lodging facilities has increased. Most of these properties are smaller, with 250 to 500 rooms and limited banquet space. Many suburban hotels offer a selection of casual and fine dining restaurants to appeal to the general population in the area and frequent business travelers. Such hotels also provide some of the amenities found in the downtown hotels, such as health clubs, valet service, and lounges, but in a more convenient location.

Employment opportunities are numerous in the suburban hotels, as they increasingly compete for qualified workers. These properties offer many advantages, including an easier commute and a less hectic yet still sophisticated environment. This market is expected to expand as the suburbs' commercial sector grows.

Airport Hotels

Hotels and motels near metropolitan airports began to crop up during the 1950s, and today this area is continuing to grow. Business travelers often prefer the convenience of *airport hotels* for brief stays, and so these properties have become a major source of competition for the downtown hotels.

Airport properties face their own set of challenges. When airports close because of inclement weather, hotels are bombarded with hungry,

View of the Westin Hotel, O'Hare, a fine example of an airport property. (Photo courtesy of Westin Hotel, O'Hare)

travel-weary guests. When this occurs, a hotel can rise from 30 percent to 100 percent occupancy almost immediately. Employees may be called on to work double shifts, and feeding hundreds of unexpected guests puts an extra strain on the foodservice staff.

As the areas around airports continue to develop, competition among these properties will strengthen, each trying to outdo the other by offering more amenities and upscale accommodations. The struggle for weekend business is another problem: Although occupancy may be high on Monday through Thursday, filling the hotel over the weekend is difficult. Most properties therefore offer discount rates and special promotions to increase traffic.

Employment at an airport property is rarely boring. Owing to the high occupancy rate and the rapid turnover of guests, the pace is fast. Typically smaller than the convention hotel, the airport property is not as overwhelming. It is a quick growth area, and opportunities for employment are numerous.

Moderately Priced Properties

As room rates climbed to all-time highs during the 1970s, moderately priced hotels began popping up in greater quantity to respond to the need for low-cost lodging. Money saved on construction and amenities is passed along to the guests. Some of the more successful chains, such as Ramada Inn and Holiday Inn, have grown quickly through *franchising*. People who want to own a hotel pay a fee for the franchise and in return are provided with a well-known name, management expertise, national advertising, and a central reservation system. For companies that franchise hotels, the biggest problem is control. Without strict standards, service may deteriorate at some properties, which hurts the reputation of the entire company.

In the past, the main market for moderately priced hotels was families. But today, as hotel rates continue to rise and companies tighten their expense accounts, many business travelers are becoming concerned about room rates. Prominent chains such as Marriott and Hilton are responding to this need by developing no-frills, good-quality lodging conveniently located but offering less expensive rooms than their other hotel properties do. A good example of this concept is Marriott's Courtyard Inns. Each inn has about one hundred rooms with a thirty-seat restaurant and lounge. The furnishings are comfortable and only slightly less opulent than the chain's typical hotel; however, several of the amenities, such as room service and health clubs, have been abolished. Many of these properties are being built in suburban business areas and appeal to both business travelers on a budget and vacationers.

Opportunities for employment in moderately priced hotels are plentiful. Though not as glamorous as convention hotels or resorts, a higher management position can be reached more quickly at a moderately priced hotel, owing to its smaller size and greater simplicity.

NEW LODGING CONCEPTS

As the needs of our society change, so does the lodging industry. To remain viable and healthy, businesses must pay close attention to trends and adjust their operations accordingly. Three emerging lodging concepts that are responding to consumers' needs are bed and breakfast (B & B) inns, all-suite hotels, and geriatric care facilities. Although the philosophy behind these operations is not new, the attention they are currently receiving is. B & B inns and all-site properties are proliferating at a rate faster than ever before. The lodging industry has not truly committed itself to geriatric care facilities at this time, but some are seeing this as a consumer need of the future.

Bed and Breakfast Inns

Bed and breakfast inns are common in England, Ireland, and continental Europe. They offer an overnight stay in a private home or small inn in

The Elizabethian Inn, a bed and breakfast owned and operated by Elizabeth Farrell, overlooks the shores of Lake Geneva in Wisconsin. (Courtesy of the Elizabethian Inn)

which the traveler is treated more like a visiting relative than a source of income. B & B's have proliferated in the United States in recent years, with the large concentration being on the East and West coasts. To be successful, the B & B operator must have several comfortable guest rooms, preferably with private baths, and a large common room where guests can relax in the evening. Most importantly, the owner must truly enjoy meeting and being with people.

Guests enjoy the change from the impersonal hotel or motel room, preferring the character and quality found in the B & B or inn. The owner in turn has the opportunity to share his or her home with others and be provided with a modest income. The following case study tells the story of one successful bed and breakfast operator.

A Bed and Breakfast Success Story

Elizabeth Farrell owns and operates the Elizabethian Inn in Lake Geneva, Wisconsin. She is a retired foodservice director who formerly worked for Saga. Not satisfied with retirement, she instead channeled her energy and business sense into making a lifelong dream come true. Although some risk was involved, Mrs. Farrell's new business has enjoyed great success.

The Elizabethian Inn is located on the shore of Lake Geneva and has five guest rooms and a lovely breakfast room overlooking the lake. Initially, business was slow, and it was not until the second year that she began making a profit. Now business is booming. The inn has a regular local following, and guests also arrive year-round from across the country. Not willing to rest on her laurels, Mrs. Farrell has renovated the old barn that stands behind the inn, adding four guest rooms, a living room, a dining area, a kitchen, and a den.

Mrs. Farrell feels that the most important aspect of the business is cleanliness, and her immaculate house exemplifies this standard. Although Mrs. Farrell is extremely busy, she is also very happy with her venture. She truly enjoys serving people: Her motto "my house is your home" is the secret of her success.

Owning and operating a B & B is not for everyone. On the negative side, most require a large initial capital investment. The charming vintage mansion might be purchased for a modest sum, but the needed improvements and renovation can be extensive. In many locations, business is seasonal, and so without another source of income, the B & B owner may find it difficult to weather the off-peak times. Some operators find that they value their privacy much more than they realized. A house full of strangers with access to treasured heirlooms and antiques can cause more stress than expected.

Before opening a bed and breakfast inn, would-be innkeepers must do their homework. Many states have regulated B & B's and require inspections to make sure that building codes, zoning regulations, and health standards have been met. Many states also limit the extent of foodservice allowed. Local and state licensing offices can provide more information.

All-Suite Hotels

All-suite hotels were developed in response to consumers' demands for more spacious accommodations and more amenities. They are cropping up rapidly in large cities, near airports, and in resort areas. All-suite properties attract both frequent business travelers and tourists.

An all-suite property usually consists of 50 to 250 separate suites containing a fully equipped kitchen, living area, and one or more bedrooms. The rooms are large, and the decor tasteful. Guests feel that they are staying in a luxurious condominium and not a hotel room. The kitchen is stocked with staples, and the refrigerator contains a variety of delicacies. The stock is inventoried just before checkout, and guests are charged for what they consumed.

Many all-suite properties also contain small meeting and banquet facilities, health clubs, and restaurants. In these hotels, guests can enjoy the same luxury and convenience found in a regular hotel, for only a slightly higher price.

The all-suite properties are another excellent source of employment. The pace is not as fast as in a large hotel, but the standards are high. Housekeeping in an all-suite property is particularly challenging. Attendants must clean several rooms, and each site must be spotless. Soon the all-

A view of the lobby of the Hotel Sofitel, an all-suite property located near Chicago's O'Hare Airport. (Photo courtesy of the Hotel Sofitel)

suite properties and the existing hotels will be competing not only for guests but also for trained employees.

Geriatric Care Facilities

As the baby boomers continue to age and life expectancies lengthen, there will be more people over the age of sixty-five than ever before. More than fifty million Americans will retire over the next forty years, and the health care industry is expected to grow proportionately.

Who better to develop high-quality *geriatric care facilities* for the aged than a major hotel chain known for quality, service, and location? Marriott has applied its skill in lodging and foodservice to geriatric care and in so doing has joined other nonlodging corporations expanding into the life care services industry. Marriott is planning to begin construction of its first project in 1987 in San Ramon, California, and eventually to develop and add fifteen to twenty more such communities.

Each community will consist of one- and two-bedroom apartments built in a scenic environment. A community center will house full-service restaurants, private dining areas, meeting rooms, shops, a bank, and a library. There will also be extensive recreational facilities and a large health center. Should residents require additional care, they will receive it at the health center.

Marriott has encountered many obstacles to its community development plans. It requires residents to pay an initiation fee of $125,000, which will be refunded if the resident leaves the facility or when he or she dies. This fee has caused difficulties in regulating lifelong contracts. Marriott has also had problems with local zoning restrictions and in gaining certification as a health care provider.

But once Marriott overcomes these difficulties, it will have the initial control of a market that is sure to expand. Upscale retirees share many of the same needs as hotel guests have, and it is only logical that a lodging giant would be most able to meet them. Should Marriott be successful in this market, other major chains will likely follow.

So-called life-style communities will require trained health care workers; yet the facilities will be managed like a resort property. The communities will still need restaurant managers, chefs, housekeepers, and other lodging professionals. Although working with the aged will present special challenges, the concepts of quality and service will be the same as those found in other aspects of the hospitality industry.

OWNERSHIP OF HOTEL PROPERTIES

All the hotels belonging to a particular chain may seem at first glance to be similarly operated. That is, many untrained observers simply assume that all of Sheraton's or Holiday Inn's properties are owned by the company whose name they bear, but this is not so. There are several kinds of ownership of hotel and motel properties, such as full ownership, a management contract, or a franchise.

A fully owned porperty is one in which all of the hotel's rights are held by the chain that operates it. All profits or losses revert to the owning corporation. New systems and procedures are often installed and tested at these properties before being adopted throughout the corporation.

When a company desires accelerated growth, it looks to a *management contract* with a group of investors that might include construction contractors, insurance companies, or other large businesses. But because they know nothing about the hotel's operation, they enter into an agreement with Hilton or Hyatt or another chain that has responsibility for managing the property. The chain usually receives a management fee and a percentage of the profits. It is given full responsibility for staffing and operating the hotel, using its employees and its procedures.

Another way for a chain to expand quickly is to franchise, or sell, its name and technical expertise to an investor. Unlike a management contract agreement, in which the property is completely operated by the lodging chain, the franchised hotel is managed by the investor. The investor is trained and supported by the parent company, which usually has strict quality standards. If the franchisee does not maintain the company's standards, the franchise contract can be revoked and the owner forced to sell the business. It thus is important that the company be selective in awarding franchises because its good name is at stake. Several poorly run franchised properties can give the whole company a bad reputation. Advantages to the franchisee include extensive training, access to national advertising, brand recognition, and a central reservation system.

THE OPENING OF A HOTEL

There is a nothing more exciting than helping open a new property. Although it requires a great deal of work and long hours, participants truly feel that the operation's success or failure rests on their shoulders. An opening also provides an in-depth look at the workings of a hotel. It is amazing that such an enormous task can be achieved so smoothly with teamwork.

Table 6-3 shows a typical schedule for a hotel opening. Although it may vary from hotel to hotel, it will indicate what must be accomplished before the grand opening.

Preopening Challenges

Murphy's law can certainly apply to preopening management: Whatever can possibly go wrong, will. Proper planning can do much to alleviate some of these concerns; yet the nature of the task lends itself to unexpected calamities. For instance, problems often arise with labor unions: A strike can cause severe delays in the construction schedule. The grand opening date was changed six times during one project with which I was involved. These constant delays resulted in public relations problems and lost convention business. There may also be problems with faulty design or poor building materials that can later cause electrical failure or a partial building collapse. One can only hope that these problems will occur and be resolved before grand opening.

Staffing may also be a problem. Labor markets in different parts of the country vary and may not always offer the caliber of employees needed. For example, should a hotel open in a rural part of the country, it may be almost impossible to find waitpersons experienced in French service for the fine dining facility. But seasoned hotel openers view these and the many other problems as just part of the excitement of creating a new hotel.

Table 6-3   Preopening schedule.

Before Opening	Activity
2 years	Complete architectural design Meet all local zoning regulations Review bids and choose contractor Obtain financing
18 months	Have key executive staff in place Request bids on furniture and equipment Begin construction Set up working sales and project planning office
16 months	Devise rate structure Aggressively market property Make contact with community groups and officials
12 months	Expand sales staff Decide on opening date Develop organizational chart
6 months	Begin recruiting department heads and key managers
4 months	Have management staff in place Recruit hourly employees
2 months	Complete opening-day activities Begin "punching out" or inspecting completed section of property Bring in key task-force managers Organize new departments
1 month	Complete hiring of new employees Fit new employee uniforms Train and orient new staff Bring in task-force employees Practice with dry runs
1 week	Hold soft opening Complete training
Opening day	Hold grand opening celebration

SUMMARY

The lodging industry is one of today's most varied and challenging businesses. Employment opportunities abound and will be even more numerous in the future. As the lodging industry continues to evolve, its scope will broaden. At first, most hotels were found in urban areas, but now they are being built near airports, suburban office complexes, and rural areas. Bed and breakfast inns, all-suite properties, and geriatric care facilities are some of the newer concepts. The challenges presented by the lodging industry are many, especially in preopening management. But the excitement of being involved in building a new business far outweighs its difficulties.

KEY TERMS

Convention hotels	Moderately priced hotels
Resort hotels	Bed and breakfast inns
Suburban hotels	All-suite hotels
Airport hotels	Geriatric care facilities
Franchises	Management contract

CASE STUDY

J. R. Hotels, Inc., is planning a new property in a growing suburb of a major city. The following is a brief summary of the area's demographical situation.

Population

The suburb has a population of sixty thousand people. The median income is $20,000, and 60 percent of the area's residents live in single-family dwellings.

Business

This suburb houses two corporate headquarters, employing a total of three thousand people. The suburb is also planning to build two high-rise and one low-rise office complex in the next five years.

Competition

To date, there are several moderately priced properties in the area and one large resort hotel. The average occupancy rate is 85 percent.

Discussion Questions

Working within the limits of the information provided, discuss the following questions:

1. Can this area support another hotel? Why or why not?
2. Based on the information provided about the competition, discuss the pros and cons of building a convention hotel, resort property, moderately priced hotel, suburban hotel, B & B, and all-suite property here.
3. Before committing itself to the area, what additional information should J. R. Hotels consider?

Chapter 7

Lodging Operations

I f you enjoy variety, travel, and excitement but do not mind hard work and constant change, a career in hotel management may be the right choice for you. It provides the opportunity for extensive travel and brings you in contact with many interesting people. There are rarely dull moments in the hotel business. As a catering manager, you might be called on to organize a reception for two hundred Swedish truck drivers, none of whom speaks English, or as a restaurant manager, you might have the opportunity to serve the president of the United States. It is an exciting business.

Major hotel chains require that their managers be willing to relocate. At the beginning of your career, you will have little say about when or where you move. After a year in New York and a year in Hawaii, you might be offered a great opportunity in East Overshoe. But as you gain seniority in the company, you will have more control over this aspect of your job.

One advantage found in the lodging industry is the variety of positions it offers. Hotel employees have a wide range of skills—from an executive chef with an extensive culinary background to a director of security familiar with the latest advances in electronic surveillance. The job requirements of each department are different, but each department must be able to communicate if the hotel or motel is to function properly.

KEY DEPARTMENTS AND THEIR FUNCTIONS

The organizational chart depicted in Figure 7-1 is typical of a major hotel with seven hundred or more rooms, indicating the top-down management system found in most operations. Information from the general manager flows down the various lines of communication, eventually reaching the lower-level employees. Although this chart depicts the departments commonly found in a major hotel, this organization may differ somewhat from property to property.

Hotel Executives

The *general manager* of a hotel must have a thorough knowledge of accounting, administrative functions, food and beverage, and guest services. The best general managers are those able to make quick decisions under stress. They also must be able to lead and inspire their staff. The general manager's attitude determines the climate of the entire hotel. Some are authoritative leaders, whereas others use a more participative management style, encouraging employees to become involved in the decision-making process.

The hours are long and the stress can be overwhelming, but most general managers find that the benefits of the position far outweigh the drawbacks. General managers have an excellent salary, stock options, bonuses, an automobile, and the use of the hotel facilities. Many corporations also provide luxurious living quarters, meal service, and maid service.

The general manager has the overall responsibility for operating the hotel profitably and providing the best possible service for its guests. Typically, general managers have had at least ten years of hotel experience, hold a bachelor of arts or science degree, and have demonstrated their ability to lead and motivate others.

Reporting directly to the general manager are the *resident manager* and the *executive assistant manager*. They supervise the department heads within the hotel and work closely with the general manager to solve problems and establish goals. By promoting an employee to executive assistant, the corporation is indicating that it believes that this person will eventually be able to run an entire hotel. An executive assistant can expect to move up to resident manager and, later, general manager of a smaller property.

Sales Department

The *sales department* is responsible for soliciting and booking convention groups and frequent business travelers. Its main goal is to sell guest

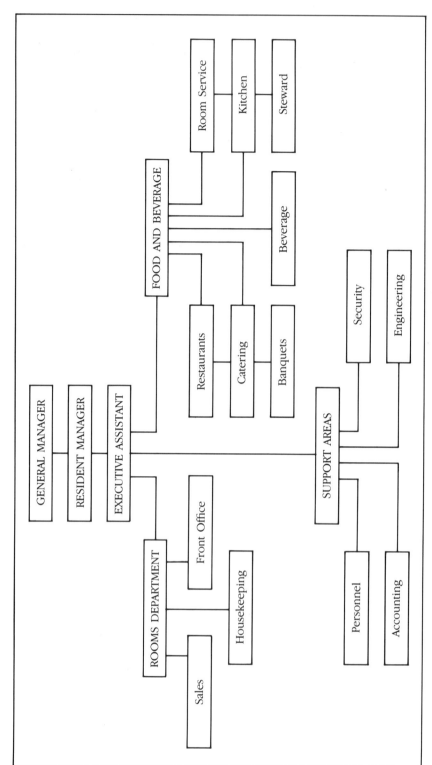

Figure 7-1 *Organizational chart for hotel with 700 or more guest rooms.*

The beautifully appointed Penrose Suite at the Broadmoor in Colorado Springs. (Bob McIntyre)

rooms and meeting space to large groups. If a convention is booked and food is also required, the *catering department* will help plan the banquet. The catering department is composed of a director and several sales managers. In addition to coordinating the managers' work, the director of sales is responsible for setting room rates, designing packages, and marketing special events. Each manager is given an area of responsibility based on seniority and experience. New managers are generally responsible for local or transient business, such as designing special weekend packages to attract couples in the area. At the next level is the sales manager responsible for executive business travelers, who solicits accounts with local companies and major corporations in return for a reduced corporate room rate. The third and most demanding account is *convention* bookings, which involve planning large meetings that last for several days and generate a great deal of revenue for the hotel.

When a large convention group is interested in booking at a particular hotel, the sales manager's first move is to try to obtain headquarters status, which means that the convention group will hold most of its meetings and food functions at that property. Once the hotel has been

One of fourteen meeting rooms located in the Ritz-Carlton in Naples, Florida. (Courtesy of the Ritz-Carlton, Naples)

filled, any "overflow" will be sent to nearby hotels. Most major convention groups have their own meeting planners who work with the sales managers. These planners prefer to do business with properties that are organized, well located, and offer the best room rate. The sales manager must make sure that the quantity of rooms desired is available, negotiate a special group rate lower than the published room rate, and then, through the reservations department, block or book the rooms needed. But the sales manager's responsibility does not end here: Follow-up is important. If food functions are needed, the sales manager will help the catering manager book banquet space and plan large events. The convention service managers, responsible for the physical setup of banquet rooms, work closely with the sales and catering managers. When the convention group arrives, the sales manager must be available to solve any problems with check-in, to inspect the rooms, and to ensure that the proper billing procedures are followed. The sales manager also attends large events to make sure they are run smoothly.

Good sales managers must be organized administrators and must also be able to deal effectively with guests and have a good working relationship with the front office, housekeeping, and catering.

Spacious suites with private balconies at the Ritz-Carlton in Naples, Florida, overlook the Gulf of Mexico. (Courtesy of the Ritz-Carlton, Naples)

Front Office Operations

The front office performs several functions, all relating to guest service. Hotels now have become more automated, and most have a computer system linking the front desk, reservations, housekeeping, and sales. Therefore, to progress in this department, employees must become familiar with the particular company's system. The front office is headed by the director of front office operations, who is responsible for hiring and supervising the managers and employees. To reach this position, an employee must have had several years of experience in this department, typically having worked up from a desk clerk position.

Reservations

The reservations department is overseen by a reservations supervisor or manager and is responsible for reserving guest rooms. Reservations can be made in several ways: through a central reservations office with an "800" number, locally through a hotel reservation clerk, or through the sales department. The reservations department employs several clerks who take reservations by telephone. It is important that these clerks be familiar with the hotel's guest rooms so that they can describe to the customers the accommodations available and handle special requests if necessary.

During a hotel's busy season, when convention groups are in town, management attempts to achieve as close to 100 percent occupancy as possible. Because of the great number of no-show reservations, some hotels overbook to reach this percentage. Overbooking is accepting more reservations than there are rooms available, a practice that does

*One of 463 guest rooms at the Ritz-Carlton in Naples,
Florida. (Courtesy of the Ritz-Carlton, Naples)*

have risks. Management attempts to estimate the number of no-shows
likely. But should it overestimate this number and more guests arrive
than there are rooms available, problems will occur. A guest will become
very annoyed when he or she arrives with a confirmed reservation and
is then told the hotel is full. When this happens, the hotel must pay for
the guest's first night at another lodging facility and provide transportation
there. Overbooking occurs infrequently, but when it does, it is an in-
convenience for the guest and an expense for the hotel.

Front Desk

When guests arrive at the hotel, they check in at the front desk. The
clerk verifies the guest's reservation on the computer terminal, his or
her method of payment, and length of stay. When a guest is ready to
check out, the cashier presents the bill, having posted, or added, any
recent charges.

Front desk clerks do need a fair amount of technical knowledge, and
the following are some terms with which they must be familiar:

Open: There are plenty of rooms available for guests arriving without
reservations.

Closed: There are no rooms available for people without reservations.

Restricted: There are rooms available only to those willing to pay the
full price assigned to the room.

Rack rates: The full price is assigned to each guest room.

Group rate: A discounted room rate has been assigned by the sales
department.

Walk-in: A guest arrives without a reservation.

Guaranteed: A room will be honored until check-out time the next day, regardless of when the guest arrives.

No-show: A guest does not arrive and fails to cancel the reservation.

Desk clerks report to one or more front desk managers or supervisors. Aside from technical knowledge, the most important requirement of employees at the front desk is courtesy. These individuals represent the front line, and when problems arise, the guest will look to them first for a solution.

The Concierge

The *concierge,* long a mainstay of European hotels, has finally become an important staff member in many of the larger American lodging operations. This individual, sometimes also called the assistant manager, has a desk in the lobby and is asked to solve a variety of guest problems, ranging from the relatively simple, such as making restaurant reservations, to the more complex. For example, one concierge was asked to locate a pound of ox gallstone used to make a heart medication, and another managed to find two games of Scrabble in Russian. A concierge in a major hotel was even called on to lend his desk to a visiting Moroccan

Crystal chandeliers adorn the lobby of The Breakers. The hotel's Italian frescoed ceilings add to its charm and help recapture the spirit of the Italian Renaissance in Palm Beach. (Courtesy of The Breakers)

dignitary (Austin 1987). Requirements for a position as a concierge include fluency in one or more foreign languages, familiarity with the city, ability to deal effectively with guests, and, of course, resourcefulness.

The Bellstand

The bellstand is staffed by a captain and several guest service attendants, who are responsible for handling the guests' luggage, escorting the guests to their rooms, and providing information about restaurants and entertainment in the area. An able attendant will point out the particular features of the guest's room, answer any questions the guest might have, and also take the time to promote the hotel's food and beverage facilities. Once again, courtesy is the most important job requirement in this department.

Housekeeping

The housekeeping department is responsible for cleaning all guest rooms and public spaces in the hotel. It is a big job and, if not done properly, can diminish the guests' satisfaction with their stay. It is important that all guest rooms be spotless and high standards be met.

The housekeeping department is headed by the director of house-keeping who is assisted by one or more managers. Supervisors are assigned to one or more floors and are responsible for checking the work of the guest room attendants in their area. The room attendants have a heavy work load, with as many as eighteen rooms to clean each day. The nature of this job, combined with less than extravagant pay, can lead to morale problems, and so many operations have developed creative systems for motivating their employees. For example, a major hotel chain thought up a particularly successful contest: Room attendants accumulate points for attendance and thoroughness of cleaning. They receive bonus points if they can find a small stuffed animal hidden in often overlooked spots, like closet shelves or under the bed. The persons with the most points at the end of a fixed period of time win cash prizes.

Housekeeping works closely with the front desk. It must give the desk a room status report indicating whether a room is available. Many hotels have adopted a computer system linking the front desk and housekeeping to transmit this information. The following are some terms used to refer to room status:

Vacant in order: A room is vacant and clean, ready to be booked.

Vacant out of order: A room is vacant but has not yet been made up.

Occupied: The room is occupied by a guest.

Occupied baggage: The room contains the guest's luggage, but the guest is currently out of the room.

Occupied person: The guest is in the room.

Sleeper: The guest is scheduled to depart today but has not yet checked out.

Out of order: Repairs are needed in the room, and until its status is changed, it cannot be sold.

Food and Beverage Department

The food and beverage department consists of several separate areas, all relating to the purchase, preparation, and sale of food and beverages. It is headed by the food and beverage director who oversees all operations. The director must have extensive knowledge of each of these areas and must make sure that they are up to standard. He or she must have expertise in food cost control, menu development, marketing, and the selection of managers. Typically this individual has moved up the ranks, having worked in several different departments.

Food Production

The executive chef is in charge of all aspects of food purchasing, production, and storage. He or she must have excellent culinary skills and, in addition, be a good administrator and leader. Some executive chefs possess little formal training, having worked their way up from the bottom, but others have risen more quickly, having earned a culinary degree. Many hotels are seeking to upgrade their culinary reputations by hiring prestigious chefs. According to Lydia Shire, chef at Seasons, in the Bostonian Hotel, the emphasis on top-quality chefs is escalating. She observed a "change in attitude among hotel general managers. They are looking for really bright, super-duper chefs who will add something special to the dining room" (Niepold 1986, p. 21). In the February 27, 1986, issue of the *Boston Globe,* Robert Levy awarded Seasons four and a half out of a possible five stars, thereby rating it as one of the best restaurants in town.

Today's hotel chefs must be creative and also have sound management skills. The days of the temperamental chef are numbered. Instead, chefs must be able to lead and motivate their employees using current management techniques.

The executive chef is assisted by the *sous chef,* which means "under chef" in French. Some hotels also employ one or more food production managers, who supervise the cooks and prepare some of the food. Also reporting to the chef is the executive steward, who oversees the entire washing operation, including dishes, silver, and glassware. In larger properties, the executive chef also has a purchasing agent and a receiving clerk who handle the purchase and storage of all food.

Restaurants

Hotels today offer their guests a variety of dining experiences, from fine dining to quick service. Each is operated as a separate entity overseen by its own manager. The restaurant manager, like an independent operator, is responsible for scheduling, payroll, hiring, training, and purchasing of supplies. Yet the hotel restaurant manager is part of a larger operation and must abide by all hotel guidelines and procedures. This manager reports to the director or assistant director of food and beverage. The restaurant manager works with his or her supervisor to set an annual budget, forecast sales, and develop special promotions.

Each restaurant employs its own servers, buspersons, hosts or hostesses, and, if large enough, dining room supervisors. Most restaurant managers have had several years of experience in lower-level positions and, more frequently today, hold a degree in foodservice management. Restaurant management is an excellent position for advancement and can lead to positions in catering, banquets, beverage, and eventually higher-level management.

Beverage Department

The beverage manager is responsible for the purchasing and service of all liquor in the hotel. In a larger property with more than one bar and possibly a nightclub, the beverage manager is assisted by a lounge supervisor and a storeroom clerk. The beverage manager is also in charge of banquet liquor service and oversees the banquet beverage operation.

One of the most important aspects of this manager's job is installing tight control systems to avoid theft. Storerooms must be kept locked at all times, with access to the keys strictly controlled. Guest checks must be used for all liquor service, and each bar's liquor must be inventoried at the end of each day, with the count compared with the sales records.

Beverage managers work their way up, usually starting as bartenders. They are well paid, receiving a salary and a percentage of the liquor sales. Although this position can lead to higher management, many beverage managers prefer not to cross over to foodservice, being happy to remain in this position for a long period of time.

Room Service

At best, most hotel room service departments break even. The costs of labor, equipment, and food are high, making it difficult to show a profit in this area. But guests enjoy the convenience of room service and would certainly be disappointed if it were not offered.

The room service department is headed by a room service manager or supervisor. In larger properties, this manager is assisted by one or more captains who supervise the servers. Room service operators take orders over the telephone and so must have good communication and sales skills.

The key to a successful room service operation is organization. Food must be delivered promptly and at the correct temperature. Guests will become annoyed if their breakfast order arrives an hour late. Incorrect orders also complicate the system, as it takes a geat deal of time to return an incorrect order to the kitchen, have it redone, and transport it back to the guest's room.

Room service management provides excellent training in food and beverage and can lead to a position in catering or banquet management.

Oz nightclub high atop the thirty-two-story tower of the Westin St. Francis in San Francisco. (Courtesy of the Westin St. Francis)

Catering Department

The catering department is responsible for booking and planning all banquet foodservice events. When a convention group is booked in the hotel, the sales manager blocks guest rooms, and the catering manager plans the food functions.

This department is headed by the director of catering who supervises the work of the catering managers. As in sales, each catering manager is responsible for a particular area, with the more experienced individuals planning functions for large convention groups. Catering managers must have extensive knowledge of food, wine, table settings, and menu development. They may also be asked to arrange for flowers and entertainment.

When a guest is interested in holding a food function in the hotel, the catering manager records the function date, attendance figures, type of function, food preferences, size of the budget, and billing procedures. The manager then checks the *catering diary,* or logbook, to make sure that space is available. After the banquet room has been reserved, the next step is to plan the menu. Although each hotel has standard menu offerings, some clients prefer to use their own. In this case, the catering manager must confer with the executive chef or the banquet chef to make sure that the hotel can prepare such a menu. A banquet event order listing all the specifics regarding the function then is prepared and circulated to the departments involved. Two days before the function, the catering manager must confirm the *guaranteed attendance number,* or final guest count. The client will be charged for the guaranteed number of attendants even if not all come.

The banquet manager is responsible for service at all catering functions. He or she hires and schedules waiters, oversees the banquet setup, and carries out the service. The catering manager also attends the larger functions and handles any last-minute problems or guest requests.

The proper execution of catering functions involves a great deal of teamwork. The catering manager, sales manager, executive chef, banquet manager, and banquet beverage manager all must work together. To avoid errors, the catering manager must be organized and check and double-check the arrangements; otherwise, major problems can arise. For example, at a recently opened convention hotel, a catering manager double-booked the ballroom, meaning that there were two groups scheduled to hold dinners in the same room at the same time. All other space was reserved that evening, and so one group was forced to hold its function in the lobby area of the ballroom. Needless to say, the guests were not pleased, and the hotel was forced to "comp" the function, or not charge for it. Errors of this kind are rare, but even small problems can result in lost business.

Hotel catering is exciting. The hours are long and the job can be stressful, but the rewards are many. Many catering managers have previous experience in restaurants, banquets, or room service. They can advance to director of catering and then are in an excellent position to become director of food and beverage.

Support Areas

A hotel has several departments that are not directly responsible for serving the guests or producing revenue but assist the operating areas. Most heads of these departments have had special training or education in their field. And most do not progress according to their general hotel management experience but often are promoted to corporate positions in which they are assigned a region and oversee the operation of their specialized area in several hotels.

Engineering

The engineering department is responsible for the building's physical upkeep. The chief engineer has an extensive background in building maintenance and, in a large property, supervises the plumbers, painters, electricians, and carpenters.

When a department manager notices a problem or needs a job done, he or she fills out a work order and sends it to the engineering department. Jobs are prioritized, and employees are assigned by the chief engineer or his or her assistant.

This department is especially important when a hotel is being built or renovated, as the general manager depends on the chief engineer to oversee the work being done.

Accounting

The accounting department is headed by the *controller,* or comptroller, who is assisted by specialized managers and clerks. The accounting department is divided into accounts payable, which is responsible for paying the hotel's bills, accounts receivable or the credit department, which collects fees, and payroll, which determines employee wages. The accounting department also helps with budgeting, or setting the hotel's spending limits, and forecasting or projecting expected sales revenues.

The controller generally has a degree in accounting and may be a CPA. In addition to overseeing the department's operation, the controller acts as a financial adviser to the general manager.

Personnel Department

The personnel department is responsible for hiring and training new employees. Some departments also handle insurance administration and payroll. The personnel department is headed by the director of personnel, who may be assisted by a manager, recruiter, benefits administrator, and training coordinator, depending on the operation's size.

Personnel has become quite complicated, particularly in the area of selection. Strict federal guidelines have been established regarding preemployment inquiries and discrimination. Employees in this area thus have usually had formal training in personnel management.

MANAGEMENT TRAINING PROGRAMS

All of the major hotel chains offer some type of comprehensive training program for new managers. Most trainees are recent graduates of hotel management programs but have had limited experience in the industry. Corporate recruiters visit college campuses and interview senior students. When selecting trainees, they look for flexibility, ambition, good communication skills, and dedication.

Employees are trained at established hotels and have little say over which geographical area they will be assigned to during this period. They are paid a minimum salary while in training but receive an increase when assigned to a permanent position. The training program might begin with an intensive, week-long session at the company's corporate headquarters, followed by assignment to a property. The trainees spend three to six months at a particular hotel, rotating from department to department. Most of the programs are well organized and train the participants in all pertinent areas in each department. The trainees are supervised by the personnel director or training manager at the hotel, and their progress is monitored closely. The trainees are required to do a great deal of studying and to make a report at the end of each departmental rotation.

At the end of the training program, the new managers are assigned to a permanent position and property. The hotel chain will attempt to place them in their preferred geographical location but cannot guarantee it. If a new manager is interested in the front of the house, his or her first job might be front desk manager. A new back-of-the-house manager might begin as a food production supervisor or restaurant manager. There is opportunity for advancement, and a new manager's success depends greatly on his or her performance in this first position.

SUMMARY

The essential ingredient of hotel management is teamwork. The various departments that make up the organization must work together closely to serve its guests. Each department has a specific task and must rely on other areas in order to perform it effectively.

The general manager oversees the entire hotel operation and is assisted by the resident manager and the executive assistant. Each department is led by a director who supervises several mid-level managers. As a result of this multilevel management structure, hotels offer many opportunities for advancement.

Perhaps one of the best ways for a recent college graduate to begin a career in hotel management is to be accepted into a management training program. The trainee is rotated to each department in the hotel, thereby gaining expertise in the overall operation in a short period of time. At the end of the program, the trainee will be assigned a permanent entry-level management position.

KEY TERMS

General manager	Convention services
Resident manager	Concierge
Executive assistant manager	Catering diary
Sales department	Guaranteed attendance
Catering department	Controller

—————— CASE STUDY ——————

A.T.A. Industries is planning to hold a major convention in Los Angeles next year. Its meeting planner, Joan Reynolds, would like to assign the convention's headquarters to the Ventura Palace Hotel. It has an excellent reputation, extensive banquet facilities, and adequate exhibit space. The convention will last for several days, and in addition to guest rooms and meeting space, the group will require breakfast, lunch, and dinner each day. A.T.A. Industries is also planning to have a large party on the last evening, at which the food, decor, and entertainment all will have the same theme.

Discussion Questions

1. When Joan contacts the sales department, what questions should the manager ask her regarding the group's needs?

2. Joan is referred to a catering manager to plan the food functions. What information will the catering manager need to reserve space and begin planning the event?
3. What factors might cause Joan to look elsewhere for a convention headquarters?

REFERENCES

Austin, Beth. 1987. "Guardian Angels." *Chicago Tribune,* January 14, sec. 7, p. 21.

Niepold, Cecelia. 1986. "Hotel Chefs Are Cooking up New Reputations for Their Restaurants." *NRA News* 6(5): 21.

Chapter 8

Travel and Tourism

When we think of the tourism industry, travel, vacations, and recreation immediately come to mind. But the scope of tourism is much broader than this, encompassing travel agencies, bus lines, taxicabs, air carriers, restaurants, hotels and motels, gas stations, cruise ships, local attractions, and many other businesses that produce travel-related products. All of these fields create millions of jobs. According to the U.S. Travel and Tourism Government Affairs Council, tourism is among the top three largest employers in thirty-nine states.

This chapter will look at some of the many facets of travel and tourism, particularly their relationship to the lodging and foodservice industries.

THE HOSPITALITY INDUSTRY AND TRAVEL

People travel for a variety of reasons: for a visit to friends, for business purposes, or for pleasure. The hospitality industry, incorporating food and lodging operations, is closely linked to tourism. Travelers often stay at hotels and tend to dine out more often. Local attractions such as Disney World in Orlando, Florida, or Union Station, in St. Louis, include numerous foodservice operations. When travel and tourism are prospering, the hospitality industry also benefits.

Many hotel and restaurant operators have recognized this link and have begun to promote tourism in their area by joining their local chamber of commerce and visitors' bureau. When business operators and local government work together, they can revitalize a dying tourist

Perhaps the most distinctive and best-known feature of St. Louis Union Station is the Bedford limestone Headhouse with its 230-foot-high clock tower, visible throughout downtown St. Louis. Built in 1894 to resemble a medieval bastioned gate, the Headhouse covers two city blocks along Market Street. St. Louis Union Station, a National Historic Landmark, was once the largest and busiest passenger rail terminal in the world. (Photo courtesy of St. Louis Union Station)

market. For example, around 1980, St. Louis was experiencing serious economic problems, which were made worse by a lack of travel and convention business. So, with the cooperation of the city government, local business owners worked to change the city's image. Several new attractions were developed, including Laclede's Landing, which houses restaurants and shops in renovated historical buildings, and Union Station, which includes a luxury hotel and mall. Several chains have built large downtown hotels in the city, and a convention center was established. Recently, the St. Louis Convention and Visitors Commission stated that visitor expenditures in the metropolitan area amounted to more than $1.3 billion annually and had provided more than 33,000 jobs. When business and local government join forces to increase tourism, everyone benefits.

THE ECONOMIC IMPACT OF TOURISM

According to the U.S. Travel Data Center, in 1986, tourism generated $269 billion in sales, which amounted to 7 percent of the United States' national product. In hearings held by the House of Representatives

The spectacularly restored Grand Hall, which once served as a waiting area for train passengers, is now the lobby and the lounge of the Omni International Hotel at St. Louis Union Station. The Grand Hall features Romanesque arches, a 65-foot barrel-vaulted ceiling, elaborate stencilwork, plasterwork highlighted in gold leaf, and antique stained-glass windows. (Photo courtesy of St. Louis Union Station)

relating to tourism and small businesses, a prominent Arkansas resident stated that if travel suddenly ceased, the number of jobs in Arkansas would fall by as much as 10 percent, and each resident would have at least a $125.00 reduction in income. Travel and tourism indeed have an important local and national economic impact. Tourism also has a *multiplier effect;* that is, when tourism increases, local business increases too. In addition to more jobs, tourism indirectly affects the health of the economy by stimulating the production of goods and services needed to support these businesses. For instance, the textile and wholesale food and equipment industries must raise production to supply new restaurants and hotels, which means more jobs and also more tax revenue for local and state governments. In a tourism hearing before the House Small Business Subcommittee, Rick Dantzler, a Florida state representative, described the multiplier effect caused by Cypress Gardens. In 1935, Cypress Gardens was a "cypress swamp," but after Dick Pope's development of the area, it has become a 223-acre "national treasure," providing jobs for an average of seven hundred people each year.

On an international level, tourism can acutally help the economy. For several years, America has been importing more goods than it has exported, thereby causing a *trade deficit.* International tourism actually helps reduce this trade deficit by bringing "new" money into the system from foreign countries. According to the U.S. Travel and Tourism Government Affairs Council, expenditures from a West German couple traveling to the United States for vacation might total $2,200, an amount equivalent to exporting five refrigerators or 293 pairs of jeans. We can also lower the trade deficit by encouraging Americans to travel in their own country rather than going abroad. This keeps American dollars in this country and increases the health of its small businesses.

Many factors affect the health of the travel industry, both nationally and abroad. When the price of gasoline declines, as it did in recent years, Americans are more apt to travel in the United States and Canada. The European and Mediterranean market was threatened by the surge of terrorism that began with the hijacking of a Trans World Airlines jet in 1985. Coupled with the fall of the U.S. dollar against several foreign currencies, these two factors made travel abroad less attractive to Americans, which meant that more people stayed home and spent their vacation dollars here, resulting in increased profits for American businesses.

TRAVEL SEGMENTS

The tourism industry is enormous and continues to grow. According to the U.S. Travel Data Center, tourism is supporting 5.2 million jobs in a variety of skilled and nonskilled professions across the country.

The essence of the tourism industry is to advise and serve those who are traveling or are planning to do so. Tourism includes sales agencies, transportation, activities for vacationers, and lodging and camping accommodations. This section will examine these areas and especially the career options they offer.

Travel Agents

The first travel agency was started by an Englishman, Thomas Cook, in the mid-1800s. Since then, the primary mode of travel has changed from steamship to airline, but the *travel agents'* job is basically the same. They serve clients by arranging transportation, lodging accommodations, escorted tours, packages, and individual itineraries (Figure 8-1). Travel agents do not usually charge clients for their services but receive their income from commissions paid to them by the airlines, hotels, steamship companies, and railroads. This amount is from 7 to 10 percent of the sale.

Wholesale travel agents also organize tours and packages but do not usually deal directly with clients, instead selling vacation packages to travel agencies and groups. Wholesalers sponsor familiarization or "fam"

The Homestead, a four-season resort hotel located on a 15,000-acre wooded estate in the heart of the Alleghenies in Hot Springs, Arkansas. (Photo courtesy of The Homestead)

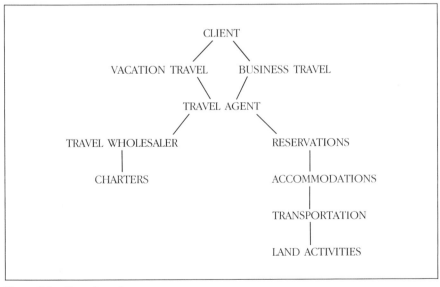

Figure 8-1 *Travel services.*

trips for travel agents, which give them an opportunity to sample the tours they will be selling to their clients. For many agents, the opportunity to vacation in exotic parts of the world while they work makes them overlook the long hours and sporadic pay that comes with the job. Fam trips allow travel agents to recommend tours to clients and to gauge the worth of such tours. To qualify for a fam trip, the agent must have been a full-time employee with his or her particular agency for at least one year and have a minimum of six months' tariff/ticketing experience. Figure 8-2 describes an itinerary for a typical fam trip.

It is also the travel agent's responsibility to protect clients from unreliable packages. Sometimes, unreliable wholesalers go bankrupt without warning; hotels are overbooked; or there are last-minute price increases on packages. An experienced, well-informed agent can prevent these problems.

Travel agents provide a multitude of services. All the client needs to do is make one phone call, and the agent will make reservations for

---

San Francisco Tour (FAM)

Cost: None

Host Property: The Golden Palace

ITINERARY HIGHLIGHTS

Thursday: Afternoon arrival at San Francisco International Airport and transfer via Golden Gate Tours to the Golden Palace Hotel; welcome reception and dinner at the hotel. Balance of the evening free.

Friday: Breakfast seminar at host property; depart the Golden Palace for a visit to Chinatown and Fisherman's Wharf. Lunch on your own at Fisherman's Wharf. Dinner and evening free.

Saturday: Breakfast seminar at host property. Tour of Alcatraz and the Presidio. Luncheon on Telegraph Hill. Afternoon visit to museums and Japanese Garden in Golden Gate Park. Dinner in Chinatown.

Sunday: Breakfast at leisure; check-out of hotel and depart for a tour of Stanford University in Palo Alto followed by return to San Francisco International Airport and return flights home.

Note: Air fare paid by carrier.

Figure 8-2 *Familiarization trip.*

various means of transportation, lodging, local attractions, and sight-seeing tours. The agent also counsels clients and recommends appropriate services.

The initial contact between travel agent and client is important. The agent must first listen carefully to the individual, sum up his or her needs, and then provide information. A good travel agent is also a salesperson. The agent does more than just answer questions; he or she must also describe the benefits of each service presented.

Once the initial contact is made and the client's needs are assessed, the next step is to make travel reservations with hotels, airlines, railways, or steamships. Travelers are value conscious today, and so it is important that agents find the best prices available.

Because most long-distance travel today is by air, agents work closely with the commercial airlines. To advise clients and make reservations, they must have a complete copy of the tariff structure for each carrier. The *airline tariff* includes the cost of the transportation and all rules covering such passage. Owing to deregulation, fares are constantly changing, and the agent must note all revisions on the tariff as they are transmitted. After reviewing the tariff, the travel agent contacts the airline and books the flight. After verifying the fare with the airline, the agent is ready to ticket the flight. The agent may also be asked to make steamship, railway, bus, or hotel reservations, either in coordination with air travel or separately.

Another option is the charter vacation, which allows individual travelers to take advantage of lower group rates. Charter vacations are typically sold on a round-trip basis and operate on fixed schedules. The *charter* or package may include transportation, lodging, sight-seeing, meals, entertainment, and transfers between hotels and airports. Packages offer advantages to both the travel agent and client. They are economical, and the agent needs to make only one reservation for an entire trip. In the past, most charters were affinity based, meaning that travelers had to be part of a common-interest group in order to take advantage of the special rates. But today there are many nonaffiliated, or public, charters that do not have this stipulation. Many charters require that a complete tour package be purchased, but others allow the client to purchase only the airfare at the special rate. It is the agent's job to filter out the unreliable charters and steer clients toward packages that are not likely to include long delays or misleading information regarding accommodations.

Many travel agents have developed their skills while on the job. More frequently today, agents complete college-level training programs where they learn the basics of the job. In addition to frequent travel, other job responsibilities include

Office sales: This includes greeting customers, determining their travel needs, planning and presenting possible travel arrangements, assisting in making decisions, and attending to details.

Telephone sales: Often the travel agent has little face-to-face contact with clients but must sell and make travel arrangements by telephone.

Reservations, fares, and ticketing: These are the agent's technical duties and include making transportation and hotel reservations, writing tickets and vouchers, and computing fares and charges.

Clerical: There is a great deal of paperwork to be done, which requires filing and typing skills.

When hiring agents, most employers look for people who have had extensive travel experience, communicate well, and have a good appearance. Organizational skills are a must, and fluency in one or more foreign languages is a plus.

Standards for the industry are set by the Institute of Certified Travel Agents. Individuals who have completed their courses are Certified Travel Counselors and have the right to use this title after their names.

Travel Wholesalers

Travel wholesalers design and operate tours around the world and market them through retail travel agencies and airlines. Travel wholesalers investigate lodging accommodations, transportation, and cruise lines to create exciting vacation packages. The travel wholesalers' job also involves selling, but rather than dealing with individual vacationers, wholesalers sell to the retail travel agencies. Travel wholesalers employ representatives whose job duties are similar to those of an agent. Some also employ *tour guides* who personally escort groups visiting foreign countries. Nearly all guides are foreigners well versed in the language and culture of the country being toured.

Tourist Attractions

As disposable incomes increase and travel costs decrease, the world is becoming smaller and more accessible to the average American. In the past, travel was a luxury reserved for the affluent, but today the family vacation can be enjoyed by middle-class Americans. Accordingly, many new travel destinations have been developed to appeal to them, providing vacationers with a reason to visit a particular area and with a source of entertainment and activity.

Theme Parks

Today when we think of an amusement park, the most spectacular of them all, Disney World, immediately comes to mind. But amusement parks have been around for hundreds of years. One of the earliest was Vauxhall Gardens in England, dating back to the 1600s, and Coney Island opened in the United States in 1895 (Powers 1984).

The first modern theme park, Disneyland, opened in 1955 in a rural area of Orange County, California. Skeptics said that it would never be successful, but all now realize how wrong those early critics were (Dickson 1984, p. 285). Most of today's amusement parks followed Walt Disney's lead and are directed toward a particular theme. Some parks adopt a historical theme, whereas others, like Busch Gardens in Florida, recreate an African safari. Another successful Florida attraction, Sea World, is both exciting and educational. The successful theme park of today offers family entertainment, a place where children of all ages can relax, enjoy themselves, escape from reality, and even be educated.

But as the population ages, theme parks must adjust to appeal to the

Designed to resemble an ornate Moorish temple, the new 1,200-seat Moroccan Palace theater at Busch Gardens, The Dark Continent, in Tampa, Florida, features pointed archways, turreted rooftops, and elaborate tilework. Artisans from Fez and Marrakesh spent months decorating the theater inside and out with colorful mosaic panels and etched friezes. (Photo courtesy of Busch Gardens, The Dark Continent)

Fearless riders of the reptilian Python coaster at Busch Gardens, The Dark Continent, in Tampa, Florida, rocket through the revolutions of two 360-degree loops and travel at speeds of up to 50 mph. The Python ranks as one of the most thrilling rides in the South. (Photo courtesy of Busch Gardens, The Dark Continent)

More than 500 animals representing a variety of species coexist on the Serengeti Plain at Tampa's Busch Gardens, The Dark Continent. The park exhibits a total of more than 3,000 birds, mammals, and reptiles (most in natural habitat displays) and is currently ranked among the nation's top zoos. (Photo courtesy of Busch Gardens, The Dark Continent)

Great America has four of the greatest roller coasters in the Midwest. Thrill seekers can challenge these white-knuckle favorites: (top left clockwise) the American Eagle, the park's giant wooden racer; the Demon, featuring two vertical and two corkscrew loops; the Whizzer with its quick spirals and high-banked turns; and the Tidal Wave, a 55-mph trip forwards and backwards through a 76-foot-high vertical loop! (Photo courtesy of Six Flags Great America)

older audience. Once again, Disney broke new ground with the development of its Experimental Prototype Community of Tomorrow, better known as the *EPCOT Center,* which gives visitors a glimpse of the food, life-style, and industry of tomorrow.

Career opportunities at theme parks are numerous and varied and can be categorized into three areas:

Attractions management: These managers are responsible for the smooth operation of the entire park. They manage transportation, ticketing, individual attractions, and parking, and their primary job is selecting, scheduling, training, and supervising employees.

Food management: Most of today's theme parks offer a wide range of dining choices, from fast food to fine dining. Foodservice managers in theme parks share similar responsibilities with those in other hospitality operations. There is one difference, though: volume. Some theme park food outlets must serve nearly 100,000 people per day and must do so quickly and efficiently. Theme park foodservice managers thus must be systems oriented to meet this tremendous volume.

Merchandise management: Theme parks earn much of their profit from their retail outlets, providing weary guests with a welcome respite from the weather and crowds. The key to success in this area is the product, for customers want unusual souvenirs that offer quality and value.

Theme parks have a huge management structure and frequently have openings for both skilled and unskilled employees. Most of their managers have college degrees and have worked their way up through the ranks. At Disney, each employee's job is viewed as equally important. All entry-level employees, whether in sanitation, foodservice, or one of the other many departments, are called *hosts* and *hostesses.* Disney has a theatrical environment, and appropriately, instead of personnel, central casting does its hiring. Employees do not wear uniforms but are fitted for costumes, no matter which position they hold. Disney employees are reminded that when they deal with customers they are on stage and must always play the role of service representative.

Urban Centers

Cities across the nation are competing for tourist dollars by developing and marketing their own attractions. New facilities are being built to give vacationers a reason to visit their community. San Francisco has Fisherman's Wharf; San Diego has its famous zoo; St. Louis has Union Station; and New Orleans has the Superdome. Other cities, like Las Vegas and Atlantic City, New Jersey, have legalized gambling and are designed almost solely for entertainment. Such development also leads to the growth of both food and lodging operations, thereby increasing the need for employees in these and other businesses that serve tourists. Such development requires a strong link between local government and the business community. City officials can do much either to facilitate or deter the creation of a tourist market. By working together, urban

The colorful pushcarts located throughout St. Louis Union Station create a festival atmosphere around every corner. Shoppers can browse among an ever-changing array of goods—from handmade puppets, pottery, and handblown glass to snowcones, balloons, and chocolate sculptures. (Photo courtesy of St. Louis Union Station)

and rural areas can promote tourism without detracting from the year-round residents' quality of life.

Parks and Recreation

Camping has been popular for many years. In 1864, Yosemite, in California, was established as the first park, and in 1916, the National Park Service was established. The demand for outdoor recreation is growing, and now many sophisticated camping facilities offer power hookups for large recreational vehicles. Other parks are building their own lodging facilities to appeal to visitors not interested in camping. Some national parks also offer convention facilities. Asilomar, located near Monterey in northern California, provides the best of both worlds, by featuring lodging accommodations that rival those found in luxury facilities in a setting complete with nature trails and wild animals. Of course, rustic settings are available in national parks for those whose idea of roughing it does not include a queen-size bed.

There are also numerous privately owned campgrounds scattered across the United States. Some of them, such as Kampgrounds of America (KOA), are franchise operations. After the initial investment, operating costs are minimal. If the location is good, a campground owner can make a comfortable living, even though the business is usually only seasonal.

The Airlines

The airlines have experienced tremendous growth since 1970, a trend that is expected to continue. The airlines offer a broad range of positions, good pay, and excellent benefits, including free airfare. Career opportunities can also be found in the foreign carriers maintaining facilities in the United States, such as KLM (Netherlands) and SAS (Scandinavia). Some of the typical job offerings include

In-flight chefs: Supervise the preparation of meals for airline passengers. Some airlines, such as United, have their own foodservice operation, but others contract from private caterers.

Customer service representatives: Book flight reservations, secure hotel and car rental reservations, and ticket passengers. Customer service representatives perform many of the same duties as do travel agents, but they work for a particular airline.

Passenger service representatives: These representatives have much contact with the public. Their responsibilities include providing passengers with information, arranging ground transportation, directing flights, and giving special attention to the elderly, disabled, and children.

Reservations agents: Make telephone reservations for customers through the airline's computerized system. They quote fares, help passengers choose flights, give flight information, and reserve hotel and car rentals.

Ticket agents: These agents do basically the same work as do reservations agents, but instead of telephone sales, they have direct contact with customers and work at airports or city ticket offices.

Flight attendants: These attendants are responsible for performing all phases of customer service on board the aircraft. Their job is physically taxing and also highly stressful. The future outlook for employment is good. Applicants who have completed two years of college with previous customer service experience have the best chance of being hired.

Steamship and Cruise Lines

Employment on an oceangoing vessel offers a variety of rewarding careers and the opportunity to travel to foreign lands. Although few positions are available, it is possible for both skilled and unskilled workers to find them. Passenger ships usually have three departments:

Deck department: Mates are responsible for directing the ship's speed and course and maintaining the deck and hull. Deck officers supervise the work of the sailors, who comprise the crew.

Engine department: Employees in this department operate and maintain the engines and machinery on board the ship.

Steward department: The steward department is responsible for cooking and serving food and maintaining living quarters aboard the ship. This department has the most employment opportunities for individuals with a hospitality-related background.

In addition to these departments, cruise ships also employ hairdressers, social directors, entertainers, salespersons, and clerical workers.

It is difficult to gain employment aboard foreign-flag ships, but there are some opportunities with American lines. The Delta Queen Steamboat Company, with offices in St. Louis and San Francisco, is an American line featuring both river and ocean cruises.

MARKETING TOURISM

Tourist trade would not exist if someone were not marketing and selling the services to would-be travelers. Each segment of the industry depends on marketing to maintain its share of the vacationing population. The hotels must sell their properties to wholesalers who design packages; the wholesalers then sell to the retail travel agencies, which market directly to the consumers.

Many businesses find that the best marketing approach is a group effort. A region's lodging, foodservice, and travel-related operations often join forces to promote tourism in that area. Many strategies can be used to capture the leisure market (Go 1984, p. 271), including the following:

1. Sell tourism to local civic leaders and politicians by demonstrating its economic significance to the community. Back up ideas with facts and figures.
2. Describe the area's local and regional features to prospective visitors. Use a variety of media channels, including television, radio, newspaper, and magazine advertisement.
3. Promote the area by sending news articles to both local and national newspapers and television stations. A feature story in a local paper might even be picked up nationally and provide extensive exposure, free of charge.
4. Sponsor special events and festivals to attract different groups and encourage repeat visits.
5. Make tour operators, convention bureaus, and transportation companies aware of the area.

6. Consider developing a multiattraction passbook in cooperation with other local operators.
7. Become involved in the local chamber of commerce and work with it to promote tourist-related businesses.

By combining resources, local businesses can greatly increase the number of tourists and help their operations grow.

SUMMARY

Tourism affects almost every aspect of society, and countries depend on it for economic growth, jobs, and recreation. Tourism has given Americans a higher quality of life, more employment opportunities, and lower taxes. It encompasses a wide variety of ventures, from the huge airline or lodging corporations to the many small travel- and food-related operations serving tourists. By generating spending, especially that resulting from foreign travel in the United States, tourism helps reduce the national trade deficit. Tourism also has a multiplier effect: When travel dollars increase, the financial well-being of many related businesses improves, new jobs are generated, and disposable income rises.

Tourism offers many career opportunities to both skilled and unskilled employees. Many jobs in the industry are attractive, especially those in travel agencies and transportation, because of their liberal travel benefits.

The hospitality industry, particularly its foodservice and lodging segments, is closely linked to travel and tourism. Today's operators must become aware of tourism and the impact it can have on their business. By forming a partnership with the travel industry and working together to promote tourism, hospitality operations can ensure greater profitability, both now and in the future.

KEY TERMS

Multiplier effect
Trade deficit
Travel agent
Wholesale travel agent
Airline tariff

Charters
Tour guide
EPCOT Center
Yosemite
In-flight chef

—————— CASE STUDY ——————

Susan Johnson recently purchased a one-hundred-room motel in a small town in northern California. The area was once a popular resort community, but over the past ten years, tourism has decreased significantly. Many businesses have closed, and currently only a few motels and restaurants are still operating. This drop in tourism is primarily the result of an image problem the town has had. It is located on a river that is quite scenic but several years ago had a pollution problem. It has since been solved, and testing has indicated that the water is now clean. But during this time another problem also arose: The number of families visiting the area gradually decreased, and a rougher clientele began coming up from the nearby metropolitan area.

Susan hopes to revitalize the area and win back the tourist trade it once had. The town has many advantages: It is located between two major cities, is surrounded by national parks, is on the outskirts of the California wine country, and is only about a half-hour from the Pacific Ocean. The town itself also is interesting, having several historic buildings and an old covered bridge.

Susan has convinced several local business owners to meet with her and formulate a plan to bring tourists back to the area.

Discussion Questions

1. What particular attractions might be developed to appeal to tourists?
2. How should the local businesses market their community?
3. Where should their marketing efforts be directed so as to ensure reaching a higher-quality clientele?

———————————————

REFERENCES

Dickson, Duncan R. 1984. "A General Overview to Theme Parks." In *Introduction to Hotel and Restaurant Management,* ed. Robert A. Brymer. Dubuque, Ia.: Kendall/Hunt, pp. 285–288.

Go, Frank. 1984. "The Hospitality Tourism Connection: A Cooperative Plan of Action." In *Introduction to Hotel and Restaurant Management,* ed. Robert A. Brymer. Dubuque, Ia.: Kendall/Hunt, pp. 271–280.

Morrison, James W. 1980. *Travel Agent and Tourism.* New York: Arco.

Powers, Thomas F. 1984. *Introduction to Management in the Hospitality Industry.* New York: John Wiley.

Stevens, Laurence. 1981. *Your Career in Travel and Tourism.* Wheaton, Ill.: Merton House.

PART 2

Service:
The Cornerstone
of the Hospitality
Industry

Chapter 9

Guest Service

The American economy has evolved into a *service economy,* and the service industry is likely to account for two-thirds or more of the U.S. economy by the year 2000. Leading this boom will be the hospitality industry. The service-driven America of the future will be much different from the industrialized society of our past. During the industrial era, the product was tangible. Quality control depended on following procedures and then testing and double-checking the commodity for accuracy. But the product of the future, customer service, is not so easily controlled. Although company policy is still important, service depends largely on people.

In the hospitality industry, service is a commodity. It is a basis for competition, with those companies providing the best service coming out on top. During their rigorous orientation program, Disney trainers ask new employees, "What do we make here at Disney?" Some might think the answer would be a better theme park, money, or entertainment, but the answer the trainer is looking for is "We make people happy." This is Disney's product, and it is making it better than anyone else. This is the basis of its five decades of success. But unfortunately, many other members of the hospitality industry pay only lip service to the importance of customers. They say, "the guest is number one" but continue to ignore the methods their employees are using to serve guests and even develop policies that dampen the guest's satisfaction.

SERVICE VERSUS HOSPITALITY

Today's definition of service has changed. In the past, service meant driving up to a gas station and having four attendants filling the tank, checking oil, washing the windshield, and checking the tires. Today it means prepaying an attendant who sits behind bullet-proof glass, filling your own tank, and washing your own windows. We have traded all the extras for cheaper prices and a quicker turnaround. But is this what the American consumer really wants? One successful gas station has returned to its old full-service format with great success. Customers pull up and leave their car with the attendant, and while they enjoy free doughnuts and coffee, their auto is refilled, checked, and groomed by the employees. Because the station depends on volume for its profit, it offers all the extra frills for only a little more than the cost of just gas at a self-service station.

Many companies today feel that the key to service is offering a quality product efficiently and quickly. New computerized systems have been devised, but unfortunately, many customers find the electronic employees more amiable than their human counterparts. For example, when visiting fast food operations, most people prefer the convenience of the drive-up window where they are greeted by a huge talking menu board. And the most efficient method for checking into a hotel is to use its computerized system.

In this book *Megatrends* (1982), John Naisbitt observes a formula by which we respond to technological development. He believes that when a new technological advancement is made, it must be counterbalanced by a human response. Thus we are a *high tech/high touch* society. We want the greater service delivered by new systems, but at the same time we still need the human element. Perhaps increased automation in hotels has been offset by the revitalization of the country inn and the bed and breakfast. As observed by authors Albrecht and Zemke in *Service America!* (1985), the few contacts that guests do have with employees are more important than ever before. As the food and lodging industries continue to create more efficient systems for providing guest service, the role of old-fashioned hospitality will become more important. Guests will have less contact with people, but they will place added emphasis on the experiences they do have. Companies in turn must place the same emphasis on guest relations that they are giving to systems development. As we enter the age of service, we must not lose sight of the guests' need for hospitality.

IMPACT OF POOR SERVICE

According to a 1985 Gallup poll on eating out, 83 percent of the individuals surveyed stated that they would avoid a restaurant with poor service. Compounding this, 34 percent stated that they would pass on their gripes about a restaurant to a friend. Thus while it is becoming more and more difficult for restaurants and hotels to find experienced employees, at the same time, consumers are becoming more and more particular about service.

Corporations such as Hilton Hotels, Disney, and McDonald's are addressing this issue and have instituted companywide customer-service training programs for both management and employees. Yet even though an enormous amount of time and energy is being spent on improving guest relations, this whole process can be destroyed by employees who commit a *30-second blunder* (Magnesen 1985). That is, although a hotel sales manager may have spent months grooming a new client, the entire account can be lost in just a few seconds by a surly desk clerk at check-in.

Can This Customer Be Saved?

When we enter a hotel, restaurant, or other service establishment, we expect to deal with polite, knowledgeable, well-groomed employees, but unfortunately this is not always the case. How often have we contacted the customer "service" department of a business, expecting help, only to be met by an apathetic representative? A great deal can be learned about guest service by examining both our positive and negative experiences with it. As you review the following blunders, try to determine what went wrong and think of a way to remedy the situation.

Blunder 1

A diner in a restaurant ordered an appetizer to be followed by a steak entrée. He requested that a glass of milk be served with his steak. The waitress quickly returned with his appetizer and the glass of milk. The customer said, "I wanted to have the milk with my steak." The server responded, "Well, don't drink it until your dinner arrives."

Blunder 2

At a wedding reception in a fine hotel, the banquet waiter was serving an expensive French champagne at the head table. As he poured a glass for one of the bridesmaids, a large, black bug came out of the bottle with the champagne. The waiter apologized profusely and immediately reached for a clean glass and proceeded to pour her another serving from the bottle.

Blunder 3

As reported in the *Wall Street Journal* (Hughes and Landro 1986) a gentleman made a luncheon reservation for three at a prominent Los Angeles restaurant. He and another member of the party arrived on time and were seated. They ordered drinks, but after ten minutes, the third person in their party had not arrived. The hostess then asked that the two individuals move to the bar to wait for their friend. When one of them said he saw his tardy friend drive by looking for a parking space, he was accused of lying. "Pardon me?" the gentleman asked. "You're lying," the hostess repeated. Fortunately, the third member of the party arrived just at that moment.

Blunder 4

A hotel guest called room service at 6 A.M. to order breakfast. She showered and dressed, but by 7 A.M. her breakfast still had not arrived. She phoned room service to inform them of the problem and was told that the orders were backlogged. After asking when her breakfast would arrive, the operator said possibly by 8 A.M. The guest told the operator that she had an 8 o'clock meeting and could not wait that long. The operator then said, "Well, you should have known better than to order room service if you're in a hurry."

Blunder 5

A diner in a family-style restaurant ordered a salad with vinegar and oil dressing. When the salad arrived, there was no dressing accompanying it. The guest reminded the waiter that he wanted vinegar and oil and was told, "The vinegar and oil are busy on another table. You'll have to wait until they're done."

Above and Beyond

Though service glitches are all too frequent, occasionally employees have been known to go that extra mile to help guests. Just as we can learn from the errors of others, so we can learn from their successes. It is true that a 30-second blunder can alienate a customer, but a 30-second triumph can also win loyalty. As you read the following positive service encounters, determine what was done to turn a potential problem into a success.

Triumph 1

A European guest in a large Chicago convention hotel followed a familiar custom and placed his dress shoes out in the hallway overnight, expecting them to be shined. After dressing the next morning, he opened his door to retrieve the only pair of shoes he had brought on the trip, only to find that they were gone. He was very angry, and immediately called housekeeping. The clerk then explained that American hotels do not offer the same shoe-shine service as European hotels do and that his shoes had probably been stolen. The gentleman explained that he had an important meeting that morning and had no other shoes. The clerk was very helpful and went out and purchased another pair of dress shoes for him.

Triumph 2

A man was attending a convention at a major hotel for the second year in a row. During the convention's opening night reception, he stepped up to one of the banquet bars to order a drink. As he walked up, the bartender had a manhattan waiting for him. Amazed, he asked, "How did you know that's what I wanted?" and the bartender replied, "I remembered your drink from last year."

Triumph 3

At a small country restaurant, locally famous for its sumptuous desserts, the pastry chef has become something of a celebrity. After finishing her morning baking, the gray-haired, grandmotherly woman goes into the dining room and, moving from table to table, asks the guests how they are enjoying their meal. She offers suggestions for dessert and, when asked, shares her recipes and offers advice to novice bakers.

Triumph 4

A couple on vacation was staying in a large downtown hotel with their five-year-old and seven-year-old sons. The woman was in the gift shop with the boys and stopped for a moment to choose a magazine. When she looked back up, her sons had disappeared. In a panic, she searched the lobby area and, unable to find them, went to the front desk for help. The desk clerk calmly notified the police and hotel security. Every available employee pitched in to help search the entire building and surrounding street. An hour later, one of the maintenance workers found the children in a restaurant storage closet, happily tearing open packets of sugar and emptying them on the floor.

Triumph 5

A hotel guest had forgotten to make dinner reservations for his and his wife's twenty-fifth anniversary. It was 4:00 P.M. when he finally remembered to call the hotel's fine dining restaurant. Unfortunately, there was a large convention in town, and the dining room was booked for the evening. When the guest explained the situation, the hostess volunteered to make a reservation for him at one of the local restaurants outside the hotel. After calling eight of the better restaurants with no luck, she finally located one that had had a cancellation. The grateful guest went down to thank her, but she refused the twenty-dollar tip he offered, saying that she was only doing her job.

Lack of Respect

Many service employees feel that they just cannot get any respect from management or the company they work for. This is the most commonly cited reason for the nosedive that service as a profession has taken. Customers, restaurant owners, and managers do not consider serving a highly skilled or prestigious occupation (Lydecker 1986), and regard service jobs as lower-level positions relegated to unskilled, inexperienced employees. And unless employees hold a tipped position, their pay is relatively low.

But serving customers can be a complex job. Employees are called on to sell, to coordinate the customer's experience, to promote goodwill, and also to be creative. But management often fails to give its employees the credit they are due. If service is to improve, it must be viewed as a profession.

MANAGING SERVICE

Perhaps the best way to improve service in a company is to look at the way that the business itself is managed. The focus of most planning and policy setting in lodging and foodservice organizations is financial. Few good managers would attempt to run a restaurant without drawing up an annual sales forecast and budget. But how many also formulate a service strategy? It is easy to get caught up with day-to-day concerns and lose sight of the business's primary purpose: guest service.

The Company Mission Statement

The first step in creating a service management system is to make a *company mission statement*. This can actually become the business's theme and should encompass all that the organization hopes to accomplish.

McDonald's statement, "Quality, Service, Cleanliness, and Value," shortened to QSC&V, exemplifies its high standards.

Service As Policy

Next, the theme of a company's mission statement must become part of its policy. Just as a business develops policies to be followed for purchasing, employee conduct, and department functions, it must also develop a service policy. McDonald's has put into practice its QSC&V standards. For example, it uses only prime beef; if a burger is not sold in exactly ten minutes, it must be thrown out; and cashiers must make eye contact with and smile at every customer.

The service establishment must develop a working definition of service quality. Guest expectations should be defined, and the behavioral objectives for meeting them should be identified. Table 9-1 lists some common service standards and the actions required of employees to meet them. Notice that the behavioral objectives are specific. Rather than just noting that service should be speedy, a time has been assigned. When these standards are communicated to employees, there will be little confusion about what is expected of them.

Beyond Charm School

The service policy must be communicated to employees at all levels of the organization. Service procedures manuals and job descriptions in-

Table 9-1   Standard procedures for guest service.

Standards	Objectives
Provide speedy service	Seat guests within two minutes of arrival when possible Take order within five minutes after seating guest
Provide courteous service	Servers smile when greeting guests Servers use guest's name when possible Servers thank guests for their patronage
Provide accurate service	Servers repeat all orders back to guests Servers return to check on guest three minutes after serving food
Use suggestive selling	Servers recite daily specials Servers are familiar with menu and can answer all questions about it Servers suggest wine and dessert
Handle problems correctly	Return improperly cooked food to kitchen promptly and give priority to correcting problem Servers first attempt to resolve problems; then, if necessary, contact the dining room supervisor

corporating the information listed in Table 9-1 should be written. Through proper training, there is much that service organizations can do to foster good guest relations. Unfortunately, many companies simply send their employees to customer service workshops, feeling that by doing so, they have done their duty. Unfortunately, many employees view their experience with "charm school" as unrewarding and irrelevant to their problems.

Still other companies fail to look at the organization as a whole when designing this training. For example, one major hotel chain developed an excellent program. It set standards and developed training materials addressing guest relations. Unfortunately, this material was geared to only front-of-the-house service employees; management and back-of-the-house employees were left out. The service employees enjoyed the training program and found it beneficial. They learned more effective ways of dealing with guests. But when they returned to their departments, they found that their managers and supervisors—not familiar with the new program—felt somewhat threatened and so did not reinforce the service employees' new behavior. Improvement as a result of the program thus was short-lived.

Rather than offering service training to only one group, organizations should follow Disney's example: Its service training program extends from top-level management to newly hired dishwashers. The employees attend a rigorous three-day orientation and later return periodically for more "fairy dusting." Employees are encouraged to attend seminars, which will help their chances for promotion.

Training may also be ineffective if employees have underlying concerns that are not being considered. Perhaps employees are not motivated to provide good service because they want to retaliate against a poor supervisor. Or they may feel that they will provide only the level of service that their poor pay warrants. Marriott does an excellent job of dealing with the entire picture: It spends more than $20 million annually on training and reinforces this by providing regular performance reviews and allowing each employee to participate in Marriott's profit-sharing plan. Marriott also gauges morale at each hotel by surveying the employees' satisfaction. Guest relations training is important, but alone it is simply not enough.

Rewarding Service

After service standards are in place, and training has been given, the new behavior taught to employees must be reinforced. Many companies in the hospitality industry use incentive programs to accomplish this. But to be effective, the program must reward the desired behavior.

Employee-of-the-Month programs are popular, but all too often, the criteria for selection are vague. Specific guidelines for selection must be established and communicated to all employees so that they will know exactly what is needed for them to be chosen. Other operations award employees for receiving positive guest comment cards. If administered properly, this can be an effective way of reinforcing good service. Still other operations give guests tokens to be dispersed to employees who provide good service. The employees can then exchange the tokens for money or prizes.

Service can be reinforced if it is made part of the performance review process. If providing good service is a performance criterion, it will affect the employee's pay increase and eventual eligibility for promotion.

The One-Idea Contest

It is also important that service employees be given a voice in running the operation. Rather than being viewed as peons who must be managed, service employees must be viewed as sales representatives. Service employees are closer to the customers than anyone else is and can give management valuable suggestions on improving guest satisfaction.

Stew Leonard, owner of a dairy store made famous by Tom Peters and Nancy Austin in *A Passion for Excellence* (1985), has mastered the art of customer relations. He has made his employees an integral part of his program and relies on them for insight. Periodically, he takes fifteen employees, including hourly workers and new hires, to survey the competition. He challenges them to come up with one idea to make Stew Leonard's better as a result of the visit. His employees are inspired to improve the business. They feel they can make a difference and are motivated to become enthusiastic sales representatives. Leonard's *one-idea contest* could certainly be used in the hospitality industry. Why not send employees to a new hotel or restaurant to look at the competition? The ideas they bring back may be worth a great deal more than the cost of a meal or a room for a night.

Service-illiterate Management

In addition to fostering customer service awareness in front-line employees, management must also be concerned with guest relations. Many managers today have received excellent technical training at the college or university level, and after being hired by a company, they continue to develop by completing a management training program. As a result, however, the new managers become experts at cost control and department administration but are not prepared to deal with customers. The new managers are *service illiterate*. Rather than going out on the floor and talking with customers, they hide in the office, completing their paperwork. On the rare occasion when the manager must deal with an irate guest, he or she is unprepared. Unfortunately, some of these technically competent managers just cannot deal with people. Thus it is important, especially in hospitality-related operations, to give to management the same care and concern about service as is given to line employees.

Managers must get closer to the customers. They must become front-line supervisors and actively deal with guests' problems themselves. Employees will use their supervisors' behavior as a model and can learn just by seeing how they handle a problem. Management also needs to communicate more frequently with guests, asking them, "How was your meal?" or "Is there anything we can do to make your stay more pleasant?" If more formal contact is needed with customers, a focus group can be held, inviting in customers to talk about how they view the business. The focus group leader covers a list of topics, ranging from menu offerings to the employees' friendliness. Or it may be best to hire a professional marketing representative to act as the group leader, as customers are more likely to give this person honest answers.

Another way to assess an operation is to try to view it from the customer's perspective. What is the guests' first impression? How are the employees treating them? If you can see problems, so can your customers.

SUMMARY

Customer service is the responsibility of everyone in an operation, from top management downward. Service is the number one commodity in the hospitality industry. Although many technological advances will make service smoother and faster, guests still want old-fashioned hospitality. They expect a lot when dining out or staying in a hotel, and it takes a companywide commitment to meet these high expectations. Organizations must devote as much time and effort to planning service as they do to the business's financial aspects. Too many managers are technically proficient but service illiterate.

A company can be only as good as its employees. Service workers must receive the respect and pay that their key positions deserve. Training is not enough to promote good guest relations but must be accompanied by fair pay, incentive, regular performance appraisal, and supervisors sensitive to the needs of both the employees and the guests.

KEY TERMS

Service economy
High tech/high touch society
30-second blunder
Company mission statement
QSC&V

Employee of the month
  programs
One-idea contest
Service-illiterate management

─────────── CASE STUDY ───────────

Bill Hendricks is with a major hotel chain and has just completed its management training program. He has been assigned to be the front desk manager at a small property and has been told by the general manager that the department has a lot of problems and that he hopes Bill can solve them.

After a few weeks on the job, Bill realizes that the administrative aspects of the department are fine. The paperwork is up to date and the budget is being met; yet complaints keep coming in from other departments and customers. He realizes that the problem lies with the employees and so he takes a close look at the desk, trying to see it as the guests do, and what he observes is unsettling. The clerks are sloppily dressed; their uniforms are wrinkled; and their hair is unkempt. Not only do they not smile at customers, but they fail to make eye contact. When guests ask questions, they are met with disdain. Lines are long, and the clerks seem to make little effort to speed up service.

Bill knows that he must improve the employees' attitude and guest service but is overwhelmed by the task.

Discussion Questions

1. What is causing the service problems at the front desk?
2. Where should Bill look for solutions to the problem? To whom should he talk?
3. What steps should Bill take to improve service at the front desk?
4. What type of support will Bill need from higher management to solve this problem?

REFERENCES

Albrecht, Karl, and Ron Zemke, 1985. *Service America!* Homewood, Ill.: Dow Jones–Irwin.

Hughes, Kathleen A., and Laura Landro. 1986. "A Lot of Restaurants Now Serve Rudeness with the Rigatoni." *Wall Street Journal,* p. 29.

Lydecker, Toni. 1985. "Handling the Problem Customer." *NRA News* 5(10): 14–19

——— . 1986. "Crisis in Service: A Look at the Problem." *NRA News* 6(3): 13–16.

Magnesen, Vernon A. 1985. "And Then ... The 30-Second Blunder." *Training* 22 (10): 126.

Main, Jeremy. 1981. "Toward Service Without a Snarl." *Fortune,* pp. 58–66.

Mill, Robert. 1986. "Managing the Service Encounter." *Cornell H.R.A. Quarterly* 26 (4): 39–46.

Naisbitt, John. 1982. *Megatrends.* New York: Warner Books.

Peters, Thomas J., and Nancy Austin. 1985. *A Passion for Excellence.* New York: Random House.

——— , and Robert Waterman, Jr. 1982. *In Search of Excellence.* New York: Harper & Row.

Russell, George. 1987. "Pul-eeze! Will Somebody Help He?" *Time,* pp. 48–55.

Chapter 10

Communication Skills

In the future, businesses will base competition not just on product quality but also on service. Although there is a great deal that management can do to improve customer relations, the personnel responsible for making or breaking an operation's reputation are the service employees. Many managers assume that their employees know how to deal with people. When faced with a problem guest, employees are expected to use their own judgment. But all too often, they handle the situation poorly and lose the customer. In the past, employees were taught the technical, but not the interpersonal, skills required to perform the job. But today, the number of operations providing guest relations training is increasing. We can no longer assume that good communications skills are inborn. Service employees can and must be taught how to deal with guests.

COMMUNICATING VERBALLY AND NONVERBALLY

Just as carpenters and plumbers must have the right tools to do their job, so must service employees. In addition to tangible supplies, they must be armed with basic communication skills. Ideally, only people-centered individuals concerned with the welfare of others should be hired. Yet even if you are fortunate enough to have only warm, compassionate, outgoing employees, you cannot assume that they know how to deal with angry guests. Today's employees must be able to do more than just smile and say thank you; they must be able to understand their behavior and recognize its effect on others. Before employees can be expected to provide service, they must be able to listen to others, use proper language, be aware of their tone of voice, read the guest's body language, and, perhaps most importantly, empathize with or place themselves in the guest's position. Without these basic tools, guest service will be forced and mechanical.

Listening

According to Nichols and Stevens in *Are You Listening?* (1957), 40 percent of our interpersonal communication is listening, even though we receive little formal training in this communication skill. We often equate listening with hearing, but listening also includes the interpretation and integration of and the response to what was heard. If a diner says to his waiter, "I have an important meeting in a half-hour," and the waiter fails to infer the guest's need for quick service, there will be a problem. We all are guilty of occasionally hearing without listening; overcoming these errors requires awareness and discipline. The following are common listening errors:

Interrupting
Jumping to conclusions
Changing the subject
Thinking about what you want to say
Thinking about something else
Rushing the speaker by saying "umhm, umhm, umhm"
Failing to maintain eye contact
Ignoring nonverbal cues

We first must acknowledge our failure to listen and then force ourselves to concentrate on what the sender is communicating. Remember to let the speaker finish his or her thought and to avoid reacting until you have heard the whole story. It may also be helpful to ask relevant questions, which will allow you to gain additional information and, at the same time, will let the speaker know that you are paying attention.

Active versus Passive Listening

The *passive listener* hears what the other person is saying but fails to respond appropriately. For example, a guest is checking out and says to the desk clerk, "The room was very dirty. It hadn't been dusted, and the carpet wasn't even vacuumed. I'm really surprised that such a well-known hotel wouldn't be more concerned with cleanliness." The clerk hears what she says but responds passively by saying, "Oh, I'm sorry to hear that. Will you be paying cash or using a credit card?"

On the other hand, *active listening* is a sincere attempt to understand what is being communicated; it is more than just hearing what the person says. The following are three components of active listening:

Sorting: Sorting is focusing on important information and disregarding unimportant information. If a guest states that there is a leak in the ceiling of his room and then goes on to describe similar problems in his summer home, it is up to the listener to stay on track by asking questions about the problem at hand.

Responding: We let people know that we are paying attention by using both verbal and nonverbal cues. We say things like "Hmm, tell me more about that" and "Yes." Nonverbal cues include nodding, smiling, and eye contact.

Reflecting: Reflecting is letting the speaker know that we understand, by reflecting or restating what was said. If a diner says, "This steak is terrible," you reflect back, "You're unhappy with your steak and can't eat it." This lets the diner know that you are listening and encourages him to provide additional information.

A good listener *empathizes* with the speaker, or responds to both the words and the feelings transmitted. Empathy does not signify agreement, but it does mean that the listener understands what was said. If a guest tells a server, "I just had a terrible day. I lost a million-dollar account that I thought was all sewed up," the empathic response would be, "That's really rough. You must be very disappointed." A less empathic server might just say, "That's too bad" or talk about how bad her day was too.

Listening is a communication tool that can be developed. We can increase our listening skills by becoming more aware of our listening habits. Another strategy that will facilitate listening is to talk less. Good advice can be found in an old proverb: "Listening provokes wisdom; speaking provokes repentance."

The Power of Words

The words with which we communicate can have a positive or negative effect on the listener's perception of our message. Some people sound critical, although this might not be their intention. For example, a guest wants to cash a check at the front desk and the employee says, "Our policy states that you must have two major credit cards and a driver's license to cash a check." Although this statement gets the message across, it does sound rather rigid. Instead, the clerk might have said, "I'll be happy to cash your check. I'll need to see two major credit cards and your driver's license for verification." Try to avoid using the critical and blaming statements listed in Table 10-1, and instead choose the more neutral alternatives.

Other words can have more than one meaning or interpretation and so also block communication. If a room service operator tells a guest, "Your meal will arrive soon," the guest might assume that this means he will have his meal in ten minutes, when the operator's definition of soon was more like twenty or thirty minutes.

What do we mean by

Occasionally
Usually occurs
Soon
Those are the rules
Often
Sometimes
Probably
I'll see what I can do
In a little while

When dealing with guests, be sure to communicate your definition of these and other vague words, so as to avoid confusion.

Another communication error is the use of "cop-out" words or phrases. By using these, we attempt to shift the focus or blame to someone else, avoiding responsibility for our statements or actions. For example, statements by a server such as "This isn't my station" or "I'm just following

Table 10-1   Critical statements and their neutral
alternatives.

Avoid	Use Instead
Always	I believe
Never	Who, what, when, where, how
You ought to	Alternatively
You're wrong	I can
Now listen	Here are the facts
You'll have to	Tell me more
I must have	What do you think

orders" are cop-out statements. When we use these statements, we are shifting the focus of responsibility to someone else and making ourselves appear weak and ineffectual. Customers then will feel that they are getting the runaround and cannot find anyone who will solve their problem.

Tone of Voice

The old adage that it is not just what you say but how you say it contains a great deal of truth. The tone of voice used when communicating with others can often reveal more of your true meaning than can the words you use. For instance, a desk clerk might say, "I didn't realize you wanted a double room," using a very critical, blaming tone of voice, thereby sending the message that the customer somehow failed to impart the proper information. Another clerk might use the same words but utter them apologetically, thereby implying that more information should have been requested of the guest. Our tone of voice almost always reveals our true feelings. Although management may be able to control the words used by guest service employees, it is difficult to control their tone of voice. If they feel superior to or critical of a guest, their voice will reveal this.

Empathy

Empathy is a powerful tool for guest service employees. Angry or disappointed customers will be at least partially mollified if they feel that the employee can at least see why they are upset. Empathy does not mean that you must always agree with the guest, just that you can see his or her side of the problem. If a customer calls a busy restaurant at 4:00 P.M. asking for a reservation for that evening and the hostess says, "I'm very sorry to disappoint you, but all of our tables are reserved until 10:00 P.M. this evening," he will feel much better about being refused than if the hostess says, "You should have called sooner. We're always booked solid on Saturday night." The first statement implies that the hostess is genuinely sorry that the request cannot be honored, whereas the second statement conveys the hostess's feelings of superiority.

Perhaps one of the most difficult characteristics to foster in guest service employees is empathy, as it is not easily taught. Some people simply are more sympathetic than others are. One way to encourage hotel employees to be more empathetic is to have them compare their daily commute to work with that of a guest traveling one thousand miles or more to arrive at the hotel. If employees are grumpy because of delays in public transportation or inclement weather, they can imagine how a guest must feel after dealing with busy airports, cranky taxi drivers, and late buses. So if a guest who just traveled from San Francisco to New York is in a bad mood, perhaps the employee will be understanding.

Body Language

We communicate not only with words and tone of voice but also with our facial expression, gestures, and posture. This nonverbal communication is called *body language.* To a certain extent, we all are able to read the physical messages sent by others. A frown means dissatisfaction; a smile signifies pleasure; and a clenched fist conveys anger. The ability to interpret body language correctly is a valuable tool for the guest service employee. If a concierge observes a man approaching her desk and notes that he is frowning, his shoulders are tense, he is tightly clenching his briefcase, and he is leaning slightly forward and walking very quickly, she will immediately realize that he is angry and so be prepared to deal with him.

Social scientists estimate that about 80 percent of our communication is nonverbal. The words used actually account for very little during our interaction with others. Almost unconsciously we observe others and make inferences based on their body language. Nonverbal signals are often clustered with the several cues used to send a message (Lydecker 1985). The following are some commonly observed attitudes and the gestures used to communicate them:

Openness: Opens hands, uncrosses legs, unbuttons coat, raises head, and assumes relaxed facial expression.

Defensiveness: Crosses arms on chest, clenches hands, leans back, and crosses legs.

Evaluation: Rubs nose, rests face on hand, leans forward, tilts head, and slightly squints eyes.

Suspicion: Covers mouth with hands, avoids eye contact, turns slightly away, crosses arms, rubs nose or eyes, and clasps hands behind back.

Readiness: Puts hands on hips and sits on edge of chair.

Needs reassurance: Brings hand to throat, pinches fleshy part of hand, and chews on pencil.

Frustration: Rubs back of neck, takes short breaths, and tightly clenches hands.

Confidence: Assumes erect stance, steeples fingers, raises chin, and leans back with hands laced behind head.

Self-control: Grips hand behind back, locks ankles, and clenches hands.

When dealing with guests, develop the habit of observing nonverbal cues. If the customer appears tense, with his or her feet crossed at the ankles, this person may want something but be too shy or too controlled to ask. If a guest approaches the front desk and brings her hand slowly to her throat, picks at her cuticles, glancing around uncertainly, it is obvious that she feels insecure and needs reassurance. If a diner is leaning forward, tapping his foot, and looking toward the door, he is in a hurry and wants the check right away.

In customer service, it is also important to become aware of the signals sent by employees. When dealing with guests, it is best to send signals denoting confidence and readiness for action. Stand erect, lean slightly forward, maintain eye contact, and raise your head slightly to show that you are interested and in control of the situation. If you frown, lower your head, slump, and tap your fingers, the guest will assume that you do not like your work, are not friendly, and are unwilling to help.

DEALING WITH GUESTS

After acquiring the necessary communication tools, the next step is to use them when dealing with customers. The best teacher is experience. The more often you must deal with angry, difficult people, the easier it will become. Also, as you gain experience, you will gain confidence. Guests are much more likely to trust a self-assured employee than an insecure one with their problems.

When faced with an angry guest who is criticizing you, shouting at you, or blaming you for something you did not do, you can react in one of three ways. You can become submissive and give the guest a long, drawn-out explanation and apology. You can react aggressively and defend yourself by shouting back. Or you can react assertively by letting the guest know that you empathize with him or her but also express you own point of view in a rational manner.

Suppose a guest becomes belligerent when making a reservation and finding the suite he wants is not available. The reservationist can react

Submissively: We're booked solid that week. There's a tool-and-die convention in town; then the Veterans' Association is holding its annual convention; and we have several weddings. I'm so sorry that we don't have a suite for you. I wish there were something I could do.

Aggressively: You must be kidding. This is our busiest season. There's no way you're going to find a suite anywhere in the entire city.

Assertively: I'm sorry, sir, but all of our suites are reserved. We do have double rooms available, or I could suggest other downtown hotels that might have suites available.

People that behave submissively lack self-confidence and avoid conflict by escaping confrontation. They use many words and phrases like *maybe, but,* and *you know.* The lack the confidence that it takes to stand up to an angry, belligerent person and to deal with the problem at hand.

Aggressive individuals look for opportunities to release their own pent-up frustrations and to enjoy the sense of power that comes from telling someone else off. They use threats, put others down, and may become sarcastic when blaming others for their shortcomings.

Assertive people avoid rambling apologies, and rather than attacking others, they look for ways to resolve the problem. They are brief and to the point, and rather than wasting energy by looking for a scapegoat, they seek a solution.

When dealing with others, avoid submissive or aggressive behavior. Instead, respond assertively when problems arise. Rather than being controlled by others, you will be in charge of the situation. When you respond assertively, no one loses. The guest wins because he or she feels treated fairly, and you win because you have presented opinions and suggestions that lead to the achievement of your goal, pleasing the guest. Remember the following five components of assertive behavior:

1. Empathize with the guest.
2. Ask questions.
3. Suggest solutions.
4. Be honest about the situation.
5. Take responsibility.

Difficult Situations

Often situations arise that are more difficult to deal with than are day-to-day problems. Examples are a guest who is forced to wait forty-five minutes or more for lunch because the server forgot to put in his order, the desk clerk who must inform the customer with a reservation that the hotel is overbooked, or the guest service attendant who must tell the customer that he has lost his luggage. All of these are service errors that are likely to make the guest extremely angry. Five steps in dealing with critical situations are

1. *Apologize:* Make the apology brief and to the point. Do not waste time by saying over and over again how sorry you are.
2. *Empathize:* Let the guest know that you understand how upsetting the error is.

3. *Actively listen:* Ask questions and repeat and rephrase what the guest says.
4. *Offer solutions:* Let the guest know exactly what you can do to solve the problem and when you will do it.
5. *Ask for solutions:* If the guest rejects your alternatives, ask, "What would you like me to do?"

Is the Customer Always Right?

Many guests have unrealistic expectations about service. They might make requests that are impossible to fulfill or expect the same hovering service in a busy coffee shop as they would receive in a fine dining restaurant. Service employees are called on to deal with all sorts of difficulties, from a customer who finishes his entire meal and then refuses to pay for it, to the person who becomes angry when forced to wait ten minutes for a table on a busy Saturday night. Guests can be unreasonable, and even though the server may not be at fault, the guest must still be treated politely and respectfully. The best technique for dealing with the unreasonable guest is assertion. By staying calm and standing your ground, you can avoid further difficulties and defuse a potentially volatile situation. An example of how one experienced maître d' dealt assertively with an angry guest is as follows:

MAÎTRE D':   Good evening sir, welcome to Cafe Versailles.

MR. JONES: My name is Jones, and I want a table for four, overlooking the lake.

MAÎTRE D':   I'm sorry sir, but those tables are reserved. I can seat you in a very comfortable booth near the fireplace.

MR. JONES: What do you mean I can't have a table with a view? I'm an important attorney in this town. I have clients to entertain. How dare you try to shove me in a corner booth?

MAÎTRE D':   I'm sorry sir, but the other tables are already taken.

MR. JONES: What's your name? I'm going to let the owner of this restaurant know what an incompetent he has working for him!

At this point, it would be easy for the maître d' to take a submissive role and avoid confrontation by either giving Mr. Jones the table he wants and inconveniencing another guest or simply continuing to apologize. Or the maître d' might also become aggressive and shout back at Mr. Jones. But the most effective way to deal with the problem is to remain assertive. Let us see how the maître d' handles the situation.

MAÎTRE D':   We'll need to continue this discussion over here. (The maître d' leads Mr. Jones to a more private area.) Now, as I've said, the lake view tables are reserved. Our next available time slot is 9:30 P.M.. I can seat you elsewhere now, or you can have drinks in the bar and wait for the window table.

MR. JONES: I've told you that I have clients to entertain. I can't expect them to sit in the bar all night waiting for a table. Can't you make an exception?

MAÎTRE D':   I can certainly understand your predicament. But all of the lake view tables are reserved, and people have even left deposits to hold them. If you had gone to all that trouble, you wouldn't want to come in and find your table had been given to someone else, would you?

MR. JONES: No, I guess not. You can give me a booth by the fireplace now?

MAÎTRE D':   Yes, Mr. Jones. I can seat you right away.

By staying calm, listening to the guest, being honest, asking questions, and offering solutions, the maître d' was finally able to arrive at a compromise with Mr. Jones.

Another problem customer might reject the food, service, or hotel room by trying to avoid paying the bill. It is difficult to determine whether the person's complaint is valid. Most operations are forced to provide either a refund or a substitute at no extra charge. But if a diner finishes an entire steak, she can hardly refuse to pay for it because it was overcooked. One restaurant owner faced a similar situation: A woman ate a serving of roast duck "down to the bone" and then refused to pay because she said it was really chicken. He then called the police, who forced the woman to pay. But she caused such a disturbance that he advises against this strategy, even though the customer was wrong (Lydecker 1985). Forcing a guest to pay for a meal with which he or she is dissatisfied is a no-win situation.

SUMMARY

Employees need good communication skills if they are to deal with guests effectively. They must be able to listen, choose the proper words, read a guest's nonverbal cues, and empathize.

Good communication includes self-understanding and insight. By becoming aware of how others see them, guest service employees will be able to take the correct action when faced with problem situations. Rather than reacting submissively or aggressively when faced with a difficult situation, the employee should react assertively. This will let the guest know that the employee is willing and able to resolve the problem.

Some of the problems with which employees must deal are caused by the server or the operation, whereas others are created by the guest. Both must be handled calmly and confidently. Guests expect much from service employees, and through selection, training, and feedback, management can make sure that they are not disappointed.

KEY TERMS

Passive listening
Active listening
Sorting
Responding

Reflecting
Empathy
Body language
Difficult situations

———————— CASE STUDY ————————

It is a very busy day at the front desk. Mr. Sims walks up to Eleanor, one of the desk clerks, to check in:

ELEANOR: Hello sir, welcome to the Chicago Palace. (He smiles, nods, and leans slightly forward.)

MR. SIMS: Thank you. My name is Sims, and I have a reservation. (Mr. Sims smiles back and appears to be relaxed.)

ELEANOR: (Eleanor checks the computer, looks through the reservation cards, and begins to frown.) I see that you have your reservation confirmation, but I can't find any record of it. Evidently it's been misplaced.

MR. SIMS: Well, I'll just take whatever is available. (Although he's still smiling, his shoulders become tensed.)

ELEANOR: I'm sorry, Mr. Sims, but I'm afraid that we're booked solid. There are no rooms available. (Eleanor remains erect and maintains eye contact.) I'll have to send you to another hotel. Of course we'll pay your cab fare and your first night's lodging.

MR. SIMS: (He is frowning now with hands clenched.) I don't understand this. I have a confirmed reservation, and it was your error. I don't want to go to another hotel. I want a room here.

ELEANOR: (She leans farther toward Mr. Sims, frowning and clutching her pen tightly.) Well, it's just not possible. We have nowhere to put you. I can send you to the Excelsior in River Park.

MR. SIMS: Just forget it. I'll never stay at another one of your hotels. You better believe that your general manager is going to hear about this! (Mr. Sims turns and stomps off.)

Discussion Questions

1.   What were the first nonverbal cues sent by both Mr. Sims and Eleanor?
2.   What clue did Mr. Sims later give Eleanor that indicated his displeasure and mounting anger?
3.   What mistake did Eleanor make that led to Mr. Sims's anger? How should she have dealt with Mr. Sims's displeasure over being sent to another hotel?

REFERENCES

Lydecker, Toni. 1983. "Can You Read Between the Lines?" *NRA News* 3(10): 5–8.

———. 1985. "Handling the Problem Customer." *NRA News* 5(10): 14–17.

Nichols, Ralph, and Leonard Stevens. 1957. *Are You Listening?* New York: McGraw-Hill.

PART 3

Management Skills That Motivate

Chapter 11

Supervision

The transition from line employee to manager can be difficult. After years of being led and instructed by others, suddenly the former line employee is in charge. This can be exciting and satisfying, but it also brings new challenges. In addition to gaining the commitment and respect of his or her employees, the new supervisor may have to solve problems created by the previous management. But these and other difficulties are certainly not insurmountable. Entering into the position with sound knowledge of good management practices can be an advantage if it is accompanied by experience. There are risks involved, and a new manager often makes mistakes, but each error is an opportunity for learning. As the manager gains experience and develops his or her own management style, leadership will become almost second nature. A supervisor is called on to wear many hats. He or she must lead the employees, motivate them, and help them become a winning team. A person's ability as a manager will determine how well his or her employees function. This chapter will examine some of the key components of supervision.

MOTIVATING EMPLOYEES

Motivation is the reason for our actions, the force that makes us behave as we do. Many American companies today are overburdened by un-motivated employees, resulting in lowered productivity, poor product quality, and a companywide feeling of malaise and apathy. Unfortunately, there is no real cure for a lack of motivation. Many sociologists and psychologists have developed theories of motivation but have not yet discovered one method applicable to all situations. We shall examine several promising motivational theories: If you are faced with poor productivity, one of these methods might solve the problem.

Achievement Motivation

David McClelland and David Winter (1969) found that some people have a greater *achievement motivation* than others do, and so such people will consistently outperform low achievers. It follows that one simple way to solve motivational problems is to hire employees with a high need for achievement. But the solution is not that simple, as high achievers cannot be readily identified.

Another way to improve productivity is to teach low achievers to become high achievers. McClelland states that this is possible in some instances but will not always increase motivation in all cases. Sometimes the job itself may act as a barrier to achievement. That is, if the job is not challenging and offers little opportunity for creativity, a high achiever still will not be motivated. To obtain outstanding performance among high achievers, the work itself must contain the following characteristics:

Success through individual effort
Tasks that are challenging but not impossible
Clear, concise feedback
Involvement in the problem-solving process
Future orientation

If these conditions are not met, achievement-oriented employees will not perform at their highest level. Hiring an achievement-motivated employee and then placing him or her in a repetitive, boring job such as that of dishwasher will not result in increased motivation.

If you want someone to work independently and creatively and to solve his or her own problems, hire either a high achiever or offer achievement-oriented training. But if you are looking for someone to do a repetitive task and follow orders, achievement will not affect productivity.

Goal Setting

Many companies today have successfully incorporated *goal-setting* techniques into their management system. They have found that by setting specific, difficult goals for employees, they improve their performance.

Goal setting is often part of the performance appraisal system or the planning process. For example, Marriott uses a comprehensive top-down Management by Objectives (MBO) system of strategic planning, which sets goals at the highest level and communicates them to all employees.

Goal setting is especially effective at an individual level. For years, Lee Iacocca (1984) has been using this system to motivate managers. Each quarter he and other top-level supervisors meet with managers and ask them a few basic questions about their objectives, plans, priorities, and hopes for that period and also how they plan to achieve them. After the supervisors and managers agree on the goals, they put them in writing. At the end of three months, the goals are assessed, and new goals are set for the next period.

The advantages of setting goals include greater employee involvement in the job, increased motivation to achieve goals, the development of new ideas, greater employee visibility, and more open lines of communication among managers.

Behavior Modification

B. F. Skinner, a noted psychologist, developed the theory of *behavior modification,* that states that behavior is shaped by reinforcement and punishment. For example, the frequency of a particular behavior will increase if the behavior is rewarded. Likewise, undesirable behavior can be extinguished by either ignoring or punishing it. Frederick Luthans and Robert Kreitner (1975) used Skinner's ideas to devise a behavior modification system applicable to organizations and created the following five-step program that allows managers to motivate their employees' performance:

1. *Identify critical behavior.* Specify those observable actions that are crucial to high performance.
2. *Set the baseline.* Measure the average rate at which these actions occur.
3. *Determine triggering conditions.* Identify those factors that lead to the critical behaviors and those that punish or reinforce the desired actions.
4. *Create an intervention.* Create a way to reinforce desired behavior and either to ignore or punish undesired behavior.
5. *Evaluate.* Compare the baseline frequency of the critical behavior's occurrence at the start of the program with that at the end of the program, so as to determine improvement.

One hotel used this system in an effort to improve the excessive frequency of its employees' accidents. First, it established its goal, which was to decrease the frequency of accidents in one year by at least 50 percent. Next, it measured the baseline or current average and identified the safe and unsafe work habits that were causing the accidents. Next, the hotel thought up a safety contest that rewarded employees for practicing safe work habits. Each employee in each department that did not have an accident during a month's time received either two cases of beer or a ham. Employees in departments that had accidents were not rewarded. After a year, the accident rate had been reduced by 80 percent.

Another way to motivate employees is to tie pay to performance. Rather than giving an across-the-board pay increase, outstanding employees are rewarded with a larger raise than are poor performers. When employees realize that their raise depends on their performance, they will be more motivated to improve. An alternative is to reward employees for the individual task performed. For example, one restaurant gives each server a 5 percent commission on each bottle of wine sold. This can also be applied to dessert sales or daily specials.

When using behavior modification, it is important to communicate the performance criteria clearly and thoroughly. Each employee must know exactly what must be done to acquire the specified reward.

Behavior modification is most applicable to lower-level jobs whose tasks are readily measured, such as housekeeping or dishwashing. It is not good for management positions, however, because of its emphasis on precisely measured performance.

Motivation–Hygiene Theory

Frederick Herzberg (1982) constructed the *motivation–hygiene theory,* or two sets of factors that affect employee performance. The first of these he called hygiene factors, which include compensation, supervision, working conditions, and company policy. If these are inadequate, dissatisfaction and thus a lack of motivation will be the result. If they are adequate, employees will be satisfied but still not motivated to work harder.

For performance to improve, motivators must be offered. Herzberg defined these as opportunities in the job itself for growth, achievement, recognition, responsibility, and advancement. But employees can be motivated by these factors only if the hygiene components such as fair pay and good supervision are present.

For example, one hotel motivated its housekeeping room attendants by developing a retraining program and placing the best room attendants in charge of implementing it. The trainers received an increase in responsibility, pay, status, and an opportunity for advancement. They were motivated by having more interesting and rewarding work, and the other room attendants who wanted to become trainers worked harder also. At the end of the retraining period, the trainers either became responsible for orienting new employees or were promoted to supervisory positions. Although the employees did receive a pay increase, the main source of motivation was the job itself.

Responding to Employee Needs

No one motivational technique will work with all employees at all times. One person might be motivated primarily by money, but another individual might have little desire for a pay increase. Before adopting a motivational method, you must first assess the needs of your employees and then choose the right incentive. Individuals whose jobs are very routine must be motivated extrinsically, or by factors in their environment such as incentives and compensation. As the job becomes more complex, the more intrinsically motivated, or self-starting, employees will become.

LEADERSHIP STYLE

The leadership style you adopt will determine the atmosphere or work climate in your department and will affect the way you communicate with and motivate your employees. No one style of leadership has emerged as superior to all others: The style that will work best for you depends on your personality, your employees, and the type of work for which your department is responsible.

The Theory X Leader

Douglas McGregror (1960) felt that management made assumptions about their employees that affected the way in which the employees were treated. According to him, *Theory X* managers made the following negative assumptions about their employees:

Employees do not like to work and are basically lazy.

They must be "coerced, controlled, directed, threatened with punishment" to get the job done.

Employees avoid responsibility and want only security from their jobs.

Theory X assumes that employees cannot be intrinsically motivated and that the only way to improve their performance is through extrinsic incentives and punishment.

The Theory Y Leader

McGregror proposed *Theory Y* as a more productive orientation to management. Theory Y managers assume that

Employees do not inherently dislike work.

Employees are motivated by a desire for achievement.

Employees not only will accept responsibility but also will seek it.

Employees are capable of creativity and innovation.

Organizations must allow employees to reach their potential.

Employees are capable of self-motivation when their goals and those of the organization are the same. Managers' assumptions or preconceived notions about people affect how they lead their employees: Theory X managers prefer close, controlled supervision, whereas Theory Y managers are more likely to delegate responsibility to employees.

Bureaucratic Leaders

Bureaucratic leaders are well organized and always do things by the book. They depend on policy and rules to make decisions. If the company's policy states that an employee should be fired after three times failing to report for work, this is exactly what a bureaucratic leader will do. This style is most effective in operations that do not change over time. It does not encourage the creativity and flexibility required by businesses faced with many problems or rapid growth.

Autocratic Leaders

Autocratic leaders believe that they are always right. They closely supervise their employees and constantly provide direction. They want tight control over their department and are not interested in their employees' problems or concerns. Autocratic leaders are like sergeants directing their troops. An autocratic style of leadership can be effective when an emergency arises or employees have had little training. But this leadership style stifles communication between employees and management, thereby leaving both groups unsure of what is really going on in the organization.

Laissez-faire Managers

Laissez-faire managers are the exact opposite of autocratic leaders. Laissez-faire managers are nondirective and place all responsibility for decision making on their employees, providing little advice or direction. This leadership style can be effective when employees are extremely motivated and self-directed and do not require supervision. But it can be disastrous in situations in which employees require direction or in instances in which decisions must be made quickly.

Participative Leaders

Participative leaders encourage open communication between management and employees. Decisions are not made individually, but by the work group as a whole. Participative leaders foster a sense of team spirit and encourage the development of their subordinates. They encourage their employees to solve their own problems but offer advice and direction when needed.

Although somewhat similar to laissez-faire managers, participative leaders help in the decision-making process. This style is most effective when employees are well trained and experienced, but it is not good when employees are unfamiliar with their jobs or when there is a crisis.

Choosing a Leadership Style

There is no ideal style of leadership. Research has shown that a more autocratic style of leadership works best when emergency situations arise or employees are unfamiliar with the work at hand. A more participative style is best when employees are experienced and deal with situations requiring problem solving and creativity. If you are faced with opening a new restaurant or hotel and have to lead a group of unskilled workers, obviously you cannot leave the decision making up to them. On the other hand, if you are supervising a group of servers who have been on the job for many years, allowing them to participate in the decision-making process will improve the overall operation. Good managers must choose a style consistent with their personalities but then be flexible enough to adapt to the requirements of the particular situation.

MONITORING EMPLOYEES' PERFORMANCE

Managers are responsible for monitoring their employees' performance and giving them feedback about how they are doing. Some supervisors find it very difficult to tell an employee that he or she is doing poorly. But although this may be an unpleasant task, without honest feedback employees cannot be expected to improve their behavior. Information about performance might be provided during an informal counseling session, an annual or semiannual performance review, or a disciplinary interview. Each of these situations must be handled professionally, but the requirements they place on the supervisor and the employee are different.

The Counseling Session

The informal employee counseling session gives management an opportunity to resolve employees' problems before they get out of hand. The following four signs indicate potential problems that must be addressed before they become more severe:

1. The employee fails to meet deadlines.
2. The employee often is absent or late.
3. The employee's work is sloppy.
4. The employee complains to co-workers.

By dealing immediately with these and other minor difficulties, the chances of their developing into situations requiring disciplinary action are reduced.

When holding a counseling session with an employee, choose a private place, and make sure that the time is convenient for both of you. Do not schedule a session when you are pressed for time or you are angry. The following four steps can lead to effective counseling:

1. Establish a good working relationship with your employees—especially those who are doing poorly.
2. During a counseling session, avoid dwelling on past problems or feelings—stick to the facts.
3. Have the employee evaluate his or her own performance.
4. Negotiate a plan of action.

The counseling session is not a time for lecturing the employee, but for uncovering difficulties and exploring solutions. Keep the interaction on a professional level. The less emotional you are, the less emotional the employee will become.

After the counseling session, send the employee a memo outlining the agreed-upon action plan (Figure 11-1). Not only will the memo document the session, should difficulties arise in the future, but it will remind the employee of what behavior changes you expect. Always state a follow-up date when you will meet with the employee again to discuss progress.

The Appraisal Interview

Most companies review their employees' performance annually or semi-annually. This review gives management a scheduled opportunity to provide feedback, assign a pay raise, and to discuss career development. Four components of an effective review session are

TO: Joe Williams, Busperson   DATE: October 1, 1987

FROM: Mary Smith, Supervisor   RE: Counseling

During our meeting on September 30, 1988, we discussed some improvements to be made in your performance. We agreed that you would abide by the following guidelines in addition to performing your regular job duties:

1. Attend work from 9:30 A.M. to 4:00 P.M. and perform sidework during the half-hour period in the morning to make up for leaving early in the afternoon.

2. Perform job duties as requested by the servers in exchange for a daily tip. Report any failure of waiters and waitresses to tip you.

3. Limit breaks to half hour as specified in company policy.

We will meet again on October 15 to discuss your progress. If your performance does not improve and you fail to follow these guidelines, disciplinary action will be necessary.

Figure 11-1 *Performance memorandum.*

1. *Participation.* Employees are encouraged to discuss their performance and to become involved in setting goals.
2. *Critical elements.* The appraisal is based on specific job requirements, not vague dimensions such as quality or quantity of work.
3. *Goal setting.* The best review systems set goals for improved performance and monitor the employees' progress.
4. *Advance warning.* It is best to let employees know ahead of time when they will be reviewed and what will be discussed.

Each organization has its own method for appraising employees. Some use Management by Objective or goal setting, whereas others use a rating instrument. Figure 11-2 is a typical appraisal. Note that it lists several criteria and requires the manager to rate the employee on each one. The problem with this instrument is that it is not based on behavior or on those activities required for successful job performance. That is, an employee might be rated outstanding on Quality of Work but not know exactly what he or she is doing right. Figure 11-3 is a rating form using basic job requirements. Once again, the manager must rate the employee on each criterion, but it is a much more specific and accurate appraisal form than that in Figure 11-2.

THE PALACE HOTEL

RATING FORM

Employee Name: _____   Date: _____

Supervisor: _____   Dept: _____

5 = Outstanding, 4 = Above Average, 3 = Good, 2 = Below Average,
1 = Unacceptable

RATING

Quality of work   _____

Quantity of work   _____

Job knowledge   _____

Attitude   _____

Work habits   _____

Dependability   _____

Hygiene   _____

Comments: _____
_____

Overall Rating: _____

Employee's Signature: _____

Supervisor's Signature: _____

Figure 11-2 *Employee performance appraisal.*

Try to create a nonthreatening atmosphere for the appraisal interview. The more relaxed the employee is, the more open he or she will be to your feedback. As you go through the rating form, discuss each item thoroughly. If your company uses an appraisal similar to that in Figure 11-2, it is especially important that you explain the reasons for your assessment of each criterion. Ask the employee for input about both additional strengths and measures to overcome weaknesses. If appropriate,

```
┌─────────────────────────────────────────────────────────────────┐
│                                                                   │
│                          Hotel Excelsior                          │
│                                                                   │
│                  Secretarial Performance Appraisal                │
│                                                                   │
│  Name: _____    Position: _____    │
│  Supervisor: _____    Department: _____    │
│  Review Date: _____                                  │
│                                                                   │
├───────────────────────────────────────────────────────────────────┤
│                                                                   │
│  Rating Factor:  Always         5     Rarely  2                   │
│                  Frequently     4     Never   1                   │
│                  Occasionally   3                                 │
│                                                                   │
│      1.  Maintains organized work flow in supervisor's   _____  │
│          absence                                                  │
│                                                                   │
│      2.  Is able to prioritize work                      _____  │
│                                                                   │
│      3.  Keeps up with the department's demands          _____  │
│                                                                   │
│      4.  Reminds supervisor of upcoming events           _____  │
│                                                                   │
│      5.  Meets assigned deadlines                        _____  │
│                                                                   │
│      6.  Uses correct greeting when answering phone      _____  │
│                                                                   │
│      7.  Asks for caller's name and refers calls correctly _____  │
│                                                                   │
│      8.  Provides complete and accurate telephone messages _____  │
│                                                                   │
│      9.  Answers the telephone before the fourth ring    _____  │
│                                                                   │
│     10.  Can compose own letters as instructed by supervisor ___  │
│                                                                   │
│     11.  Maintains an accurate and up-to-date filing system ____  │
│                                                                   │
│     12.  Maintains confidentiality                       _____  │
│                                                                   │
│     13.  Corrects spelling and grammatical errors when typing __  │
│                                                                   │
├───────────────────────────────────────────────────────────────────┤
│                                                                   │
│  Goals for next six-month period:                                 │
│                                                                   │
│      1. _____         │
│                                                                   │
│      2. _____         │
│                                                                   │
│      3. _____         │
│                                                                   │
│  Employee's Signature _____   Date: _____          │
│                                                                   │
│  Supervisor's Signature _____   Date: _____          │
│                                                                   │
└─────────────────────────────────────────────────────────────────┘
```

Figure 11-3 *Behavioral performance appraisal.*

discuss the employee's career aspirations and help him or her set goals to reach them. If dealing with a poor performer, schedule a counseling session in the near future to discuss improvement.

Disciplinary Action

Sometimes, counseling a problem employee is not enough, and disciplinary action must be taken. There are two positive results from disciplining an employee. First, it is another form of feedback and provides the employee with an opportunity to improve his or her performance. Second, it documents your efforts to help the employee improve and, if termination later becomes necessary, will help you avoid claims of discrimination.

A good disciplinary system first lets your employee know what rules you expect them to follow when they are hired. Give all new employees a handbook outlining the company's policy. Next, use a system of progressive discipline, basing the severity of the action taken on the severity of the offense committed. For example, you would not fire someone the first time he or she comes in late, or give only a verbal warning to an employee who attacks a co-worker. Many companies use a three-step system:

1. *Verbal warning.* Used for a first-time or minor infraction of company policy. Although the warning is documented in writing, it is not severe.
2. *Written warning.* Used for more serious infractions of policy or recurring problems. If the employee receives three or more written warnings during a twelve-month period, he or she may be fired.
3. *Termination.* Used for extremely serious first-time offenses such as fighting or theft or for documented, recurring problems.

You must also be impartial in disciplining employees. If your best waitress fails to call in when absent, you must discipline her in the same manner as you would your worst waitress.

Employees should always be disciplined in private. Begin the session by stating the problem. Next, ask the employee to describe the circumstances that are blocking his or her performance improvement. With input from the employee, outline the steps that must be taken to resolve the problem. Describe the disciplinary action to be taken, and let the employee know what the next step will be if he or she violates the policy again. End the session by assuring the employee of your interest and support.

Figure 11-4 is an example of a written warning notice. Complete this form, describing in detail the infraction of policy. Be sure to include

WRITTEN WARNING NOTICE

Employee Name: _____   Position: _____

Supervisor: _____   Department: _____

Date of Warning Notice: _____

Date of Policy Infraction: _____

Describe in detail the policy infraction:

_____

_____

_____

Goals for improvement of employee's performance:

1. _____

2. _____

3. _____

Next disciplinary step if infraction recurs:

_____

_____

Employee's comments:

_____

_____

Date of Follow-up Meeting: _____

Employee's Signature: _____

Supervisor's Signature: _____

Witness: _____

Figure 11-4   *Written warning notice.*

the next, more severe, action that will be taken if the problem continues. At the bottom of the form is space for both you and the employee to sign. If the employee refuses to sign the warning, have another manager sign it in the employee's presence. This is a very important step and documents the fact that the employee has knowledge of the disciplinary action taken. In the past, warning notices were placed in employees' files without their knowledge, but now disciplinary action provides legal documentation only when the employee is aware of it.

THE MANAGER AS COACH

Capable supervisors often view themselves as coaches responsible for helping their work team become winners. Rather than focusing on what their employees are doing wrong, they focus on what must be done to achieve success. Kenneth Blanchard, in *The One Minute Manager* (1982), defines coaching as a combination of both direction and support. Although the decision-making responsibility still lies with the supervisor, he or she requests input from the employees. Coaching requires open communication between management and employees. The two groups work together to make the right decisions. The coach is also responsible for fostering team spirit in the work group. When employees cooperate with one another, the customers will benefit through improved service.

Team Building

Florence Berger and Rachel Banger (1986, p. 82) define *team building* as "the process of establishing trust and opening communication channels in a group." Some benefits from team building are better interdepartmental relations, greater group cohesion, and higher productivity. Team building is most effective when it is used throughout the company. But if the organization you work for is not ready to make such a commitment, there is still a great deal you can do in your department to create a team spirit. Team building is more than simply creating a group of cheerleaders; it also is identifying and dealing with problems that occur in the work group.

Identifying the Problem

The first step in any team-building effort is to pinpoint the problems you want to solve. These might relate to service, morale, motivation, productivity, or some other aspect of departmental performance.

Gaining Employee's Commitment

Once the problem has been identified, you must next gain support from your employees. Their role in team building will be to discover problems and concerns and to propose solutions. Employees may initially be skeptical and fear that any negative views they present may be used against them. You must reassure such employees that you will respect their opinions.

The Team-building Session

The next step is holding your first team-building session. If time is limited, this can be incorporated into your regular weekly departmental meeting. During this session, problems will be identified, and the group will propose solutions for them. If you feel that your employees may be somewhat hesitant when asked to identify problems, you can pass around an anonymous survey ahead of time. The results of the survey can be tabulated, and the information generated can be presented to employees during the first meeting.

During the team-building session, you will act as the coach and encourage the employees to make suggestions. Use brainstorming to gather information, and write down on a flip chart the problems and solutions that the group mentions.

Action Planning

Once problems and solutions have been identified, the group should formulate a plan of action. This step may require one or more meetings and input from other departments. The plan of action should be detailed and put in writing. As shown in Figure 11-5, responsibility for carrying out the plan must be indicated and deadlines set for its completion or for further discussion.

Evaluation

During each subsequent meeting, review the plan and assess the progress. As new problems arise, continue to discuss them as a group and to generate solutions. Also, ask the group to evaluate the effectiveness of the team-building effort. Has it improved communication, service, and the like? Discuss ways to improve the team-building sessions and to make them more productive.

Team building is not a cure-all for an ailing work group, but it does promote communication and cooperation among both workers and management. Employees will feel greater responsibility for their de-

RESTAURANT ACTION PLAN		
Date of Last Meeting: _____		
Date of Next Meeting: _____		
Action Plan	To Be Completed By	Completion Date
1. Rotate server's stations	Host/Hostess	November 1
2. Change menu	Chef	December 15
3. Improve sidework	Servers	November 1
4. Keep kitchen floor clean	Janitors	November 1
5. Quicker food preparation	Expediter	December 1
6. Remodel employees' lockers	Manager	January 15
7. Quarterly performance review	Manager	January 1
8. Customer service training	Personnel	January 1

Figure 11-5 *Team-building action plan.*

partment when working to make it better and will feel that their opinion is valued. Management will also reap benefits. Employees who have been on the job for some time often have ideas that could benefit the entire operation. But management never hears these because it never asks. Team building is a way of gathering valuable advice and creative input from employees.

SUMMARY

Your first position might be managing a group of employees who are much more experienced than you, or you might be asked to solve morale problems created by the previous supervisor. A combination of theory and experience will help you develop the skills you will need to overcome such difficulties.

One responsibility of managers is motivating their employees. There are many effective motivational techniques, ranging from behavior modification to goal setting, that will help improve your employees' performance. Some techniques are better than others in given situations, and so you must find those that will work with your employees.

Supervisors must also give their employees feedback about their performance, including counseling poorly performing employees, completing a formal appraisal, and, when necessary, disciplining individuals who break company rules. The last can be an unpleasant task, but necessary if the employee's performance is to improve.

Your leadership style will determine the type of supervisor that you become. You will determine the atmosphere for your entire department, whether it will be informal or more conventional. But whatever style you adopt, coach your work group and maintain open communication with your employees.

KEY TERMS

Motivation	Theory Y
Achievement motivation	Bureaucratic leaders
Goal setting	Autocratic leaders
Behavior modification	Laissez-faire managers
Motivation–hygiene theory	Participative leaders
Theory X	Team building

———————————— CASE STUDY ————————————

Greta Johnson is the newly appointed chef at a fine dining restaurant. During her first week on the job, she finds that the cooks are in the habit of drinking beer while working. The previous chef, who had been there for ten years, had allowed it. Greta does not like this practice: Besides feeling that drinking on the job is unprofessional, she is concerned that it will slow down the cooks and increase the risk of injury on the job.

Greta has presented a new policy to the cooks, forbidding the consumption of alcoholic beverages on the job. The cooks are very upset and have threatened to quit if the policy is put into effect. If they do, this will cause serious problems for Greta, as all the cooks are experienced and will not be easy to replace.

Discussion Questions

1. Should Greta reconsider and allow the cooks to continue drinking on the job?
2. If she backs down, what problems will this create for her?
3. How could Greta have avoided this situation?

REFERENCES

Berger, Florence, and Rachel Banger. 1986. "Building Your Hospitality Team." *Cornell H.R.A. Quarterly* 26(4): 82–90.

Blanchard, Kenneth. 1982. *The One Minute Manager.* New York: Morrow.

Herzberg, Frederick. 1982. *The Managerial Choice: To Be Efficient and to Be Human.* Salt Lake City: Olympus.

Iacocca, Lee, with William Novak. 1984. *Iacocca.* New York: Bantam Books.

Luthans, Frederick, and Robert Kreitner. 1975. *Organizational Behavior Modification.* Glenview, Ill.: Scott, Foresman.

McClelland, David C., and David S. Winter. 1969. *Motivating Economic Achievement.* New York: Free Press.

McGregor, Douglas. 1960. *The Human Side of Enterprise.* New York: McGraw-Hill.

─── Chapter 12 ───

Selecting the Right Employee

Because of the high turnover rate in the hospitality industry, it is essential that managers become experts at selecting employees. Much of a supervisor's job is recruiting, interviewing, and hiring new employees. Choosing the right person for the job is perhaps one of the most important decisions a supervisor will have to make. Making the wrong decision can be costly in both time and money.

Many managers hire new employees arbitrarily. They insist on relying on only their instincts when choosing new employees. But in recent years, the rise in litigation in this area has made selection much more complicated. Several laws have been passed that protect the rights of applicants, and even an unwitting violation of these can lead to expensive legal battles for employers. Therefore, all managers responsible for recruiting and hiring must become familiar with and follow these laws.

Errors in hiring can also result in more direct expenses to the company. Much of the extremely high turnover rate, as much as 300 percent annually in some areas, is a result of poor hiring decisions. As a result, orientation and training costs rise; management time is wasted; and customer service suffers from the constant influx of inexperienced employees.

With a little knowledge and planning, problems with selection can be minimized. It is possible to hire brighter applicants, to reduce turnover, and to avoid costly litigation. This chapter will consider the selection process and the skills needed to hire service superstars.

SETTING JOB STANDARDS

Before you can begin recruiting and interviewing prospective employees, you must know the requirements of the job they will be asked to perform, as the questions you will ask during the screening and interviewing process will be based on these qualifications. First, you should write a *job description* for each position in your department. This need not be a lengthy and tedious process if you follow a standard format and use your employees as a resource. When establishing job standards, do not forget those relating to guest service. The ability to relate to guests is just as important as is the technical knowledge required to do the job. Figure 12-1 is a sample job description for a server's position. Note that it lists both general responsibilities and more specific standards of performance, including those relating to guest service. When developing a job description, delegate some of the responsibility to your employees. Who better to identify performance objectives for a cook than someone successful in that job? Your employees can give you a rough draft of a job description.

Not only is the job description valuable to the selection process, it can also help you design training programs and performance appraisal instruments.

LEGAL CONSIDERATIONS

Each aspect of the selection process, beginning with the job description and ending with the hiring decision, is affected by legal constraints. The Civil Rights Act passed in 1964, also called Title VII, prohibits discrimination in all employment decisions, on the basis of race, religion, national origin, or sex. And in 1967, the Age Discrimination in Employment Act was passed, making it unlawful to discriminate on the basis of age against those employees or applicants forty to seventy years old. The Rehabilitation Act of 1973 prohibits discrimination against the handicapped and applies to businesses that receive federal grants or contracts. Many state laws also protect the handicapped by making it illegal to discriminate against them. As a result, managers and recruiters must be careful when interviewing and hiring employees (Sovereign 1984). The Equal Employment Opportunity Commission and the courts are especially sensitive to claims of unfair treatment against groups that are often the victims of discrimination, such as minorities and the handicapped.

Bona Fide Occupational Qualifications

The best way to avoid legal problems is to use only *bona fide occupational qualifications* (BFOQs) when selecting employees. BFOQs are those

JOB TITLE: Dining room server

BASIC JOB FUNCTION: Greets guests, takes their orders, and serves meals
                              in main dining room.

REPORTS TO: Dining room supervisor, restaurant general
                              manager

RESPONSIBILITIES

1. Performs daily sidework which includes filling salt and pepper shakers, folding napkins, setting tables, and cleaning up.
2. Takes guests' food and beverage orders, using assigned suggestive selling techniques.
3. Promptly presents orders to cooks.
4. Serves food using proper techniques.
5. Clears table as guests finish their meal.
6. Presents the guest's check, takes money to cashier, and returns the guest's change.

STANDARDS OF PERFORMANCE

1. Is able to serve comfortably five tables at a time.
2. Follows guest service guidelines at all times: Greets guest by name when possible, smiles, maintains eye contact, responds to problems immediately, uses a pleasant tone of voice, and responds to guests' special requests.
3. Cooperates with managers, buspersons, servers, and kitchen staff. Acts as a team player and lends help when needed.
4. Arrives at work on time and stays until scheduled departure.
5. Demonstrates scheduling flexibility by working weekends, days, evenings, holidays, and overtime as needed.
6. Follows grooming standards which include clean and ironed uniform, neat hair style, no extreme makeup, polished shoes, proper hosiery, and manicured nails.

In addition to responsibilities and standards listed, the server will perform all other work-related job duties as assigned by management.

Figure 12-1   *Job description for dining room server.*

qualifications or attributes necessary for successful job performance. All aspects of the selection process, including the job description, recruitment efforts, application, interview questions, and hiring decision must be based on BFOQs. For instance, if you are searching for cocktail waitresses who are at least five feet seven inches tall and weigh no more than 120 pounds, you are not basing your recruiting efforts on bona fide occupational qualifications, as these requirements are not necessary for successful job performance.

Preemployment Inquiries

Be sure that all preemployment inquiries, both on the job application and during the interview, are job related. Table 12-1 lists *discriminatory questions* that should be avoided and preferable alternatives. If you do choose to ask discriminatory questions relating to such areas as age or marital status, you must be prepared to prove that they are job related.

Many managers are careful not to ask discriminatory questions during the job interview but forget to consider the job application form they are using. And because these questions are in writing, it is easier to prove discrimination. Figure 12-2 is an example of an application used by a restaurant. See if you can find the potentially discriminatory questions (see Figure 12-3).

When designing a job application, remember to keep job specifications in mind. For example, if you are hiring someone who will be required

Table 12-1   Discriminatory and acceptable questions.

Category	Discriminatory	Acceptable
Name	Did you change your name? or Is that name Arabic?	Would any of your past work records be listed under another name?
Birthplace	Where were you born? or What country are you from?	Where do you live?
Religion	What religious holidays do you observe?	Do you have any outside activities that would make it difficult for you to work evenings or weekends?
Age	When is your birth date?	The legal age to serve liquor is twenty-one. If hired, can you prove that you are at or above this age?
Citizenship	Do you plan to become a U.S. citizen?	If hired, can you prove that you have the legal right to work in this country?
Relatives	What is your father's, cousin's, or spouse's name?	Do you have any relatives that work here?
Clubs	Do you belong to any social organizations?	What professional organizations do you belong to?
Family	Are you married? or Do you have children?	Do you have any responsibilities that would make it difficult for you to work days, evenings, weekends, or overtime?
Pregnancy	Are you pregnant? or Do you plan on having children?	Do you have any physical limitations that would restrict your activity on the job?

XYZ RESTAURANT

Position: _____ Date: _____

Name: _____

Address: _____

Telephone number: _____

Social security number: _____

PERSONAL DATA

Date of birth: _____ Sex: M   F

Height: _____ Weight: _____

Marital status: _____ Dependents: _____

EDUCATIONAL BACKGROUND

Schools attended   Degree

_____

_____

_____

EMPLOYMENT HISTORY

Name of company   Position   Dates   Reasons for leaving

_____

_____

_____

Did you ever serve in the U.S. military? _____

Dates of service: _____ Discharge: _____

Are there any reasons that you might not be able to perform all reasonable
job duties assigned? _____

Have you ever received worker's compensation? _____

Have you ever been arrested? _____

Have you ever been convicted of a felony? _____

Do you speak any foreign languages? _____

Are you willing to work on Saturdays? _____

What is your religion? _____

Are you willing to work overtime? _____

Have you ever been fired? _____ Why? _____

Are you pregnant? _____

If hired, can you prove that you have the legal right to work in this country?

_____

Figure 12-2 *Application form.*

Position, Date, Name, Address, Telephone Number, and Social Security Number: All safe questions.

Personal Data: All risky.

Date of Birth: Can lead to age discrimination. But if the position requires handling liquor, it is acceptable to ask if the applicant is of legal age to serve liquor in the state and able to prove it.

Sex, Height, or Weight: All can be discriminatory unless you can prove they are required for successful job performance.

Marital Status and Number of Dependents: Avoid questions of this nature. Typically, women are discriminated against if they are married and have children. Single males thought to be homosexual may also be affected by questions about marital status.

Education: Acceptable only if you can prove that the job requires a high school degree.

U.S. Military: Safe.

Type of Discharge: Risky and not related to successful job performance.

Performance of Job Duties: Safe.

Worker's Compensation: May be risky: You cannot refuse to hire someone because of a previous, on-the-job injury.

Arrests: Arrests are not conclusive and should not be considered when making a hiring decision.

Felony Convictions: Safe. Restaurant and hotel owners are responsible for the safety of their guests and other workers. Depending on the nature of the felony and how long ago it occurred, you do not have to hire potentially dangerous applicants.

Foreign Languages: Safe as long as you do not ask where and how the applicant learned them, in an attempt to identify his or her national origin.

Saturday Work: Safe if the job requires Saturday work.

Religion: Illegal to discriminate against applicants on the basis of religion.

Overtime: Safe if the employee might be required to work overtime.

Past Job Record: Safe.

Pregnancy: Should be avoided. Instead, ask the applicant if there are any reasons that performance of job duties might be limited.

Right to Work: It is your responsibility to verify that all employees have a legal right to work in this country.

Figure 12-3 *Analysis of application form questions.*

to travel and speak a foreign language, questions relating to this are acceptable. But if you are interviewing dishwashers, asking about travel and foreign language may be discriminatory. To be safe, base all written and verbal questions on the job description.

SELECTING SERVICE-ORIENTED EMPLOYEES

Service quality in a hospitality operation depends on the employees' customer service orientation, and concern for the guests begins with the selection process. Employers must hire individuals who possess the qualities that will allow them to deal effectively with customers. Although subsequent training can certainly enhance these qualities, it is important to select service-oriented employees initially. It is relatively simple to gauge an applicant's technical knowledge during a job interview, but how can you tell if he or she has the necessary qualities needed to serve guests? Most interviewers rely on their "gut feelings" or intuition, and there are some other approaches that can be used to select service-oriented employees.

Work Sampling

Work sampling is a relatively new approach to personnel selection and involves testing applicants in situations like those they will experience on the job. The interviewer describes a situation to an applicant and asks how he or she would respond, or the interviewer may administer a written test. A new approach to work sampling was developed by Casey Jones and T. DeCotiis (1986) using video-based tests to select hotel guest–contact employees. They videotaped guest service situations and developed a questionnaire to accompany the videotape. Applicants watched the tape and then answered multiple-choice questions about how they would respond. The questionnaires were scored, and the answers were used to make the selection decision.

Before you can create work samples, you must decide what you want to measure. Jones and DeCotiis administered a job analysis questionnaire to a sample of guest contact employees and found that the most important performance criterion for guest service employees was guest relations. They then noted six qualities of good guest relations:

1. Courtesy to guests
2. Responsiveness to guests' needs
3. Sales of hotel services
4. Cooperation with other employees

5. Belief in guest integrity
6. Display of good judgment

The next step was identifying the performance elements of each of these qualities. The authors made a behavioral definition of each aspect of performance and then based the work samples used to test service on them.

Observation

Work sampling may be too costly, time-consuming, and complicated for some operations. As an alternative, you can improve your chances of selecting service-oriented employees by simply becoming more observant during the interview. First, identify the qualities that you are looking for that should be exhibited during the interview. These might include

Maintains eye contact
Shakes hands
Smiles
Uses interviewer's name
Has pleasant tone of voice
Answers questions appropriately
Does not become defensive

If the applicant displays these characteristics during the interview, it probably indicates how he or she will act on the job.

If possible, it is also good practice to have more than one person interview the applicant. A second interview will either reinforce the first one or reveal problems that were not noticed initially.

RECRUITING APPLICANTS

Attracting the right applicants to your operation will also increase your chances of hiring qualified employees. Extra effort in recruitment will bring you applicants with the appropriate qualifications. But recruiting is more than just advertising in the local paper; many other sources can be tapped when you need additional staff, including

Employee referrals. Many companies post all job openings and award employees a finder's fee for referring applicants.

Advertising. Good sources are metropolitan newspapers and, for neighborhood businesses, community newspapers. Also consider trade publications that have a classified section.

College campuses. Many companies recruit managers by visiting college campuses each spring. Local community colleges are also an excellent source for both full-time and part-time employees.

Public employment agencies. Many state agencies screen and refer applicants for both skilled and unskilled positions.

Private employment agencies. Although the cost can be high, private agencies may be a good source for hard-to-fill management positions.

When recruiting, just as in other aspects of the selection process, you must avoid discrimination. If your recruiting practices eliminate minorities, women, older people, or the handicapped, you may have problems. Also, be careful when writing advertisements for job openings. For example, one restaurant ran an ad for a maître d' in a large metropolitan newspaper that read: "We are looking for a man who is as handsome as Robert Redford, as charming as Cary Grant, and as sexy as Don Johnson." Obviously this ad discriminates against women, minorities, the handicapped, and just about everyone who does not look or act like a movie star. It is difficult to believe that companies can make such obvious mistakes, but many operators are either unaware of the legal ramifications of discrimination or choose to ignore them.

It is certainly acceptable to list job-related qualifications in newspaper ads. If you require someone with three years of experience, a college degree, and an ability to speak Spanish, you can eliminate unqualified applicants by stating this in the ad. Just make sure that all such qualifications are really needed for the job.

PRESCREENING APPLICANTS

It is much too time-consuming to interview each person who applies for employment, and if your operation has a personnel department, it will do the *screening interviews* for you. To make sure that the personnel department refers the best people for the job, tell the personnel recruiters your job requirements. They will then screen out inappropriate applicants, thereby saving you interview time.

If you work in a small operation and do not have a personnel representative to assist you, screening will be your responsibility. Begin by reviewing job applications soon after they are completed, looking at each one's qualifications and past work history. Choose the most qualified individuals, and contact them for an interview. The screening interview should last for about ten minutes. Focus on past experience, salary requirements, previous job success, service orientation, neatness of appearance, and availability for work. If the individual is obviously inappropriate or unqualified, end the interview quickly. If the candidate seems like a possibility, either continue with an in-depth interview at that time or reschedule it for later.

THE INTERVIEW FORMAT

The purpose of an in-depth interview is to gather the information you will need to make the hiring decision. The interview will usually last for twenty to thirty minutes. If you find that your interviews are much shorter than this, you are not gathering enough information. If they are much longer, you may be talking too much. As the interviewer, your goal is to spend at least 75 percent of the time listening and only 25 percent talking. This will allow you to explore the applicant's background and make better hiring decisions.

Preparing for the Interview

Whether you are preparing for a screening or an in-depth interview, plan the questions you will use. Review the applications and jot down concerns you want to cover during the interview. Look for breaks in work history, omitted information, and reasons for leaving previous positions. Next, review the job description, paying attention to key performance standards.

As you review this information, make a list of questions to ask the applicants. There are two types of questions that you will need to ask. Begin with general, *open-ended questions* to encourage discussion, and then use *closed-ended questions* to elicit specific information. Open-ended questions encourage applicants to discuss their goals, interests, previous jobs, and preferred working conditions. Figure 12-4 lists some interview questions that will help you generate information. Closed-ended questions allow you to focus on a particular topic to get specific information you need regarding, for example, salary history, dates of employment, or years of experience.

Establishing Rapport

After planning the interview, the next step is to meet with the applicant. During the first three to five minutes, put the person at ease by making small talk. Avoid the mistake made by one high-level hotel manager, who began all of his interviews by discussing the applicant's marital status, family, and place of birth. He was quite shocked to find that all of these topics are taboo. Instead, focus on the applicant's hobbies, experiences at school, or other safe areas. An excellent question to ask at this time is, "Did you have any trouble finding us?" This is not only

WORK EXPERIENCE

What did you enjoy most about your assignments?
What did you enjoy least?
At what aspects of your job were you especially good?
About what areas would you have liked to have learned more?
Describe your ideal job.

SUPERVISION

What were your supervisor's strengths and weaknesses?
Describe your ideal supervisor.
What type of supervisor would you be?
What would you have changed about your supervisor?

EDUCATION

What subjects did you enjoy the most?
What would you change about your schooling?
What motivated you to seek a college degree?
In what subjects were you best? Worst?
In what extracurricular activities were you involved?

GOALS

What are your short-term and long-term goals?
What qualities do you have that will make you successful?
What are some things you want to avoid in future jobs?
What are your educational goals?
If you could have any job you wanted, what would it be?
In what areas do you need to develop to meet your goals?

SERVICE ORIENTATION

What do you like and dislike about working with people?
How can you tell if a guest is unhappy about service?
What can you do to meet a guest's needs?
What kinds of people bother you?
What should you do if a guest complains about the food?
What can you do to help remember a guest's name?
Describe poor service that you have received in the past.
What can be done to improve it?

Figure 12-4 *Interview questions.*

a risk-free subject but will give you valuable insight into the applicant's tolerance of the commute.

After a few moments of small talk, describe the interview format that you will follow. Say to the applicant, "I'll begin by asking you questions about your work experience and education. When we're finished, I'll give you time to ask any questions you might have about our company or the job." By being the one to set the tone, you will be in control of the interview. If you skip this step, some experienced applicants will begin by pumping you for information about the job and then later use this to their advantage when answering questions. It is best to keep the applicant uninformed about the position and required qualifications while you collect information about his or her background.

Body of the Interview

Begin the body of the interview by gathering data about the applicant's previous work history. Start by asking the individual to describe the job duties of the last two or three positions held. Investigate any omissions. Next ask, "What did you like about the job?" and "What did you find less satisfying about it?" Explore the applicant's reasons for leaving and inquire about the salary received. Continue by asking general questions about the applicant's preferred job duties, strengths, weaknesses, and the type of supervisor he or she most enjoyed working for. It is a good idea to take notes during the interview on a separate sheet of paper. Never write on the job application itself, as it is a legal document, and any blank areas should be filled in by the applicant. After making the hiring decision, discard your notes, as you might have unwittingly written down information that could be used against you should a claim of discrimination be made.

If the applicant is a recent college graduate or has a short work history, ask about his or her educational background. Ask questions about grades, extracurricular activities, and preferred courses. Ask about what was covered during more pertinent courses and what the applicant learned. If your hiring decision will be based on the person's educational background, it is a good idea to ask him or her to provide a transcript from the college attended so you can verify the information provided.

A third important area to investigate during the interview is the applicant's service orientation. Even if the individual is applying for a back-of-the-house position, good human relation skills should still be a job requirement. He or she must be able to interact effectively with management and co-workers and might one day rotate to a guest service position. Begin by asking questions about the individual's previous experiences with co-workers and customers. If the individual held a guest contact position, ask, "How did you sell or promote the (hotel, food, and the like) to the guests?" and "What did you do to respond to the guests' needs?" You may want to continue exploring this area by using the work-sampling techniques discussed. Describe a situation that occurs frequently, and ask the applicant how he or she would respond. For example, propose to an applicant for a server's position: "You served the guest his food and, after a few moments, notice that he has stopped eating it. What would you do?" The applicant's answer to such a question will tell you a great deal about how he or she will react to your guests.

Answering the Applicant's Questions

After examining the applicant's past history, allow time for his or her questions, being thorough but brief in your answers. Also, pay attention to the applicant's questions, as they also will provide insight into the individual's main concerns. Questions about the job or company are a good sign. But if all the questions pertain to vacation, sick leave, and insurance, they will indicate that the applicant is more concerned with fringe benefits than the actual work itself.

Describing the Job

Before you describe the job, evaluate your reaction to the applicant. If it is unfavorable, cut short this portion of the interview. But if it is favorable and you see the applicant as a viable candidate, thoroughly describe all aspects of the job, department, benefits, schedule, and work environment that were not covered previously. But even if you want to present the operation favorably, do not oversell the position. After training and orientation, the new employee might realize he or she has been deceived and quit, and so you should present both the positive and negative characteristics of the job and work environment.

Closing the Interview

No matter how positively you feel about an applicant, never offer the individual a job on the spot. You need time to review the information and check references. At this time, let the person know you will be talking to other applicants and state when you will be making the hiring decision. Most positions are filled within one to two weeks, but if you need more time, be sure to say so to the applicant. It is good practice to notify the applicants either way, by mail or telephone. But if your time is limited and this is not possible, allow the applicant to call you by a certain date to check on his or her status. If the position has been filled by someone else when the person calls, say so, but avoid offering additional details. Many uninformed managers have been served with discrimination suits by giving such answers as "you were just too old" or "we really needed a man for that position." Be cautious and simply say, "We chose the best qualified person for the job."

Making the Hiring Decision

Immediately after completing the interview, while it is still fresh in your mind, analyze your impressions of the applicant. This portion of the selection process should be fairly easy if you planned the interview carefully and encouraged the applicant to talk freely. Review the job description and your notes taken during the interview. Assess the applicant's answers to the questions you asked. For example, if you asked the applicant, "What did you like about your last job?" and the applicant responded, "I liked the people I worked with and having weekends off," this will tell you that the individual did not particularly enjoy the work itself and may not be happy if scheduled to work on Saturday or Sunday. But do not draw conclusions from one or two responses; look for trends in the individual's answers. Did the applicant tend to have problems with supervisors, co-workers, or guests? Based on his or her responses, will this applicant fit in and be satisfied with your organization? If the person had a difficult time adjusting to an operation similar to yours, the chances are that he or she will again.

Review the information generated during the interview, choose your final candidates, and check their references. A study by a New York executive search firm, Thorndike Deland Associates (Boyle 1985), found that 25 percent of applicants conceal information regarding job performance; 22 percent hide their compensation history; 11 percent lie about their academic history; and 11 percent falsify their employment history. Thus, checking the applicants' references is important. Contact past employers and college instructors, and ask them to verify the information the applicant provided. Although this can be done by mail, checking references by phone will be more timely and actually hearing the person's tone of voice may give you a more accurate impression.

Recent court rulings have indicated that past employers who supply negative information about an employee's work history may be guilty of slander. As a result, many employers are becoming much more careful about giving out information: They may require written permission from the applicant before responding to any request for verification and then may be willing to supply only the applicant's dates of employment and position held. The risks of checking references are fairly high to past employers, but they are minimal to prospective employers. Verifying the factual data provided and asking about the applicant's past work history can be time-consuming, but the information generated can be of value to you when making the hiring decision.

Another tactic to apply during the interview that may discourage false information is to convince the applicant that you will check references. Do this by informing all persons requesting an application that it is your policy to verify all information they provide and have them sign a waiver allowing disclosure of their past work record. During the interview, make a point of asking when and where each supervisor can be contacted, and ask the applicant what type of reference the supervisor will provide.

SUMMARY

Your success as a manager will depend on your staff. Many of the problems experienced today with high turnover, poor performance, and low productivity could have been avoided with proper attention to the selection process.

Hiring new employees today is a complicated task. Not only must interviewers generate as much information as possible from the applicant, but they also must do so without discriminating. It is unlawful to base your hiring decision on anything other than bona fide occupational qualifications. Today's employers must be prepared to prove that their recruiting and hiring practices are unbiased.

Proper planning can help managers avoid discriminatory practices and get the most information out of the employment interview. Following an interview format and listing questions to be asked ahead of time will make it less likely that an inexperienced interviewer will inadvertently explore a risky topic.

In addition to investigating past work history, education, and future goals, managers in the hospitality industry must also consider the applicant's service orientation. This area is not as clear-cut as the others, and it may require some creativity on the interviewer's part. The interviewer must be aware of the applicant's behavior and look for signs that might indicate the individual's service orientation. Simulated situations can be presented to the applicant verbally, in writing, or on videotape, and his or her responses assessed. Hiring new employees need not be the risky, hit-or-miss situation it has been in the past. Knowledge of current legal issues regarding selection and proper planning can help managers avoid costly mistakes. With a little effort, it is possible to find and hire the right person for the job.

KEY TERMS

Job description

Bona fide occupational
   qualifications

Discriminatory questions

Work sampling

Screening interviews

Open-ended questions

Closed-ended questions

——————————— CASE STUDY ———————————

Gary has recently been promoted to manager of The Steak House, located in a suburban hotel property. He needs to fill a vacant server's position as soon as possible. Personnel will be sending up an applicant shortly to be interviewed, and this will be Gary's first interview since his promotion to management. Although he has had no formal training in selection, he has attended several interviews himself and feels that he knows the process. The following is an excerpt from Gary's interview:

GARY: Why did you leave your last position?

JILL: Business was just too slow; I wasn't making enough in tips. Oh, by the way, what type of service do your waitresses do?

GARY: Mostly American, but some dishes require tableside cooking. Can you handle that?

JILL: Sure, that won't be any problem. How big are the stations?

GARY: Each server has five tables. Will that be too much for you?

JILL: No, no problem.

GARY: Tell me a little about your situation at home. Does your boyfriend mind if you work on Saturday nights?

JILL: Well, I'm married, but my husband will stay with our son when I work nights.

GARY: You know, this place really gets hectic. I'm just not sure if a little lady like you can handle the pace.

JILL: Oh, I've worked in busy places before. I'm sure I'll be able to keep up.

GARY: Well, I guess we'll give you a chance. Come in tonight at 5:00 P.M., and we'll see how you do.

JILL: Great. I'm sure you won't regret it.

Discussion Questions

1. Was Gary or Jill in control of the interview?
2. What risky questions did Gary ask? Why were these discriminatory?
3. What open-ended questions did Gary ask? Which were closed-ended?
4. How could Gary improve his interview technique?

REFERENCES

Boyle, Kathy. 1985. "Interviewing for Superstars." *NRA News* 5(6): 31–35.

Jones, Casey, and T. Decotiis. 1986. "Video Assisted Selection of Hospitality Employees." *Cornell H.R.A. Quarterly* 27(2): 68–72.

Sovereign, Kenneth L. 1984. *Personnel Law*. Reston, Va.: Reston Publishing.

──────Chapter 13──────

Training and Development

Recently while dining in a local restaurant, we experienced a problem with service that was obviously training related. We ordered wine with our meal, and after serving the entrées, the waitress brought it to our table. Following several clumsy attempts to open the bottle, she admitted that she had no idea how to uncork the wine. This was her second week on the job, and she had not been taught how to serve wine. She was quite embarrassed when one of my dinner guests had to take over opening and serving the wine.

In this situation, it is difficult to blame the waitress for her lack of skill. Although the poor service we experienced was annoying, the consequences were not as serious as in the next example: It was opening night in a fine dining restaurant in a small midwestern city. A waiter at a table next to ours was serving Steak Diane which required tableside preparation. When the young man lit the flame on the steak, he was unable to control it, and it shot up two feet or more. The front portion of his hair was singed, but fortunately he was able to avoid any serious burns by putting it out quickly with his side towel. To make matters even worse, the waiter started to serve the overcooked Steak Diane, singed hair particles and all. Fortunately, the maître d' was standing nearby and quickly intervened. Situations like these occur all too frequently in the hospitality industry. Turnover is very high, and it is not always possible to find well-trained replacements. Insufficiently trained employees provide poor service, create dangerous situations, and eventually increase costs. Yet many managers feel that training is too expensive and time-consuming, preferring to delegate responsibility for it to other employees. Although many large chains have recognized the value of training, independent operators often lack the finances or skill needed to teach employees how to do their jobs.

The two basic components of a training system are *orientation* and *skills training*. New employees must learn about the company they are working for and be taught the skills needed to perform their jobs properly. Training current employees is also necessary when changes are made in such areas as the menu, service style, or procedures. Ideally, management should handle all training, but fortunately, time usually does not permit this. Experienced employees therefore must be relied on to train the new employees. This type of on-the-job training can be very effective if management carefully maps out the program and holds train-the-trainer sessions.

This chapter will consider effective orientation and skills training programs, including developing a training program that begins with needs analysis and ends with evaluation. Finally, we shall discuss the training systems adopted by industry giants such as Denny's, Domino's Pizza, and Marriott.

NEW EMPLOYEE ORIENTATION

Starting a new job can provoke a wide range of feelings, from anxiety to exhilaration. Although new employees may be concerned about fitting in and being able to handle the work load, they will also experience a great sense of excitement at the chance for a new beginning. On their first day on the job, they will come as close to being model employees as you can find. New employees are willing to learn and are motivated to succeed. Unfortunately, all this enthusiasm can be quickly discouraged if management is disorganized, other employees are hostile, or the first day is boring. But a well-planned, thorough orientation program can help maintain this high level of motivation and ensure the employees' success on the job. Many managers complain that they do not have time to train new employees. But they are paying for this omission with increased turnover and poor customer service.

The best time to begin the orientation program is on the employee's first day. Some companies wait until they have ten or more new hires and then train all of them together. This saves time, but some employees may have to wait weeks for orientation, and by the time they participate, they will have learned the ropes on their own.

When planning an orientation program, there are several key areas to be considered. Each of these must be addressed if the employee is to become comfortable and familiar with his or her new job. Using an orientation checklist like the one depicted in Figure 13-1 will lead to a more organized program. We shall now take a closer look at some of the concerns raised during new employees' orientation.

The First Impression

A favorable or unfavorable first impression will have a lasting effect on the employees' view of their new company. Try to look at your operation

EMPLOYEE NAME: _____ HIRE DATE: _____
SUPERVISOR: _____ DEPARTMENT: _____
TRAINER: _____

Please complete the following checklist. Indicate the completion date as each area is discussed or carried out with the new employee.

INTRODUCTION	COMPLETION DATE
Introduction to co-workers	
History	_____
Employee's rate of pay	_____
Payroll dates and procedures	_____
Employee's work schedule	_____
Department tour, including:	_____
—Washrooms	
—Vending machines	_____
—Cafeteria	_____
—Break area	_____
—Lockerroom	_____
—Employees' pay phones	_____
—Fire exits	_____
—Employees' entrance	_____

POLICY	
Hotel rules and regulations	_____
Department rules and regulations	_____
Attendance policy	_____
Call-in procedures when absent	_____
Uniforms and dry cleaning	_____
Telephone usage	_____
Schedule for breaks/lunch	_____
Signing in and out	_____
Safe work habits	_____
Vacation policy	_____

Figure 13-1 *Department orientation checklist.*

JOB TRAINING   COMPLETION DATE

    Provide overview of the hotel business.   _____
    Review employee's job description.   _____
    Describe daily/weekly/monthly duties.   _____
    Discuss performance objectives.   _____
    Set performance objectives.   _____
    Explain performance appraisal system.   _____
    Review the department's function.   _____

AT THE END OF THE FIRST WEEK:

    Discuss employee's progress.   _____
    Describe areas in which performance is successful.   _____
    Discuss areas that need improvement.   _____
    Set agenda for next week's training.   _____

SUPERVISOR'S FEEDBACK

The employee will need further training to perform the following job duties successfully:

_____

_____

This training will be completed on _____

SUPERVISOR'S SIGNATURE: _____ DATE: _____

EMPLOYEE'S COMMENTS

Cite the job duties that you feel most comfortable performing: _____

_____

Cite the job duties you feel least comfortable performing: _____

_____

_____

EMPLOYEE'S SIGNATURE: _____ DATE: _____

Figure 13-1   *(continued).*

from a fresh perspective and anticipate how the new employees will react to it. Factors that will make a good first impression include an organized training program, a friendly supervisor, a relaxed atmosphere, challenging work, and accepting co-workers. Also, look at the physical environment in which the employees will be working. Is it neat, clean, and professional looking? An unsanitary kitchen or dirty lockerrooms will take some of the bloom off the new employees' enthusiasm.

The Environment

New employees must be given information about their new environment so as to foster a sense of belonging. Although you may take for granted such things as location of the employee entrance or cafeteria, they will have no knowledge of such basic information. In addition to describing your operation, the best way to acquaint new employees with the physical layout is with a tour. In a large hotel, this can be quite an undertaking, but it will give you a chance to show off your facilities. After seeing a lavish presidential suite or grand ballroom, new employees will feel a sense of ownership and pride in working at such a fine establishment.

Policies and Procedures

To make sure that the new employees do not make any mistakes, tell them about policies and procedures on the first day. There is nothing that can make a newcomer feel worse than being reprimanded for breaking a policy that he or she did not know about. In addition to providing a written list of policies, review the rules and regulations with new employees, making sure that they understand them and have a clear idea of why they are necessary.

Fitting In

Many new employees are concerned with being accepted by their co-workers, and there is a great deal that management can do to alleviate such concerns. Make sure the employees are wearing the correct clothing and have necessary supplies. If uniforms are not worn, discuss the dress code with the new employees during the interview so that they will be sure to wear the proper clothing on the first day. If uniforms and name tags are worn, try to see that the employees have them as soon as possible.

Help the new employees ease into the work group. Have them spend time with one of the more experienced employees. Introduce the new workers to a few people each day so that they are not overwhelmed right away. Also, be sure to arrange for the new employees to have lunch with one of the other staff members on the first day.

Follow-up

One essential ingredient of an effective orientation program is follow-up. It is important that the new employees' supervisor schedule a time to discuss their progress after the first few days and then again after they have been on the job for a week or two. These meetings will give the manager and the employees a chance to talk about how things are going and to deal with any potential problems early on. At this time, the manager should also give the employees honest, specific feedback about their progress, letting them know where additional training will be needed.

SKILLS TRAINING

Skills training is another important component of a basic employee training system. Skills training is analyzing all elements of a particular job and then teaching someone else how to do them. Some of the larger restaurant chains, such as Denny's and McDonald's, have corporate trainers who design programs for use in the individual outlets. They develop written materials and videotapes and then teach managers and supervisors how to use them to train their employees. But if you work for a smaller operation, you will not have access to such resources and so must plan your training activities yourself or hire a consultant. This section will outline the five steps of planning and implementing a successful employee training program, beginning with needs analysis and concluding with the evaluation process.

Needs Analysis

Training will not solve all employee performance problems. Yet many organizations immediately assume that when difficulties arise, training is the answer, and so they arbitrarily develop programs that are unrelated to the true source or cause of the problem. When employee development fails to solve the problem, they then say that training is a waste of time. But an analysis of the situation and the identification of training needs will help you avoid this pitfall.

There are two approaches to needs analysis. If you find that your current employees are not up to par and may require additional training, you first must determine the specific problems that are causing the poor performance. In the examples cited at the beginning of the chapter, it was obvious that the waitress needed training in wine service, and the waiter in tableside preparation. Training programs should be designed to teach these specific skills.

When designing programs for new employees, you must take a more general approach. Rather than focusing on specific problems, look at the performance standards required for successful job completion, and create a program that will help your employees achieve them. A good resource when setting standards is the job description, which should specify what is expected of employees and can serve as the basis of a skills training program.

Depending on the time and financial resources available, needs analysis can be as simple or as complicated as you want to make it. You begin by observing employees at work and identifying any problems with their performance. But such quick observation may not provide an accurate account of training needs. Many companies periodically survey employees and management, asking them to pinpoint areas where development is needed. This can be done verbally or in writing. Another way to find performance problems is to have each employee complete a brief written or simulation test. For example, if you are concerned with a room attendant's bed-making skills, have her make a bed and note correct and incorrect techniques. Or have your bartenders complete a written quiz dealing with mixed-drink ingredients and preparation.

Another excellent source of service information is the customers. A simple way to generate data is to talk informally with some of your regular patrons, asking them about any service problems they may have had. Customer comment cards are another good generator of information. A more complex method for gathering data involves a focus group, in which customers discuss your operation, identifying their likes and dislikes and suggesting ways the business could be improved.

The Training Strategy

The second step in organizing a training program is to decide on a training strategy, outlining what, where, when, who, and how it will progress. By referring to the needs analysis, specify what additional training is necessary either to solve an existing problem or to elevate performance to the required level. Next, decide where the programs will be held. An unused banquet facility can be converted into a classroom, or if space allows, a permanent training room can be established. The facility must be large enough to hold video equipment, a movie screen, a table and chairs, and any other materials needed.

The length of the program also must be determined. Will the meetings be held on a daily or weekly basis, and how long will each session last? Ideally, a two- to four-hour session held daily is most effective, but busy hotel and restaurant schedules do not always allow this.

Finally, decide on the training method or methods to be used. One of the most common methods is the lecture, in which the trainees take a passive role and material is presented verbally by the trainer or visually with videotape or film. This is the quickest and easiest way to present information, but unless quizzes are given frequently, the employees' recall will be poor.

The employees' participation can be increased by incorporating structured activities into the program. For example, the leader can ask questions related to the material and generate group discussion. Another effective technique is *role play,* in which participants are given a script or specified role and then act out the situation for the group. This is followed by a structured discussion of the incident. A third method is the *case study,* on which a simulated or real life experience is documented and the trainees analyze and solve the problems presented. Examples of this method can be found at the end of each chapter. Hilton Hotels' *Priority 1* training program uses all of these methods to teach its employees customer service skills. Hilton's detailed *leader's guide* contains specific discussion questions, role plays, and case studies used to enhance the lecture material presented by the leader. This program provides a lively and interesting training session and increases the employees' retention and on-the-job application of the material covered.

Program Design

The task of designing a training program may seem monumental. If funding allows, you can save time by hiring a consultant to do this for you. Consultants' services range from presenting "canned" or previously developed materials to your employees to designing a specific program to meet your needs, with the latter being the most expensive option. Choose consultants carefully, as not all have the expertise they advertise. Contact local professional organizations for referrals, and several past clients for references. Always request a contract before engaging the consultant, and have your legal adviser review it.

If your funds are limited or you just want to gain experience in program design and presentation, you may choose to develop your own training materials. Begin by visiting the local business library and examine the current trends in training in your field. Next, meet with your trainers, and ask for their advice and assistance. Depending on their expertise, you could have them help write the training manuals and select the audiovisual aids.

For written materials, you will need to produce a *procedures manual* for trainees and a guide for leaders. The procedures manual should contain step-by-step job instructions, quizzes, role plays, case studies, and any other learning aids to be used. It should be organized in the sequence that the session will follow, beginning with the simpler tasks and progressing to the more difficult ones. It should outline the information to be taught each day. Figure 13-2 is a daily training plan used by Denny's restaurants. It lists all topics to be covered on the first day of a five-day waiter/waitress, host/hostess program. Each of these topics

Name:	Date: / / Shift:	Day: Th F Sa Su M T W

Peak Periods	What will trainee do during peak periods?

TOPIC	TRAINER	TRAINING SCHEDULE
DAY ONE Tour unit, introductions		
Orientation to Denny's		
Orientation to the unit		
Orientation to customer service		
Location and use of emergency equipment		
Cash register operation		
Greeting and seating customers		
Busing tables		

Figure 13-2 *Daily training plan.*

General description of job duties		
Discuss situations		
Review day, evaluate progress		

ADDITIONAL TOPICS (taken from next day's plan)		

DENNY'S INC. RESTAURANT DIVISION
Figure 13-2 *(continued).*

is then expanded to provide a step-by-step description of how the task is performed. Figure 13-3 is an excerpt from Denny's cooks' training manual. By reading and discussing the material with their trainer, the new cooks learn preparation techniques and sanitation principles. When the employee can successfully demonstrate the task at hand, the trainer proceeds to the next job requirement.

Your training manual should include written and verbal quizzes for each task, to give both the trainee and the trainer feedback on their progress. Learning is also retained better when visual aids are used, so

TYPE OF MENU ITEMS

A broad range of food products are prepared for the cook's line at the prep station. This includes heating soups, cooking noodles, boiling eggs and slicing and portioning meats. Many of these food products are listed below to give you an idea of the range of products "prepped."

- Au Jus
- Beef Roast
- Chicken Salad
- Coleslaw
- Gravy (chicken and brown)
- Lettuce Mix
- Onions
- Pickle Spears
- Potatoes
- Seasoned-flour
- Tuna Salad
- Vegetables (frozen)

- Bacon
- Braised Sirloin Tips
- Cocktail Sauce
- Egg Batter
- Ham
- Mushrooms
- Pancake Batter
- Pineapple Slices
- Salad Dressing
- Soup
- Turkey

- Beef Roast
- Cheese
- Coffee Creamer
- French Toast
- Lettuce
- Noodles
- Parsley
- Pineapple Sweet and Sour Sauce
- Sausage links (blanched)
- Tomatoes
- Turkey Salad

COOKING PRINCIPLES

The methods used to maintain the quality of food are the cooking principles at this station. These methods begin with the proper storage of food items to using the correct recipe during preparation.

Food products are rotated so that the first items delivered are the first ones to be "prepped" and cooked. Dating or color coding systems are useful ways to determine which food should be used first. Keeping food clean, dry and at the right temperature will prevent a loss of quality. Allowing air to freely circulate around foods in refrigerated storage areas keeps them at the correct temperature. When food products are covered, they maintain their freshness. Lettuce, for example, will stay "crisp" if properly covered after it has been prepared. Storing lighter containers or items on top of heavier ones will prevent damaging food products.

As a cook, you should practice these basic rules of food storage:
1. First in, first out
2. Keep it clean, keep it dry
3. Permit air circulation
4. Keep it covered
5. Heavy items on bottom, light items on top.

These properly stored foods now have to be "prepped" for the cook's line in the quantities needed. The unit's prep sheets or chart is used to determine what needs to be prepared and in what quantities. This planning tool allows cooks to have all the food products on the menu stocked and available for our guests. The information listed below illustrates the procedures used to efficiently work the prep station.

Figure 13-3   *Cook's training packet.*

EQUIPMENT

The stove and slicer are the major pieces of equipment at this station. The stove is used to heat, boil, and cook food products. The electric slicer allows cook's to efficiently slice and portion an assortment of meats. These two pieces of equipment are found either on the cook's line or at the back-of-the house, depending on the model of the restaurant.

A variety of tools are used to prepare food products for the cook's line. They range from knives to portion papers. Each of these tools is presented and their usage explained in the "Orientation Packet" (Orientation to the cook's line).

The freezer, walk-in refrigerator and storeroom are used during prep. Food products prepared for the cook's line are stored in these areas.

SAFETY

There's more of a chance for an accident to occur at this station since so many different tools are used. For that reason, cooks must be keenly aware of potential hazards and always practice safety standards whenever using tools and equipment.

A good example is the use of knives. When using knives always use a cutting board to prevent slippage and cut away from the body. Knives should never be left at the bottom of a sink or protruding from a counter.

Always unplug equipment such as the slicer before cleaning. This will prevent unnecessary injury because the machine was accidently turned on. Also, the blade cover should be used whenever the slicer isn't being used for prep.

The tomato tammer is a seemingly harmless tool. But it's horizontal blades are sharp and can cause sharp cuts. Be sure to prevent your hands from being pushed against the blades of this tool when slicing tomatoes.

When heating soups on the stove, be sure to turn the handles in toward the stove. This will prevent the pot and it's hot contents from being knocked off the burners.

Occasionally containers will have to be carried from their storage areas to the prep station. When carrying objects, always lift them up or set them down using your legs and not by bending your back.

Figure 13-3 *(continued)*.

APPENDIX B
Example One
Parts of the Guest Check

1. Cashier's initials.

2. Server call number.

3. Number of guests at the table.

4. Table number.

5. Appetizers or Juices. Such as: O.J., Frt., etc.

6. a. When soup is requested, write in kind of soup and whether it is a cup or bowl.
   b. When salad is requested, write in type of dressing.

7. Beverage: "coffee," "coke," etc.

8. Entree plus type of meat: "#1, bacon," "stk & shrimp," etc.

9. Temperature or style of entree: "OE," "MW," etc.

10. Potato or vegetable selection: "FF," "Whip," etc.

11. Bread selection: "toast," "muffin," etc.

12. Extended prices for all items: "beverage," "entree," "accompaniment," etc.

13. Subtotal food, non-alcoholic beverage, and reorders here.

14. Indicate tax for the total food & non-alcoholic beverage order.

15. Total 13 & 14 and record here.

16. Total of all alcoholic beverages served. Total taken from reverse side of check.

17. Sum of lines 15 and 16.

18. Signature of server.

Figure 13-4 *Writing a guest check.*

APPENDIX B
Example One
continued

19. Alcoholic beverage selection: type and price.

20. Reorders or desserts.

21. Extended prices for reorders and desserts.

22. To be completed by server.

23. To be completed by server.

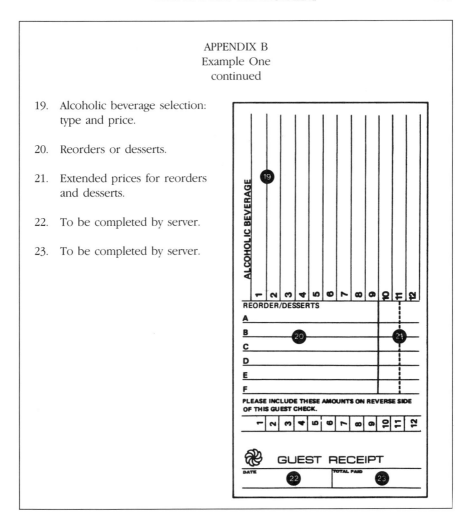

Figure 13.4 *(continued).*

include diagrams, graphics, and photos in your materials. Figure 13-4 instructs servers on the proper procedure for completing a guest check. Including both a picture of the check and an explanation of each section ensure a uniform system. Figure 13-5 is an example of a bartender's quiz. After the section on drink preparation is completed, the quiz is administered and feedback provided.

Accompanying the procedures manual is the leader's guide which contains all the information found in the procedures manual plus answer keys for quizzes and discussion questions. It also offers the leaders presentation tips and a clear statement of the learning goal at the beginning of each session.

You can supplement your in-house programs with previously developed or "canned" materials, which can be purchased from consultants, pub-

Trainer's Note: Administer after completing "cocktail service" section of manual. When the trainee has completed the quiz, grade it immediately and discuss any errors with trainee. If score is lower than 90 percent, review the material again and administer the quiz a second time.

QUIZ ON COCKTAIL SERVICE

1. What makes a Grasshopper green? _____.

2. What garnish is used for a sweet Manhattan? _____.

3. Vodka mixed with Rose's Lime Juice is a _____.

4. What ingredients are used in a Spritzer? _____
and _____.

5. A Rob Roy is a Scotch and _____.

6. What garnish is used with a Gibson? _____.

7. True or False, a Smith and Kerns is made with Amaretto:

_____.

8. What garnish is used in an Old Fashioned? _____.

9. What liqueur is used to make a Rusty Nail? _____.

10. What is the difference between a Perfect Manhattan and a regular one?

_____.

11. What goes around the rim of a Side Car? _____.

12. What garnish is used in a Black Russian? _____.

Answer Key: 1. Green creme d' menthe 2. Cherry 3. Vodka Gimlet 4. Wine and club soda 5. vermouth 6. Onion 7. False 8. Orange and cherry
9. Drambuie 10. Perfect contains both dry and sweet vermouth 11. Sugar
12. None

Figure 13-5 *Bartender's quiz.*

lishers, or professional organizations such as the National Restaurant Association. They include written manuals, films, and videotapes. If they do not address your specific problems, they can be modified to fit your program.

Training the Trainers

Most managers do not have time to train all new employees and so rely on experienced staff members to teach basic job skills. There is nothing wrong with this type of on-the-job training if done properly. Management still needs to maintain contact with the new employees by meeting with them daily to review progress and monitor performance and also to train the designated trainers before making them responsible for new employees. If this is not done, problems can arise. For example, management will have little control over what the trainers are actually teaching, who may pass on their bad habits to new employees. Trainers may also use a style of training that is not conducive to learning.

The most experienced employee is not always the best trainer, and so you should choose individuals who have mastered the job and have good communication skills, patience, and understanding. Also make certain that your trainers are loyal to the company; there is nothing worse than a trainer who instills his or her negative attitude in new employees. Make the trainer designation an honor in your company. Compensate trainers well for their time, especially if they are tipped employees who will be sacrificing part of their income.

It is a good idea to involve your trainers in the program design process, as they are more likely to use the materials effectively if they had a hand in their development.

Once a procedures manual and leader's guide have been completed, schedule several trainer-training sessions. During these sessions, teach the material to the trainers as you want them to teach it to the new employees. Make the sessions as realistic as possible so the trainers will understand exactly what is expected of them. Also emphasize the importance of acceptance and patience on the part of the trainers.

When the training begins, stay in close contact with the trainers. Meet with them daily and discuss the new employees' progress. Make yourself available to help solve problems as they arise.

Program Evaluation

The assessment of training is an ongoing process. Only through *program evaluation* will you know if it is having the desired effect. Evaluation also provides valuable feedback that will help you revise your materials when necessary.

Training efforts must be assessed both during the program and later on the job. You will need to know if the trainees are learning during the training sessions and if this new knowledge is being transferred to actual job performance.

The simplest way to assess learning during the training sessions is to administer quizzes and simulation tests. Valuable information can also be elicited by having the new employees complete a questionnaire at the end of the program, asking them to judge its success.

The best way to measure on-the-job performance is through regular evaluation. Ideally, all new employees should be reviewed after their first month on the job and then every six months after that. If serious performance problems are found during this initial review, additional training may be prescribed or disciplinary action taken. Once again, the employees should also complete a questionnaire asking whether information learned during the training sessions was useful on the job.

TEACHING CUSTOMER SERVICE

One important job skill that should receive attention during the training process is customer service. Many programs focus on technical knowledge but overlook this important prerequisite for job success. Do not assume that your employees already know how to deal with customers. All too frequently, employees lack this skill, especially those who are new to the hospitality industry.

Incorporate service into every facet of your training program. For example, when teaching servers how to take guests' orders, also instruct them to smile and to make the guests feel welcome. Include a section in your manual that deals with common problems that arise with guests, as well as several case studies as examples, and role-play situations.

Hilton Hotels' *Priority 1* training program indicates that the corporation's first priority is to please the guest. It consists of ten hour-long sessions designed first to encourage employees to empathize with the guest, then to recognize the guest's needs, and finally how to react to problem situations. After completing a rigorous trainer-training program themselves, managers from all areas of each hotel act as leaders. By tabulating customers' comment cards and surveying guests, Hilton found that the program did result in improved guest satisfaction.

CORPORATE TRAINING PROGRAMS

In addition to Hilton Hotels, several other lodging and restaurant chains have developed successful training programs, and independent operators can learn much about training from these industry giants. We shall look next at some of the methods being used by a few of the major chains.

Domino's Pizza

Domino's Pizza, with 3,800 stores in this country and abroad, takes a decentralized approach to training. Most management training takes place at its Ann Arbor, Michigan, headquarters and at regional centers (Feuer 1987), but 85 percent of all training for nonsupervisory personnel takes place on the job. Supervisors use training packages developed by their corporate staff to teach orientation, customer service, image, and job-related skills.

Domino's has rigorous job standards, and all new employees must work hard to meet them. For example, order takers must answer the phone within three rings, and pizza makers must make the pizza and get it into the oven in one minute. To reinforce these skills, Domino's holds competitive events both at each store and nationally and awards to the winners cash prizes and trips.

Domino's also has a well-organized program for supervisors, called *Management in Training* (MIT). New managers are taught both human resource development and administrative skills. The program takes about six months to a year to complete. Trainees attend classes in regional training centers or in the store itself. Domino's requires that all trainers be formally certified by completing a course entitled *Training Dynamics*, which offers hands-on experience in training, and by being approved by the regional training director.

Marriott Corporation

As the growth of the Marriott Corporation has accelerated, so has its need for training. Early in its development, the Marriott Corporation recognized the need for ongoing employee development and organized an extensive training program. Over the years, training responsibilities have changed from being centralized and mainly handled at corporate headquarters to being more decentralized with greater responsibility given to the individual properties.

When new managers are hired by Marriott, they complete an initial seminar at their corporate headquarters in Washington, D.C., or in a regional training center where they learn management skills. Seventeen human resource areas are covered, from team building to termination skills. Once this introduction is completed, the new managers begin the I.D., or *Individual Development Program*. Depending on the manager's previous experience, the I.D. program can be completed in a period ranging from six weeks to six months. The trainee is then assigned to a property and, under the close supervision of the director of human resources, rotates through each major hotel department, completing assigned tasks. For example, when training at the front desk, the new managers learn not only the job duties of the director of front office operations but also those of the desk clerk and cashier. In housekeeping, the trainees must actually practice cleaning guest rooms, and in the restaurants they wait tables. At the end of the program, the trainees should have mastered both administrative and line functions and be better able to empathize with the hourly employees.

If the need arises, corporate trainers will visit the individual properties and present special seminars to management. They also make available training programs for line employees, consisting of both written and audiovisual aids, presented by the managers at the property.

Overall, Marriott is considered to have one of the finest management training programs in the industry. Although its standard operating procedures are somewhat rigid, the administrative and supervisory functions are some of the best organized in the business. Marriott gives its managers all they will need to know to run their departments and supervise their employees, followed up by a great deal of support from the corporate staff.

Denny's Restaurants

Denny's also boasts an extensive corporate training program. Regional trainers teach managers how to orient and develop their employees, with the individual outlet responsible for teaching skills to the line workers. The restaurant managers select potential trainers who must first complete Denny's Train the Trainer program and win certification. These servers and cooks train new employees according to the *Job Code Training Program* created by corporate headquarters. New waiter/waitress training lasts for five days, and new cooks are trained for three weeks. In addition to food preparation methods, the cooks learn safety and sanitation techniques and cost control procedures. In all instances, the trainers must use the daily plan depicted in Figure 13-2. Because they cannot spend much time with the new employees during peak periods, they assign learning activities at the beginning of the shift for the breakfast, lunch, or dinner rush. Techniques used during the program include shadow training, quizzes, and case studies. At the end of three weeks, cooks must complete a lengthy test and score 90 percent or better to "graduate." Managers monitor the performance of both trainers and trainees and formally review them when the program is completed.

SUMMARY

As the hospitality industry continues to grow, the role of training becomes even more important. But with such rapid expansion, restaurants are no longer staffed by experienced, professional servers but must hire persons who have little or no background in the field. If excellence in service is to be maintained, these newcomers must be thoroughly oriented and trained.

After acknowledging the need for orientation and skills training, the company must decide whether to hire a consultant or to do the training itself. The latter choice requires careful preparation, including analyzing needs, developing a training plan, designing the program, training the trainers, and finally evaluating the program.

In the past, the major focus of training efforts was on skills, but today, with greater attention given to service, more companies are stressing customer relations.

KEY TERMS

Orientation	Procedures manual
Skills training	Program evaluation
Role play	Management in Training
Case study	Individual Development
Priority 1	Program
Leader's guide	Job Code Training

CASE STUDY

Elaine has been director of housekeeping services at a suburban hotel for three months. The manager that she replaced was very lax. She has been able to correct some of the problems she encountered, such as tardiness and poor grooming habits, but there are still too many complaints about the guest rooms' cleanliness. The room attendants are not cleaning the bathrooms thoroughly; the rooms are dusty; and one guest even found a pair of old socks under the bed.

Elaine recently attended a seminar on employee development and came away with several good ideas. She is hoping that an extensive retraining program will be the answer.

Discussion Questions

1. Does this problem sound like one that could be solved with additional training? How can Elaine find out?
2. How can Elaine sell the idea of training to her general manager?
3. Which of the training methods discussed in this chapter—lecture,

role play, case study, and so forth—would be most effective with this group?

4. How will Elaine know if her training efforts are successful?

REFERENCES

Feuer, Dale. 1987. "Training for Fast Times." *Training* 24(7): 25–32.

Warren, Malcolm W. 1969. *Training for Results.* Reading, Mass.: Addison-Wesley.

Chapter 14

Trends in the Hospitality Industry

Much of entrepreneurs' success in the hospitality industry resulted from their being in the right place at the right time, not just due to luck but, rather, to the correct anticipation of their customers' needs. Operators who have staying power are those who not only keep abreast of current developments but also have the foresight to prepare for the future.

This final chapter will examine the trends that are shaping today's hospitality industry and those expected to evolve in the future. Three major categories will be discussed: changing consumer needs, legal issues affecting the industry, and technological advances.

CHANGING CONSUMER NEEDS

Shifts in the demographic profile of America are responsible for the evolution of and change in consumer life-styles. One characteristic of the future is the so-called *graying of America*; that is, there will be more senior citizens than ever before. In 1985, there were 51 million Americans who were fifty-five years of age or older, and by the year 2000, there should be nearly 59 million people in this age group, a 16 percent increase in this category. (Conroy et al. 1986). These seniors will be more active and more health conscious than those before them. They will travel extensively and, when choosing a restaurant, look for one that serves lighter meals that are lower in cholesterol and salt and yet are still appetizing.

Another important category is working women and working mothers. Although the overall number in this group has stabilized, there now are more working mothers. Juggling home life and career is taxing and leaves little time for household chores and cooking, and so these women want the convenience of takeout or delivery service. They also demand quality and are attracted to the higher-quality fast food outlets or gourmet carryout stores. In a survey conducted by GDR Crest, the most takeout food purchases were made by females, eighteen to twenty-four years of age working full time, with children under six. Specialty restaurants are also popular with women diners. Research by the National Restaurant Association (Conroy et al. 1986) found that more working women frequented new restaurant concepts in 1986 than did any other demographic group. Thus, working women have emerged as a major source of consumer business in the restaurant industry, and their impact is expected to continue in the future. Restaurateurs must recognize this and make sure that their concepts appeal to this important group.

Children are fast becoming another prominent consumer segment in the hospitality industry. Today's children greatly influence the family's dining choice or vacation destination. Accordingly, hotel and restaurant operators must address the needs of this market segment if they are to draw their fair share of family business. First, and most important, children must be made to feel welcome, perhaps with a creative menu of their own, entertainment, activities, and celebrations of special occasions such as birthdays and holidays. As McDonald's realized years ago, a solid reputation with the children of today will mean the continued patronage of the adults of tomorrow.

FOOD

One growing need that affects all consumer groups is good nutrition. Some Americans are becoming more weight and health conscious, a concern that will have an increasing effect on their dining choices in the near and distant future. It seems that a day does not pass without another discovery about the link between eating habits and health. Of primary concern are the effects of fat, cholesterol, and salt intake, which are linked to heart disease. The American Medical Association also announced that there may be a link between diet and cancer and that by increasing our consumption of cabbage-family vegetables, fiber, vitamin A, and beta-carotene (the substance that makes carrots and other fruits and vegetables orange), we may be able to prevent this disease. Although to date, many Americans have not jumped on the nutrition bandwagon, more conclusive findings about diet and disease are sure to make believers out of more of them.

Seafood

As a result of their concern with good nutrition, Americans are consuming more seafood than ever before. Not only is it low in calories and fat, but fish oil has been found to prevent the building of cholesterol. In fact, seafood is so popular that it has been difficult for the fisheries to meet the rising demand. Indeed, many popular seafood items are no longer available commercially because they have been "fished out." For example, the blackened red fish craze in past years has made this species all but extinct in Florida. As Americans' appetite for seafood accelerates, the fisheries must respond by applying the farming techniques successful with trout and catfish to other species, and they must continue to seek out new varieties to take the place of those no longer available.

Meat

To date, the meat industry has not suffered the gloomy fate that many predicted in light of the growing concern with nutrition. Americans still enjoy a good steak, especially when dining out. But with greater interest in decreasing their intake of fat and cholesterol, the meat industry is responding by testing new breeds of cattle that produce tender meat with a lower fat content. Another process being tested is the use of electric shock to tenderize meat. Less expensive and leaner cuts can be made more palatable through this process. By staying abreast of the trend toward less fat in the diet, the meat industry will continue to retain its share of the consumer market.

Produce

Americans are also eating more fresh fruits and vegetables than ever before. Foodservice outlets first responded to this craze with the salad bar. Although popular initially, interest in this option is declining. There have been problems with freshness and sanitation, and many operators found it to be costly. Instead, restaurants now are serving more creative house salads and vegetable side dishes. The days of canned green beans are gone; fresh produce is here to stay.

Food Production

As energy costs continue to rise, the kitchens of tomorrow will be even more efficient than they are today. More self-regulating devices will be used, and perhaps the equipment of the future will be controlled by a single computer terminal.

And as labor costs escalate, foodservice operations will be seeking more efficient production methods. One technique used successfully throughout Europe is now being adopted in this country. It is *sous vide* cooking, meaning "under vacuum" in English. *Sous vide* uses some basic preparation techniques and allows portioned food to be chilled for up to three weeks with no loss of quality. The steps in the *sous vide* production method are as follows:

1. Season and brown the item.
2. Place each portion in a separate vacuum-sealed pouch.
3. Heat it in a convection oven to retard bacteria growth.
4. Place the items in ice water to chill.
5. Hold for up to three weeks at just above freezing.

When guests place their orders, or just before a banquet, kitchen workers remove the food pouches and heat them for a few moments on a steam table before serving. This method has been used successfully with lamb chops, scallops, soups, blackened red fish, and prime ribs, to name just a few. The only items that cannot be produced in this way are desserts and fried foods.

According to the October 1987 issue of *Restaurant Insights*, the Petroleum Club of New Orleans, a private club known for its fine cuisine, has been using *sous vide* cooking successfully. The club has reduced its labor costs by 17 percent and its food costs by 12 percent, with no loss of quality or weight. And its diners have reacted favorably to the change. To enable *sous vide* cooking, the club purchased a vacuum machine for about $3,500 and an air convection oven for $6,500. But this is a minimal investment compared with the reduction in food and labor costs.

LEGAL ISSUES

We live in an increasingly litigious society, and more often than not, disagreements are being settled in court. Several areas that have received public concern apply to the hospitality industry. As new laws are passed or old ones are enforced more strenuously, adjustments will have to be made in the foodservice and lodging industries.

Third-Party Liability and Alcohol Consumption

Tavern and restaurant owners and employees are being called on to help manage intoxicated guests: They have been the target of *third-party liability* or "dramshop" cases and are being sued for damages caused by their patrons who drive while intoxicated. One of the first cases of this type involved actor James Stacy, who lost both an arm and a leg and whose companion was killed after being struck by a drunk driver. The bar that served the drunk driver was forced to pay damages of $1.9 million (Henrich 1976). As a result of this and other, later judgments, alcohol sales will never be the same. Those selling liquor must take steps to limit their guests' ingestion of alcohol. Employees must be trained to recognize drunk guests and to deal with them, and so procedures for stopping patrons' drinking and providing alternative transportation must be established.

Many tavern and restaurant owners assume that they can rely on liability insurance to protect them should they be held responsible for damages, but this actually provides little protection (Rutherford 1985). Insurance companies are becoming more reluctant to write policies covering third-party liability, and those that do charge a high premium. Businesses that serve liquor must rely instead on preventive measures.

Sexual Harassment

Employees are more aware of their rights than ever before, and in recent years, one of the hottest topics has been *sexual harassment.* Made unlawful by Title VII of the Civil Rights Act in 1964, only recently has sexual harassment become a major issue and a growing concern in the hospitality industry. Owing to the nature of the business, foodservice, liquor, and lodging operators are especially vulnerable to claims of this type, and the number of lawsuits concerning sexual harassment increases annually.

Sexual harassment is broadly defined by the Equal Employment Opportunity Commission as unwelcome sexual advances, requests for sexual favors, and other verbal or physical conduct of a sexual nature. Employers are held liable for the conduct of both their employees and their guests. A bartender using profanity offensive to cocktail servers, or a guest making unwelcome advances toward an employee are both committing sexual harassment. If management fails to take immediate action when a complaint is filed, it can be held liable for the conduct of its employees or customers. Thus the best way to avoid grievances regarding sexual harassment is to take strong preventive measures. Management needs to let all employees know that it disapproves of such behavior and to develop a strong policy statement against sexual harassment, setting up procedures for handling complaints and immediately responding to problems, no matter how inconsequential they may seem.

At Sage's Restaurants, Eugene Sage instructs servers to notify management at the first sign of a problem with a guest (Papa 1985). The manager then has three options: first, to give the customer a different server, replacing a woman with a man or vice versa; second, to accompany this change with a firm reprimand; and, third, if these measures do not work, to ask the offending customer to leave. Currently, the legal fees alone for a sexual harassment claim can run as high as $85,000. Employees in the future will be more aware of their rights and more likely to file suit against an employer. Operators with foresight will take action now to avoid future difficulties.

Smoking

With the U.S. Surgeon General's warning about the dangers of secondhand smoke substantiated by follow-up studies, arguments against public smoking are gaining strength. Although most operators in the hospitality industry oppose the legal restriction of smoking in public places, it may be difficult to avoid it in the long run. Many private businesses have adopted a no-smoking policy, and local governments are following suit. Several cities have banned smoking in government buildings, and some are even moving to restrict it in all public places. The most celebrated ordinance was passed in Beverly Hills, California, where smoking is banned in public places. Restaurants there reported losses ranging from 10 to 30 percent following the ban (Bain 1987). Other state and local ordinances are less stringent, requiring restaurants and other public places to provide nonsmoking sections. Some hotels are even responding by providing nonsmoking guest rooms.

TECHNOLOGICAL ADVANCES

As the year 2000 approaches, more sophisticated computer applications, robotics, and advances in food technology will boost productivity and lower labor costs. Many large chains have been quick to add the latest "hi-tech" gadget, but many smaller operators do not have either the financial resources or the knowledge to use them. But computers and other equipment are becoming less expensive and simpler to operate, putting them within reach of everyone.

Computers are commonly being used to record sales, control inventory, plan menus, and maintain financial data. But these uses barely scratch the surface of their application in the hospitality industry. In the near future, *computerized voice recognition* for order takers will be the next step. Computers will be able to "understand" spoken words and take food orders, answer the phone, and adjust the thermostat when instructed. IBM has reported a new model that is PC based and will be able to recognize up to twenty thousand words (Woodman 1986).

Another application is being developed by Kristian Hammond, assistant professor of computer science at the University of Chicago (Magida 1987). Hammond's program, *CHEF*, goes beyond the capabilities of other recipe software now available. It not only records ingredients but also can actually create an original recipe. When asked for a recipe that has not been programmed, the computer will search its network and create one. There is also a reference program with a vast amount of culinary knowledge built into CHEF that will predict the recipe's success. If a problem is detected, CHEF will correct it, helping cooks to produce a perfect item every time.

Other computer applications include *VIEWTRON*, developed by Viewdata Corporation of America, which stores hundreds of restaurant reviews, menus, and other dining data that can be accessed by thousands of south Floridians (Kennedy et al. 1984). The diner telephones the service, uses a minitypewriter keypad to enter data, and is given a detailed list of restaurants and their prices on a video screen. The diner can then ask to see the restaurant's menu or to read a recent critic's review. Although VIEWTRON is available only in south Florida and is quite expensive at this time, one day it may become commonplace in hotels and airports throughout the country.

"HI TECH" VERSUS HOSPITALITY

With automation invading virtually every aspect of the hospitality industry in the not-too-distant future, what will happen to service? If guests can check in and out of hotels by themselves and can order meals without human contact, our industry could become depersonalized by technology. Management thus must not be too quick to embrace the latest labor cost–saving device but must keep in mind how the new system will affect customer service. Such a device may speed up the process and make fewer errors, but will it satisfy our need for human contact? Computerized reservation systems in hotels and cash registers in food-service outlets have revolutionized the hospitality industry. Management can use the time saved and information generated by computers to address the issue of guest service. If management is aware that a machine can never be a substitute for a human being, the conflict between high-tech and hi-touch can be eliminated. Automation can be used to run businesses more efficiently, but it can never take the place of excellent service by a well-trained staff sensitive to the customers' needs. The successful operator of the future will invest not only in the most advanced equipment but also in a staff. The primary goal of the hospitality industry always will be pleasing the guest.

SUMMARY

Shifts in the United States demographic profile will result in there being more senior citizens and working mothers than ever before. Americans are also more health conscious, and are choosing fresh produce, seafood, and low-cholesterol, low-fat meals when dining away from home.

Energy and labor costs are escalating. To control these expenses, more efficient production methods are being developed. One of these, *sous vide* cooking, allows food to be chilled and held for up to three weeks without loss of quality.

Several legal issues have emerged that affect the hospitality industry. Today's industry practitioners are being held liable for the conduct of both their guests and employees. Legal action based on third-party liability, sexual harassment, and no-smoking regulations is being taken against food and beverage operations with increasing regularity.

Finally, the hospitality industry is becoming more technically sophisticated than ever before. Computerized voice recognition and artificial intelligence are applications that will be commonplace in the foodservice industry in the not-too-distant future. The hospitality practitioners of tomorrow must be well prepared to meet these and other challenges that await them, but at the same time, not lose sight of their primary goal of providing quality guest service.

KEY TERMS

Graying of America
Sous vide
Third-party liability
Sexual harassment

Computer voice recognition
CHEF
VIEWTRON

———————————— CASE STUDY ————————————

When you enter a restaurant during the year 2010, you are greeted by a control panel with a voice synthesizer. After a polite welcome, it asks about your table preferences and searches its memory for the best location. One of the few human employees directs you to your table. It is equipped with a talking menu board that not only describes the choices but also provides, on request, a list of ingredients, calories, nutritional values, and photographs. You tell the computer your order, specifying preparation and service requirements. The computer tells you exactly how long your meal will take to prepare and will allow you to adjust the time to meet your needs.

In the kitchen, most of the food is prepared using robotic equipment.

All measurements are exact, as are cooking temperatures and time. A chef oversees the operation but does little of the actual preparation.

The food is served by a human waitress. If there are any problems or if you need water or ketchup, you will simply tell the computer, and the staff will respond immediately.

When you are finished, the computer totals your bill and you pay by inserting your money card. Your bank account is charged, the entire transaction taking about ten seconds. As you leave, the hostess computer thanks you politely and asks whether you enjoyed your meal. Your response and other data regarding your meal are automatically recorded. The computer not only tabulates this information for management but also makes suggestions for improving the service and food.

Discussion Questions

1. What are some of the positive and negative aspects of "hi-tech" dining as they relate to the restaurant operator?
2. What are the benefits of automated dining for the consumer?
3. How will computerized dining affect hospitality, and what can the operators of the future do to ensure that the human element is not lost?
4. What other changes in the dining experience do you predict for the future?

REFERENCES

Bain, Laurie. 1987. "Where There's Smoke, There's Legislation." *Restaurant Business* 86(12): 122–128.

Conroy, Kate, Claire Regan, and Hudson Riehle. 1986. "Outlook for 1987." *Restaurants USA* 6(11): 12–38.

Henrich, Craig. 1976. "Third Party Liability: Why Is Bob Scura Worried?" *New York Times,* May 23, p. 1.

Kennedy, Maryellen, Chris Lamb, and Steven Tally. 1984. "High Tech: The Reviews That Would Not Die." *Tables,* October, p. 18.

Magida, Phyllis. 1987. "CHEF Cooks with Cool Calculation and an Actively Inventive Memory." *Chicago Tribune,* September 24, sec. 7, p. 9.

Papa, Ann. 1985. "Protecting Your Staff from Sexual Harassment." *NRA News* 5(10): 18–19.

Rutherford, Denney G. 1985. "Managing Guest Intoxification: A Policy to Limit Third-Party Liability." *Cornell H.R.A. Quarterly* 26(3): 64–69.

Woodman, Julie. 1986. "When Server Talks, RSVP Listens, Then Computes." *Restaurants & Institutions* 96(11): 70.

Glossary

ACHIEVEMENT MOTIVATION: McClelland's and Winter's theory that assumes that some people have a greater need for achievement than do others and will consistently outperform low achievers.

ACTIVE LISTENING: A method of encouraging the speaker by giving neutral responses or reflecting his or her feelings.

AIRLINE TARIFF: A tariff used by travel agents when booking airline reservations; contains information about costs of transportation and all rules covering such passage.

ALL-SUITE HOTEL: A property offering only suites, which usually consist of a separate bedroom, kitchen, and living area.

AMERICAN SERVICE: A type of foodservice in which items are put on plates in the kitchen and then served by waiters or waitresses.

APPRENTICESHIP PROGRAM: A formal training program in which cooks learn while working for experienced chefs.

AUTOCRATIC LEADER: A leader who exerts tight control over the department and feels that his or her way is always right.

BANQUET EVENT ORDER: A detailed list of all the information pertaining

222

to a banquet function. It is generated by the catering department and distributed to all departments involved in the function.

BED AND BREAKFAST INN: A private home that offers lodging accommodations, which usually include breakfast.

BEHAVIOR MODIFICATION: A method of changing behavior through the use of positive and negative reinforcement.

BONA FIDE OCCUPATIONAL QUALIFICATIONS: The characteristics needed by applicants for successful job performance.

BUREAUCRATIC LEADER: An inflexible leader who always does things by the book.

CAPITAL BUDGET: An itemized estimation of all the funds needed to start up a new business.

CAPTAIN: A restaurant employee who supervises waiters and waitresses and performs more complex table service when required.

CASE STUDY: A written description of a simulated or actual situation used during training sessions to encourage group discussion.

CATERING DIARY: A record book used in catering that indicates which functions are being held in various banquet rooms on each day.

CATERING MANAGER: A manager who oversees the planning and sales of banquet foodservice in hotels, restaurants, or private catering operations.

CHARTER: A travel option that allows clients to take advantage of a lower group rate. It may include airline transportation, meals, lodging, and sight-seeing for one set price.

CLOSED-ENDED QUESTION: Interview questions used to probe for specific information. They require a brief response.

CONCIERGE: A hotel employee who works at a desk in the lobby and handles special guest requests and makes arrangements for VIP (Very Important Person) customers.

CONTRACT MANAGEMENT: A company that operates a foodservice establishment within another business.

CONTROLLER: The individual who is responsible for accounting in a business operation.

CONVENTION HOTEL: A lodging operation that attracts mainly large convention groups. It usually consists of one thousand or more rooms, extensive banquet facilities, and multiple food and beverage outlets.

CONVENTION SERVICE MANAGER: A hotel manager responsible for the physical design and setup of banquet and convention facilities.

CORPORATION: A business incorporated under state laws that is owned by stockholders. It is a separate legal entity from the owners and limits their personal liability.

COST OF FOOD: The expenses incurred by purchasing food sold in order to produce revenue.

CREDIT MEMORANDUM: A memorandum issued to the buyer by the food wholesaler or purveyor when the buyer has been overcharged, resulting in a credit to or decrease in the buyer's account.

DEBT FINANCING: Capital generated by loans that is used to finance a business venture.

DEMOGRAPHICS: The study of the characteristics of people living in a particular area.

DISCRIMINATORY QUESTIONS: The questions asked during an interview that deal with issues that are not job related and may result in unfair hiring practices.

EMPATHY: The ability to put oneself in another person's position and feel what he or she is feeling.

EQUAL EMPLOYMENT OPPORTUNITY: The legal requirement that all people must be treated in the same way, regardless of race, religion, national origin, age, sex, or physical disability.

EQUITY FINANCING: The portion of a business's startup funds, consisting of the owner's or stockholders' investment.

ETHNIC RESTAURANT: A foodservice operation whose menu, decor, and service are typical of a particular region or country.

EXECUTIVE ASSISTANT: A hotel manager who reports directly to the general manager and is responsible for supervising the department heads.

EXECUTIVE CHEF: The chef who oversees the entire food production operation in a hotel or other foodservice business.

EXPEDITER: A kitchen employee who ensures that food orders are placed and filled correctly.

FAST FOOD RESTAURANT: A restaurant that offers a limited menu and either drive-up or walk-up service.

FEASIBILITY STUDY: A financial study that examines the likelihood of success of a new business venture, based on expected income and expenses.

FICTITIOUS NAME REGISTRATION: A legal requirement that businesses using a name other than the owner's be registered with the state.

FINE DINING RESTAURANT: A foodservice operation that features the best in food and service at a correspondingly high price.

FORECASTING: Projecting future sales activity based on past and present data.

FRANCHISE: The purchase by an individual business owner of the name and management expertise of a parent company.

FRENCH SERVICE: A type of foodservice in which items are partially prepared and served at the table.

GARDE-MANGER: A kitchen worker who oversees the preparation of cold food.

GENERAL MANAGER: An individual who oversees an entire hotel or restaurant operation.

GENERAL PARTNER: An investor who is also responsible for a business's day-to-day operation.

GUARANTEED ATTENDANCE: The final count of the number of guests expected to attend a catering function. The client must guarantee payment for this number, regardless of the actual number attending.

HYGIENE FACTORS: Those aspects of a job that produce satisfaction or dissatisfaction in employees but do not affect their motivation.

INCOME AND EXPENSE STATEMENT: A detailed list of all expenses and income incurred by a business during a fixed period of time. It is used to calculate net profit or loss.

IN-FLIGHT CHEF: A chef who works for an airline-catering operation and oversees the preparation of large quantities of food.

INVENTORY: A record of all the goods on hand that are available for sale. Restaurants usually calculate the value of their inventory every four weeks.

JOB DESCRIPTION: A written description of the duties and responsibilities required for a particular job.

LAISSEZ-FAIRE MANAGER: A nondirective leader who places all responsibility for decision making on his or her employees, thereby providing little direction.

LEADER'S GUIDE: Manual used by trainers to help teach employees. It contains the same information as does the trainees' procedures manual, plus instructions for the trainee, discussion questions, and the answer key for test questions.

LEADERSHIP STYLE: The way in which a manager interacts with his or her subordinates.

LIMITED PARTNER: An investor who is not involved in a business's day-to-day operation.

MAÎTRE D': The person who supervises service in a foodservice establishment. This position is usually found in fine dining restaurants or hotel catering operations.

MANAGEMENT BY OBJECTIVES: A management system based on goal setting and careful monitoring of their achievement.

MANAGEMENT CONTRACT: A contract between investors and another company to manage their business for them.

MARKET SATURATION: The condition prevailing when a particular type of business has been overdeveloped and the demand for new ventures in this area is small.

MID-SCALE RESTAURANTS: A moderately priced restaurant that offers table service.

MOTIVATION: The basis of a particular behavior or action.

MOTIVATION–HYGIENE THEORY: Herzberg's theory, which states that individuals are motivated by the work itself, not by environmental factors.

NEPOTISM: A company's favoritism to relatives of the owners or other employees.

OFF-PREMISE CATERING: Catering events not held in a particular banquet facility. Rather, the caterers travel to the location of the client's choice and prepare and/or serve meals.

ON-PREMISE CATERING: Catering events held in a particular banquet facility, to which the guests come for banquets.

OPEN-ENDED QUESTIONS: Interview questions that require a detailed response from the applicant.

OPERATING RATIOS: Financial comparisons that allow a business to assess its profitability.

ORIENTATION: A new employee's introduction to the job.

PARTICIPATIVE MANAGEMENT: A style of management in which workers participate in the decision-making process.

PARTNERSHIP: A business agreement between two or more individuals. A partnership is not a separate legal entity from the owners, and so they are personally liable for any debts the business may incur.

PASSIVE LISTENING: Listening without responding to what the speaker is saying.

PERFORMANCE APPRAISAL: The periodic review and rating of an employee's performance on the job.

PRIVATE CLUB: An operation that includes foodservice and is open only to members of a particular organization.

PROCEDURES MANUAL: A detailed guide used by trainees that outlines all methods of job performance, written quizzes, and visual aids.

PROGRAM EVALUATION: A periodic assessment of a training program's effectiveness. It may be a written questionnaire distributed to all who have completed the training or may be an on-the-job evaluation of a trainee's job skills.

PROGRESSIVE DISCIPLINE: A way of disciplining employees for an infraction of company policy that applies increasingly severe penalties for each violation.

RECRUITING: The process of attracting job applicants to a particular organization.

RESIDENT MANAGER: The hotel executive who is second in command and reports directly to the general manager. He or she is responsible for supervising department heads.

RESORT HOTEL: A lodging facility that features extensive recreational facilities, including golf, tennis, swimming, a health club, and boating. A resort might be located in a popular vacation area or outside a large metropolitan area.

RESTAURANT CONCEPT: A detailed description of a foodservice operation, including the theme, decor, menu, target market, and location.

RETAIL FOODSERVICE: A restaurant operation located in a retail store, ranging from a department store to a convenience food mart.

RETAIL TRAVEL AGENT: An individual who sells transportation, lodging, and sight-seeing activities to the general public.

ROLE PLAY: A training exercise in which two individuals act out specified roles.

RUSSIAN SERVICE: Food served to seated guests from silver platters by waiters and waitresses who place it on the guests' plates with fork-and-spoon tongs.

SALES MANAGER: The hotel employee who is responsible for selling guest rooms to large groups.

SCREENING INTERVIEW: An interview used to screen out unqualified applicants before the in-depth interview.

SEXUAL HARASSMENT: Unwelcome sexual advances, requests for sexual favors, and other verbal or physical conduct of a sexual nature.

SKILLS TRAINING: A method of teaching current employees new skills or refining their current skills.

SOLE PROPRIETORSHIP: A business owned by a single individual. As in a partnership, the business is not a separate legal entity, and so the owner is responsible for any debts incurred.

SOUS CHEF: A French term meaning "under chef." This individual is second in command to the executive chef and supervises employees and performs administrative duties.

***SOUS VIDE*:**   A French term meaning "under vacuum." This is a cooking method that uses basic preparation techniques and allows portioned food to be chilled for up to three weeks with no loss of quality.

STANDARD RECIPES: A set format followed in food preparation that, when prepared correctly, ensures consistent quality and quantity every time.

SUBURBAN HOTEL: A lodging facility, located in a suburb of a major metropolitan area, that appeals to frequent business travelers and tourists.

TEAM BUILDING: A management practice that increases the employees' participation and encourages them to work together to solve problems. It usually consists of regular meetings with members of the work group, at which problems are examined and solutions are brainstormed.

THEME RESTAURANT: A restaurant at which the menu, decor, and service all reflect a particular topic or theme.

THEORY X: MacGregor's managerial assumption that proposes that employees are basically lazy, avoid responsibility, require close supervision, and are motivated primarily by money.

THEORY Y: MacGregor's managerial assumption that employees enjoy work, will work toward objectives to which they feel committed, and do not require coercion or threats to be motivated.

THIRD-PARTY LIABILITY: The ruling that individuals who dispense or sell alcoholic beverages will be held responsible for any damages caused by those who bought liquor at their establishment.

TRADE DEFICIT: The result of a country's importing more goods than it exports.

VENTURE CAPITAL: Those funds from investors who are willing to accept a high degree of risk for a potentially high return on their investment.

WHOLESALE TRAVEL AGENT: An individual who sells travel packages to retail travel agencies that in turn market them to the general public.

WORK SAMPLING: A method of testing applicants with situations simulating those they will experience on the job.

INDEX

Age Discrimination in Employment
    Act, 176
Airlines
    customer service representatives,
        124
    flight attendants, 124
    in-flight chefs, 124
    passenger service representatives,
        124
    tariff, 117
    ticket agents, 124
Asilomar, 123
Average check, 64
Average cover, 64

Banquets
    beverage operations, 104
    chef, 63
    event order, 106
Bed and breakfast inns, 86–88
Benton, Helen, 40
Beverage operations, 62, 104. See
    also Liquor control
Bolles, Richard, 18
Bonafide occupational
    qualifications, 176–78
Budget, 54
Buffalo Statler Hotel, 6
Burger King, 12
Busch Gardens, 119–20
Business structure, 53

Cafe Ba-Ba-Reeba!, 48
Campbell, Jeff, 12
Camping, 123–24

Career
    goals, 22
    objective, 24
    planning, 22–23
Case study, 199
Catering
    department, 97, 106
    diary, 106
    hotel, 97
    off-premise, 40
    on-premise, 40
Central Park, USA, 40
Chamber of Commerce, 111
Charter
    affinity-based, 117
    public, 117
    vacation, 117
Chef. See also Kitchen employees
    apprentice, 63
    apprenticeship program, 63
    banquet, 63
    de partie, 63
    executive, 62-63, 103
    sous, 63, 103
Chez Panisse, 56
Circle K, 41
Civil Rights Act, 176
Close-ended questions, 184
Coles Ordinary, 4
Collateral, 55
Communication. See also Listening
    aggressive behavior, 149–50
    assertive behavior, 149–50
    cop-out words, 146
    critical and blaming words, 145–
        47

Communication (*Con nued*)
  empathy, 145, 147–4
  non-verbal, 148
  submissive behavior, 9–50
  tone of voice, 147
  vague words, 146
Company mission statemer 136
Competitive bids, 65
Computer
  back of the house applicati ns,
    69–70
  front of the house applicatio s,
    67–68
  menu program, 219
  recipe software, 218
  VIEWTRON, 218
  voice recognition, 218
Coney Island, 119
Consumer trends
  children, 214
  fruit and vegetable consumption,
    215
  meat consumption, 215
  seafood consumption, 215
  senior citizens, 213
  working mothers, 215
  working women, 214
Contract management, 42
Controller, 107
Cook, Thomas, 114
Corporation, 53
Cost card, 73, 75
Cost control, 64
  computer applications, 67-70
  inventory, 64–66
  labor, 67
  revenue, 66
Cost percent of sales, 64
Counseling employees, 164–65
Credit memorandum, 65
Cruise lines, 124–25
Customer comment cards, 198
Cypress Gardens, 113

Denny's Restaurants, 37. *See also*
    Training
Disciplinary action, 168
  written warning notice, 168–69

Disneyland, 119
Disney World, 111, 119, 122, 131,
    138
Domino's Pizza, 13–14, 209
Dramshop laws, 216–17
Dress code, 196

Ed Debevic's, 38
EPCOT center, 121
Epicure program, 42
Equal Employment Opportunity
    Commission, 176, 217
Escoffier, 4
Etcheber, Jackie, 12

Familiarization trips, 114–15
Feasibility study, 49, 79
Financial plan, 53
Financing
  debt, 55
  equity, 55
Focus group, 140, 198
Food cost, 64
Foodservice operations. *See also*
    Restaurants
  convenience stores, 41
  employee feeding, 44
  health care, 42–43
  institutional, 21, 41–42
  ret l, 41
  school, 43–44
  turnpike, 40
Franchising, 86, 90–91

Geriatric care facilities, 86, 89–90
Gordon Restaurant, 50, 52
Guaranteed attendance, 106
Guest check handling, 66

Hamburger University, 11. *See also*
    McDonald's
High tech/high touch society, 132
Hilton, Conrad, 7–8
Hilton Hotels Corporation, 7–8
Hilton International, 8
Hotel
  definition, 4

Hotel (*Continued*)
  opening, 91
  organizational chart, 95–96
Hotel management
  accounting, 107
  catering, 97
  convention service manager, 98
  engineering, 107
  executive assistant manager, 95
  executive chef, 103
  executive steward, 104
  food and beverage department,
    103
  food production manager, 103
  front office operations, 99–103
  general manager, 95
  housekeeping, 102
  personnel department, 108
  reservations, 99–100
  resident manager, 95
  sales department, 95, 97
  restaurants, 104
Hotel ownership
  franchise, 90–91
  fully owned, 90
  management contract, 90–91
Hotel segments
  airport, 84–85
  all-suite, 86, 88–89
  convention, 81–82
  moderately priced, 85–86
  resort, 82–83
  suburban, 83–84
Hot Shoppes Restaurants, 9
Hurst, Michael, 57

Iacocca, Lee, 159
Incentive programs, 102, 138–39
Income and expense statement, 54
Individual development program,
    209
Interview
  checklist, 27
  discriminatory questions, 178–81
  employment application, 179–80,
    186
  format, 184–88
  job, 24–28

pre-employment inquiries, 178
  questions, 26, 184–85
  recruitment, 182–83
  references, 188
  résumé, 24–25
  screening, 183–84
Inventory, 65, 69
  perpetual, 66

Jackie's Restaurant, 12
Job Code Training Program, 120
Job description, 176, 181, 184, 197–
    98

Kampgrounds of America, 123
Kitchen employees. *See also* Chef
  cook's assistant, 63
  dishwasher, 64
  executive steward, 104
  expediter, 63
  food production manager, 103
  pantry assistant, 63
  porter, 63
  purchasing agent, 63–65
  storeroom clerk, 63
Kroc, Ray, 10–12

Labor costs, 64, 67
Laclede's Landing, 112
Leader's guide, 199, 205
Leadership style
  autocratic, 162
  bureaucratic, 162
  laissez-faire, 162–63
  participative, 163
  Theory X and Theory Y, 161–62
Leonard, Stu, 139
Lettuce Entertain You Enterprise,
    14–15. *See also* Melman,
    Richard
Limited partner, 55
Listening, 144–45
Liquor control, 66, 104. *See also*
    Beverage operations
Lutece, 12, 37

McDonald's Corporation, 39, 57
  Kroc, Ray, 10–12
  McDonald Brothers, 10

McDonald's (*Continued*)
   quality, service, cleanliness, &
     value, 10, 137
Management by objectives, 22,
    158–59, 165
Management in Training, 209
Market
   research, 49
   saturation, 34
Marriott Corporation
   Marriott, Bill, 12
   Marriott, J. Willard, 9
   training programs, 209–10
Measurements, cooking, 72, 74
Melman, Richard, 14–15, 38, 47–48
Menu
   à la carte, 73
   content, 71
   design, 74, 76–77
   planning, 70–77
   pricing, 72–74
   table d'hote, 73
Mitchell, Lou, 57
Mobley Hotel, 7
Monaghan, Tom, 13–14
Motivation, 157–61
   achievement, 158
   behavior modification, 159
   goal setting, 158
   motivation-hygiene theory, 160
Multiplier effect, 113

Naisbitt, John, 132
National parks, 123
Nepotism, 28–29
Nieman-Marcus restaurants, 41
Nutrition, 214

One-idea contest, 139
Open-ended questions, 184
Operating ratios, 64
Organizational chart, 29, 53
   dining room, 60–61
   hotel, 95–96
   kitchen, 60–61
Orientation, 193–94, 196
   checklist, 194–95

Overbooking, 99–100
Owner equity, 55

Palmer House Hotel, 9
Paris Ritz Hotel, 4
Partnership, 53
Performance appraisal, 139, 163,
    168
Point-of-sales cash register, 67–68
Policies and procedures, 196
   manual, 199
Priority 1, 199, 208
Private clubs, 37
Purchasing agent, 63–64
Purveyor, 65

R. J. Grunts, 15, 48
Rehabilitation Act, 176
Restaurant employees
   busperson, 62
   captain, 62
   cashier, 62
   dining room supervisor, 62
   host/hostess, 62
   maitre d', 62
   manager, 60–61, 104
Restaurant planning
   business structure, 53
   concept, 48
   feasibility study, 49–50, 79
   fictitious name registration, 52
   financial planning, 54–55
   formula for success, 56–57
   licenses and permits, 51–52
   site selection, 50–51
   zoning laws, 50, 52
Restaurant segments. *See also*
    Foodservice operations
   commercial, 36
   ethnic, 39
   fast food, 39
   fine dining, 36
   mid-scale, 37
   theme, 38
Ritz, Cesar, 4–5
Role play, 199
Rusty Pelican, 56

St. Vincent's Charity Hospital, 42
Scoozie, 15
Sea World, 119
Service
    blunders, 133–34
    difficult guests, 150–51
    economy, 131
    illiterate management, 140
    incentives, 138–39
    performance appraisal, 139
    policy, 137
    procedures manual, 137–38
    standards, 137–38
    triumphs, 134–36
Service style
    American, 71
    family, 71
    French, 71
    Russian, 71
Service training, 138
    Disney, 138
    priority 1, 199, 203
    Rusty Pelican, 56–57
Sexual harassment, 217–18
Shire, Lydia, 103
Sinclair, Gordon, 52
Six Flags Great America, 121
Small Business Administration, 55
Smoking, 218
Sole proprietorship, 53
Soltner, Andre, 12, 37
Sous vide cooking, 216
Specification, product, 64–65
Standard recipes, 69–70, 72–73
Statler, Ellsworth, 6

Tapas, 48
Target market, 49
Team-building, 170–72
Third-party liability, 216–17
Thirty-second blunder, 133
Trade deficit, 113–14

Training
    canned programs, 205–6
    customer service, 208
    Denny's training programs, 199–
        205, 210
    Domino's training programs, 209
    Hamburger University, 11
    Hilton's training programs, 199,
        203
    hotel programs, 108
    Marriott's training programs,
        209–10
    needs analysis, 197
    new employee orientation, 193–
        97
    plan, 199–200
    program evaluation, 207–08
    skills training, 193, 197
    strategy, 198
    training trainers, 207
Travel and Tourism
    attractions, 118
    economic effect, 113–14
    marketing, 125–26
    tour guide, 118
    travel agents, 114
    travel wholesalers, 114–15, 118
Trust House, Ltd., 3
Twin Bridges Motor Hotel, 10

Underemployed, 18
Union Station, 111–12, 122–23

Vauxhall Gardens, 119
Venture capital, 55
VIEWTRON, 218

Waldorf-Astoria, 8
Waters, Alice, 56
Work sampling, 181–82, 187

Yosemite, 123

Study Guide

Hospitality Past and Present

EXERCISE 1-1: Sentence Completion

NAME: _____   DATE: _____

Test your knowledge of the material covered in Chapter 1 by completing the following sentences:

1. The oldest _____ was recently discovered in ancient Mesopotamia.
2. Historical inns throughout Europe are operated today by

    _____ .

3. _____ is credited with making European hotels fashionable.
4. _____ is known for making luxury hotel accommodations affordable to middle-class Americans.
5. The first hotelier to enter international markets was _____

    _____ .

6. _____ was called "a living example of the American dream" by President Ronald Reagan.
7. McDonald's motto is _____ ,

    _____ ,   _____ ,

    and _____ .

8. The owner of Lutèce, _____ , is recognized as one of the greatest chefs in America.
9. _____ founded Domino's Pizza.
10. Richard Melman founded the restaurant chain _____

    _____ .

EXERCISE 1-2: Matching

NAME: _____   DATE: _____

Match the following people with their achievements:

_____ 1. Ray Kroc

_____ 2. J. W. Marriott

_____ 3. Cesar Ritz

_____ 4. Ellsworth Statler

_____ 5. Tom Monaghan

_____ 6. Conrad Hilton

_____ 7. Richard Melman

a. He secured patronage of the Prince of Wales.

b. He is famous for the slogan "a room and a bath for a dollar and a half."

c. His chain owns the Waldorf-Astoria.

d. He operated the first in-flight kitchen.

e. Ninety-six percent of the American population have tried his product.

f. His corporate headquarters houses a sports medicine center and a working farm.

g. His first restaurant was R. J. Grunts.

EXERCISE 1-3: Leadership Qualities

NAME: _____   DATE: _____

Research your favorite current industry leader not discussed in this chapter, and outline the reasons for his or her success. Good sources of information are trade magazines, newspaper articles, and company literature.

LEADER: _____   COMPANY: _____

1. Briefly describe the scope of the organization. You might include information about the number of units, type of operation, annual income, and date founded.

_____

_____

_____

_____

2. Briefly describe the leader's background. How did this affect the individual's success?

_____

_____

_____

_____

3. What qualities or characteristics are responsible for this person's success?

_____

_____

_____

_____

4. What new ventures are planned?

_____

_____

_____

7

REFERENCES:
List the articles, books, or other sources you used to complete this exercise. Use the end-of-chapter references as a guide to the proper format.

_____

_____

_____

_____

EXERCISE 1-4: Common Denominators

NAME: _____   DATE: _____

As you review the information pertaining to each of the leaders described in this chapter, look for common attributes or experiences and list them below.

1. _____
   _____
   _____

2. _____
   _____
   _____

3. _____
   _____
   _____

4. _____
   _____
   _____

5. _____
   _____
   _____

Chapter 2

Choosing a Career Path

EXERCISE 2-1: Sentence Completion

NAME: _____   DATE: _____

Test your knowledge of the material covered in Chapter 2 by completing the following sentences:

1. According to Richard Bolles's book *What Color Is My Parachute*, most Americans are _____.

2. _____ foodservice is found in hospitals and schools.

3. One technique that can be used to set career goals is _____ _____.

4. Goals must have the following five characteristics:

    a. _____

    b. _____

    c. _____

    d. _____

    e. _____

5. Immediately after an interview, send a _____ _____ to the person with whom you spoke.

6. When researching a potential employer's financial security, three places to look for data are _____, _____, and _____.

7. When assessing a company's potential for growth, read _____, _____, and _____.

8. When writing a résumé, your _____ should immediately follow your name, address, and telephone number.

9. On your résumé, work experience should always be listed in _____ order.

10. When starting a new job, you should review the company's _____ to acquaint yourself with key personnel.

EXERCISE 2-2: Career Checklist

NAME: _____ DATE: _____

Some career options will be more appealing than others. Complete the following checklist to understand better the job characteristics you want. Place a check mark in the corresponding column to indicate whether you prefer a particular job characteristic, want to avoid it, or have no particular opinion.

JOB CHARACTERISTICS	PREFER	AVOID	DOES NOT APPLY
Travel	☐	☐	☐
Regular work schedule	☐	☐	☐
Relocation	☐	☐	☐
Weekend or evening work	☐	☐	☐
People contact	☐	☐	☐
Close contact with co-workers	☐	☐	☐
Wide variety of duties	☐	☐	☐
Supervises the work of others	☐	☐	☐
Lots of paperwork	☐	☐	☐
Responsibility for hiring	☐	☐	☐
Responsibility for firing	☐	☐	☐
Working alone	☐	☐	☐
Heavy telephone contact	☐	☐	☐
Clerical duties	☐	☐	☐
Bookkeeping	☐	☐	☐
Use of computer	☐	☐	☐

JOB CHARACTERISTICS	PREFER	AVOID	DOES NOT APPLY
Cash-handling responsibility	☐	☐	☐
Serving customers	☐	☐	☐
Food preparation	☐	☐	☐
Physically taxing work	☐	☐	☐
Close supervision	☐	☐	☐

EXERCISE 2-3: Investigative Interview

NAME: _____ DATE: _____

To help you decide on your career goals, interview a manager in the hospitality industry who currently holds a job that you would like to have. During your discussion, review the following areas and summarize the individual's response in the space provided:

Outline of current job duties: _____

_____

_____

Previous jobs held that led to the current position: _____

_____

_____

Educational background: _____

_____

A typical day on the job: _____

_____

_____

Interviewee's future career goals: _____

_____

Advice for success in the field: _____

_____

_____

Other information learned: _____

_____

_____

_____

EXERCISE 2-4: Résumé

NAME: _____   DATE: _____

Using the format in Figure 2-2, write a résumé detailing your background. Before sending it to prospective employers, neatly type it on medium-weight bond paper.

PERSONAL DATA: _____

_____

_____

CAREER OBJECTIVE: _____

_____

EDUCATIONAL BACKGROUND: _____

_____

_____

_____

_____

_____

BACKGROUND IN THE HOSPITALITY INDUSTRY (OR PAST WORK HISTORY): _____

_____

_____

_____

_____

_____

_____

PROFESSIONAL ORGANIZATIONS: _____

_____

_____

_____

REFERENCES
References will be furnished on request.

EXERCISE 2-5: Frequently Asked Interview Questions

NAME: _____   DATE: _____

The following questions are often asked during an employment interview. Indicate your response to each one in the space provided.

1. What do you see yourself doing in five years? _____
    _____

2. What are your greatest strengths? _____
    _____

3. Which areas require further development? _____
    _____

4. Describe an ideal supervisor. _____
    _____
    _____

5. What problems have you experienced with supervisors in the past?
    _____
    _____

6. Describe an ideal work environment. _____
    _____

7. Describe your most rewarding job experience. _____
    _____

8. Describe your least rewarding job experience. _____
    _____

9. What do you do in your spare time? _____
    _____

Chapter 3

The Foodservice Industry

EXERCISE 3-1: Sentence Completion

NAME: _____   DATE: _____

Test your knowledge of the material covered in Chapter 3 by completing the following sentences:

1. When the number of restaurants exceeds the demand, this is called _____.

2. Three markets that are expected to experience growth in the future are _____, _____, and _____.

3. More mature markets less likely to experience growth are _____, _____, and _____.

4. Growth in the fast food industry is expected to _____ _____ in the future.

5. More than _____ of institutional foodservice outlets are independently operated.

6. Marriott, Service America, and Canteen are _____ _____ companies that operate foodservice outlets in institutions and businesses.

7. To meet accreditation standards, each health care foodservice operation must be overseen by a (an) _____ _____.

8. The largest educational foodservice operation is the _____ _____.

9. _____ caterers travel to another site to serve meals.

10. The foodservice industry is helped by such economic factors as _____ and _____.

EXERCISE 3-2: Matching

NAME: _____   DATE: _____

Match the following restaurant segments with the appropriate information:

_____ 1. Fast food

_____ 2. Theme

_____ 3. Convenience stores

_____ 4. Catering

_____ 5. Fine dining

_____ 6. Mid-scale

_____ 7. Ethnic

_____ 8. Employee feeding

a. This is also called a "white tablecloth" restaurant.

b. Its appeal lies in an entertaining atmosphere.

c. This appeals to the consumer's need for adventure and diversity.

d. These are moderately priced, family-style restaurants.

e. The menu, decor, entertainment, and service all must coincide.

f. This is revitalized turnpike food-service.

g. This does not require a large initial investment to start.

h. These outlets are making headway in the fast food market.

EXERCISE 3-3: Restaurant Concept

NAME: _____ DATE: _____

Develop a concept for a restaurant that you might want to own, and describe it as follows:

NAME OF RESTAURANT: _____ NUMBER OF SEATS: _____

TYPE OF OPERATION: _____ PRICE RANGE: _____

Describe the clientele you hope to attract:

_____

_____

Describe the area where the outlet would be located:

_____

_____

What type of service would you offer?

_____

_____

Describe the decor of the restaurant:

_____

_____

_____

_____

List some of the items you would include on your menu:

_____

_____

What would be unique about your restaurant?

_____

_____

What type of ambience or atmosphere would your restaurant have?

_____

_____

EXERCISE 3-4: Market Trends

NAME: _____   DATE: _____

Choose a location in your city or town where you would like to open a restaurant. Review the following list of restaurant categories, and check the appropriate box to indicate whether you think it would succeed or fail in that location. Explain your decision in the space provided.

LOCATION:

	SUCCEED	FAIL
Theme Restaurant	☐	☐

Why? _____

_____

| Ethnic Restaurant | ☐ | ☐ |

Why? _____

_____

| Fast Food Restaurant | ☐ | ☐ |

Why? _____

_____

| Fine Dining Restaurant | ☐ | ☐ |

Why? _____

_____

| Mid-Scale Restaurant | ☐ | ☐ |

Why? _____

_____

| Catering, On-Premise | ☐ | ☐ |

Why? _____

_____

EXERCISE 3-5: Restaurant Segments

NAME: _____   DATE: _____

List the name of a restaurant in your area that corresponds to each of the categories indicated.

CATEGORY	RESTAURANT
Fine dining	_____
Mid-scale	_____
Ethnic	_____
Theme	_____
On-premise catering	_____
Off-premise catering	_____
Fast food	_____
Gourmet carryout	_____
Retail	_____

Chapter 4

The Entrepreneurial Spirit

EXERCISE 4-1: Sentence Completion

NAME: _____   DATE: _____

Test your knowledge of the material covered in Chapter 4 by completing the following sentences:

1. The first step in determining the feasibility of a location is to conduct a _____.

2. Another name for potential customers is _____
_____.

3. If a business's name is anything other than just the name of the owner, a _____ registration is needed.

4. Many cities and towns limit the number of _____
_____ they issue, making it difficult to obtain one.

5. A good rule of thumb is to have enough cash on hand to keep the business running without profit for a minimum of _____ months.

6. A _____ lists all funds required to develop a business.

7. Before applying for a bank loan, you must produce a detailed summary of your _____ and your assets.

8. A _____ partner is not involved in day-to-day operations.

9. A _____ partner helps run the business.

10. If you are unable to obtain a loan from a bank, another source that might help you is the _____.

EXERCISE 4-2: Matching

NAME: _____   DATE: _____

Match the following terms to their correct definitions:

____ 1. Market study

____ 2. Sole proprietorship

____ 3. Partnership

____ 4. Corporation

____ 5. Organizational chart

____ 6. Equity funding

____ 7. Debt financing

____ 8. Venture capital

____ 9. Collateral

____10. Demography

a. A study of the people living in an area.

b. A business that has one owner.

c. Money from investors.

d. Assets held as security for a loan.

e. Money from a financial institution.

f. A business is owned by two or more people.

g. A list of the chain of command in a business.

h. Money from investors willing to accept a high degree of risk.

i. A separate legal entity.

j. A method of determining the characteristics of potential customers, evaluating competition, and identifying traffic patterns.

EXERCISE 4-3: Testing Your Entrepreneurial Spirit

NAME: _____   DATE: _____

Answer each question by checking the appropriate box.

		YES	NO
1.	Are your parents self-employed?	☐	☐
2.	Have you ever been fired?	☐	☐
3.	Did you operate a business before you were twenty?	☐	☐
4.	Are you the oldest child in your family?	☐	☐
5.	Are you the youngest child in your family?	☐	☐
6.	Are you always on time?	☐	☐
7.	Are you very organized?	☐	☐
8.	Would you like to work in sales?	☐	☐
9.	In a business situation, do you think it is important always to know who is in charge?	☐	☐
10.	Do you get along well with your father?	☐	☐

KEY

1. y = 10, n = 0
2. y = 10, n = 0
3. y = 10, n = 0
4. y = 10, n = 0
5. y = 0, n = 10
6. y = 10, n = 0
7. y = 10, n = 0
8. y = 10, n = 0
9. y = 10, n = 0
10. y = 0, n = 10

SCORING

80–100 points: Successful entrepreneur
60–79 points: Potential entrepreneur
50–69 points: Borderline entrepreneur
Fewer than 50 points: Unlikely entrepreneur

35

EXERCISE 4-4: Hot Markets

NAME: _____ DATE: _____

Describe four hospitality-related business ventures that you feel would be successful now or in the near future. Explain your reasons for selecting them.

BUSINESS 1: _____

_____

_____

_____

_____

_____

BUSINESS 2: _____

_____

_____

_____

_____

_____

BUSINESS 3: _____

_____

_____

_____

_____

_____

BUSINESS 4: _____

_____

_____

_____

_____

_____

EXERCISE 4-5: Preopening Checklist

NAME: _____   DATE: _____

Make a checklist of the activities that must be completed before opening a restaurant. Also indicate the number of weeks or months before the opening by which each activity should be completed. Assume that you are starting from scratch.

ACTIVITY   DATE COMPLETED

1. Develop concept
2. _____   _____
3. _____   _____
4. _____   _____
5. _____   _____
6. _____   _____
7. _____   _____
8. _____   _____
9. _____   _____
10. _____   _____
11. _____   _____
12. _____   _____
13. _____   _____
14. _____   _____
15. _____   _____
16. _____   _____
17. _____   _____
18. _____   _____
19. _____   _____
20. _____   _____

Food and Beverage Operations

EXERCISE 5-1: Sentence Completion

NAME: _____   DATE: _____

Test your knowledge of the material covered in Chapter 5 by completing the following sentences:

1. The _____ does all of the hiring and firing and is responsible for the financial end of the business.

2. In a small establishment, the chef _____,

   _____,   _____,

   and _____ prepare all the food.

3. Most cities sponsor a (an) _____ program in which trainees work with experienced chefs to learn cooking and administrative skills.

4. The restauranteur uses _____ to analyze the business's success.

5. _____ provide a detailed description of the quality, size, form, and condition of food items.

6. A _____ indicates that the restaurant will not be charged for returned items.

7. An inventory of food items should be made at least each

   _____.

8. A (an) _____ inventory system is used for more valuable items.

9. In _____ service, food is preplated and then served.

10. In _____ service, some of the food is prepared at the table.

EXERCISE 5-2: Matching

NAME: _____   DATE: _____

Match the following positions with their description:

___ 1. Sous chef

___ 2. Garde-manger

___ 3. Expediter

___ 4. Storeroom clerk

___ 5. Kitchen porters

___ 6. Maître d'

___ 7. Captain

___ 8. Apprentice

a. Handles cold preparation.

b. Aids the chef in administrative and supervisory functions.

c. Transmits food orders to the cooks.

d. Helps clean up and transport food.

e. Supervises wait staff and acts as host.

f. Receives goods and distributes food.

g. Serves food and supervises wait staff.

h. Is in training.

EXERCISE 5-3: Recipe Costing

NAME: _____ DATE: _____

Cost out the following recipe and indicate the total cost, portion cost, and percent of food cost in the space provided. Refer to Figure 5-8.

ITEM: Bacon, Lettuce, and Tomato Sandwich CODE # 205
PORTION: 4 oz   YIELD: 8

INGREDIENT	UNIT	PRICE	AMOUNT USED	EXTENSION
Bacon	lb	$1.60	10 oz	_____
Lettuce	lb	.69	8 oz	_____
Tomato	lb	.59	12 oz	_____
Mayonnaise	gallon	4.00	10 oz	_____

TOTAL COST: _____ SELLING PRICE: $2.50

PORTION COST: _____ PERCENT OF FOOD COST: _____

EXERCISE 5-4: Cost of Sales

NAME: _____   DATE: _____

Calculate the cost of sales in the following examples:

EXAMPLE 1:

Opening inventory	$26,540
Purchases	+ _____
Food available for sale	52,480
Ending inventory	− 18,230
Cost of sales	_____

EXAMPLE 2:

Opening inventory	_____
Purchases	+ 1,460
Food available for sale	10,950
Ending inventory	− _____
Cost of sales	5,860

EXERCISE 5-5: Operating Ratios

NAME: _____ DATE: _____

The following data pertain to the XYZ Restaurant. Use them to calculate the operating ratios indicated.

Period Ending March 31, 19XX

Total revenue	$58,760
No. of guest checks	6,590
No. of guests	10,750
Food costs	15,400
Labor costs	10,990
Total labor hours	1,660

OPERATING RATIOS

1. Average check

   _____

   _____

2. Average cover

   _____

   _____

3. Percent of food costs

   _____

   _____

4. Percent of labor costs

   _____

   _____

5. Sales per labor hour

   _____

   _____

Chapter 6

The Lodging Industry

EXERCISE 6-1: Sentence Completion

NAME: _____ '_____   DATE: _____

Test your knowledge of the material covered in Chapter 6 by completing the following sentences:

1. Four factors that affect a hotel's success are

   _____, _____,

   _____, and _____.

2. Guests at _____ hotels want hospitality suites and large banquet facilities.

3. Guests at _____ hotels want relaxation and recreation.

4. Guests at _____ hotels want comfort and value.

5. _____ offer an overnight stay in private homes.

6. _____ hotels offer all the amenities of downtown properties, but in a location more convenient to business travelers and the local community.

7. Occupancy at _____ hotels is high on Monday through Thursday but dwindles over the weekend.

8. Accommodations in a (an) _____ hotel usually include a fully equipped kitchen and living area.

9. When franchising a business, it is important that the parent company maintain strict _____, so as to avoid losing its good name.

10. A _____ can cause severe delays in the construction schedule of a new hotel.

EXERCISE 6-2: Matching

NAME: _____   DATE: _____

Match the following terms with the corresponding statements:

____ 1. Franchise

____ 2. Management contract

____ 3. Convention hotel

____ 4. Fully owned property

____ 5. Life care services

____ 6. All-suite properties

____ 7. Moderately priced hotels

____ 8. Resort hotels

a. Typically has one thousand to two thousand guest rooms.
b. Offers geriatric care facilities.
c. Is operated by the investor.
d. Faces the problems of seasonal business.
e. Is owned by investors but is operated by a lodging chain.
f. Offers more spacious accommodations and upgraded amenities.
g. Is owned and operated by a lodging chain.
h. Is another name for Marriott's Courtyard Inns.

EXERCISE 6-3: Abstracting an Article

NAME: _____   DATE: _____

Find an article in a trade publication or a newspaper that discusses new development in the lodging industry. Summarize, or abstract, the article in the space below.

AUTHOR: _____

TITLE: _____

PUBLICATION DATE: _____

SOURCE: _____

ABSTRACT: _____

_____

_____

_____

_____

_____

_____

_____

_____

_____

_____

_____

_____

_____

_____

_____

_____

_____

_____

_____

_____

EXERCISE 6-4: Concept Development

NAME: _____ DATE: _____

Choose a location in your city or town that would be an appropriate site for a lodging operation. Develop the concept, and outline it below.

LOCATION

_____

TYPE OF OPERATION

_____

NUMBER OF ROOMS

_____

ROOM RATE STRUCTURE

_____

TARGET MARKET

_____

DECOR

_____

_____

_____

FOOD AND BEVERAGE OPERATIONS

_____

_____

_____

RECREATIONAL ACTIVITIES

_____

_____

UNIQUE FEATURES

EXERCISE 6-5: Lodging Guests

NAME: _____   DATE: _____

PART 1: Listed below are the various categories of lodging customers. In the space provided, indicate which type of lodging operation (convention hotel, suburban hotel, and so on) would most appeal to each group and which features they would most prefer (banquet facilities, health club, and so on).

CONVENTION GROUPS

Operation Preferred: _____

Features Required: _____

_____

EXECUTIVE BUSINESS TRAVELERS

Operation Preferred: _____

Features Required: _____

_____

FREQUENT BUSINESS TRAVELERS

Operation Preferred: _____

Features Required: _____

_____

TOURISTS WITH CHILDREN

Operation Preferred: _____

Features Required: _____

_____

TOURISTS WITHOUT CHILDREN

Operation Preferred: _____

Features Required: _____

_____

PART 2: List two additional categories of customers that frequent lodging operations in your area, and indicate their preferences.

Category: _____

Operation Preferred: _____

Features Required: _____

_____

Category: _____

Operation Preferred: _____

Features Required:_____

_____

Chapter 7

Lodging Operations

EXERCISE 7-1: Sentence Completion

NAME: _____   DATE: _____

Test your knowledge of the material covered in Chapter 7 by completing the following sentences:

1. The _____ and _____ report directly to the general manager and are responsible for supervising the department heads.

2. The main goal of the sales department is to sell _____.

3. The sales manager in charge of _____ solicits accounts with local companies and major corporations.

4. When a hotel is the designated _____ for a convention, the group will hold a greater portion of its meetings and food functions at that location.

5. Hotel reservations are often made through a _____ system using an "800" number.

6. When the hotel accepts more reservations than there are rooms available, it is _____.

7. A room that is _____ will be honored until checkout time the next day, regardless of when the guest arrives.

8. When a room is vacant but has not yet been cleaned, it is called _____.

9. A _____ is a guest who is scheduled to depart but has not yet checked out.

10. The _____, or under chef, assists the executive chef.

11. Catering managers prepare the _____ which lists all the details of a function.

12. The final guest count for a catering function is called the _____ _____ attendance number.

EXERCISE 7-2: Matching

NAME: _____ DATE: _____

Match the following jobs found in a hotel with their corresponding description:

___ 1. Catering manager

___ 2. Comptroller

___ 3. General manager

___ 4. Concierge

___ 5. Executive chef

___ 6. Director of front office

___ 7. Sales manager

___ 8. Director of food and beverage

a. Oversees entire hotel operation.

b. Books group food functions.

c. Solves a wide range of guest problems.

d. Oversees reservations and the bellstand.

e. Sells guest rooms to large groups.

f. Oversees food purchasing, production, and storage.

g. Is responsible for accounting.

h. Is responsible for restaurants, beverage, and food production.

EXERCISE 7-3: Hotel Positions

NAME: _____   DATE: _____

List three positions found in each of the following hotel departments:

DEPARTMENT	POSITIONS
Housekeeping	_____
	_____
	_____
Kitchen	_____
	_____
	_____
Engineering	_____
	_____
	_____
Restaurants	_____
	_____
	_____
Front office	_____
	_____
	_____
Sales	_____
	_____
	_____

EXERCISE 7-4: Catering Function

NAME: _____ DATE: _____

You are a catering manager at a large hotel and have been asked by a client to plan a theme dinner for her convention group. The evening will begin with a reception, followed by dinner and dancing. The event will be attended by five hundred guests. The client wants something unusual and exciting and is not concerned with cost. Plan the event and fill in the details below.

GROUP NAME: A.M.C. Inc.
CONVENTION DATE: September 3, 19XX

GENERAL DETAILS

Overall theme   _____

                       _____

Decor   _____

                       _____

                       _____

Entertainment   _____

                       _____

RECEPTION

Service   _____

                       _____

Hors d'oeuvres   _____

                       _____

                       _____

                       _____

Special drinks   _____

                       _____

DINNER

Service _____

_____

Appetizer _____

Soup _____

Salad _____

Entrée _____

Dessert _____

EXERCISE 7-5: You Are in Charge

NAME: _____   DATE: _____

You are the general manager of a middle-sized hotel and have recently had a series of problems. In the space below, explain how you would handle each situation.

1. Complaints about the housekeeping department have been increasing: The rooms and public space areas have not been cleaned properly. It seems that the problem stems from the extremely high turnover rate, which is more than 100 percent annually. Most of the director of housekeeping's time is spent hiring and firing room attendants. There are few experienced room attendants. What can you do to decrease this high turnover rate and increase the room attendants' experience?

_____

_____

_____

_____

_____

_____

2. Your resident manager has been performing poorly on the job. He disappears frequently during the day, fails to follow through on tasks assigned, and has difficulty getting along with the department heads. You have even smelled liquor on his breath on several occasions. Unfortunately, he is also the son of one of your company's senior vice-presidents. How should you deal with this situation?

_____

_____

_____

_____

_____

_____

3. Your food and beverage director stopped in today to let you know that he wants to fire Chef Wolfe. He claims that the chef is not doing a good job. The kitchen is disorderly; the food quality is poor; and the food cost is much higher than it should be. Chef Wolfe has been with the hotel for twenty-five years, but the food and beverage director has been on staff for only three months. How should you handle this situation?

_____

_____

_____

_____

_____

_____

Chapter 8

Travel and Tourism

EXERCISE 8-1: Sentence Completion

NAME: _____   DATE: _____

Test your knowledge of the material covered in Chapter 8 by completing the following sentences:

1. Tourism has a _____ effect, in that when it increases, so does local business.

2. Tourism helps reduce the _____ by bringing new money from foreign travelers into the system.

3. The essence of the tourism industry is to _____

   _____ and to serve those who are traveling or are making plans to do so.

4. Wholesale travel agents sponsor _____ trips that allow agents to sample the tours they will be selling.

5. The airline _____ includes air cost for transportation and all rules covering such passage.

6. _____ or _____ includes air fare, accommodations, and activities, all for one price.

7. In the past, most charters were _____ based, meaning that travelers had to be part of a special-interest group to take advantage of them.

8. Disney's EPCOT stands for _____.

9. The first park in the United States was _____

   _____.

10. On a cruise ship, the _____ department is responsible for preparing and serving food.

EXERCISE 8-2: Matching

NAME: _____   DATE: _____

Match the following travel and tourism positions with their correct descriptions:

____ 1. Reservations agent

____ 2. In-flight chef

____ 3. Flight attendant

____ 4. Travel agent

____ 5. Passenger service

____ 6. Travel wholesaler

____ 7. Tour guide

____ 8. Attractions manager

a. Performs all phases of customer service on board the airplane.

b. Provides passengers with information, ground transportation, and special services.

c. Supervises the preparation of meals for airline passengers.

d. Responsible for ticketing, transportation, and attractions in a theme park.

e. Sells transportation and accommodations to clients.

f. Sells packages to retail travel agents.

g. Escorts tour groups visiting foreign countries.

h. Makes telephone reservations for customers through the airline's computer system.

EXERCISE 8-3: Travel Itinerary

NAME: _____   DATE: _____

Plan a vacation for a client in a destination of your choice. Draw up an itinerary similar to the one in Figure 8-2, indicating the mode of transportation, accommodations, and ground activities for each day. Describe this information in the space below.

DESTINATION: _____

TRANSPORTATION: _____

ACCOMMODATIONS: _____

COST: _____

DAILY ITINERARY

MONDAY: _____
_____
_____
_____

TUESDAY: _____
_____
_____
_____

WEDNESDAY: _____
_____
_____
_____

THURSDAY: _____
_____
_____
_____

FRIDAY: _____

_____

_____

_____

EXERCISE 8-4: Environmental Factors and Tourism

NAME: _____   DATE: _____

Many factors affect tourism, including changes in society, the economy, and foreign affairs. In the space below, indicate those factors that would have a positive effect on U.S. tourism and those that would have a negative influence.

INCREASE TOURISM   DECREASE TOURISM

_____   _____

_____   _____

_____   _____

_____   _____

_____   _____

_____   _____

_____   _____

_____   _____

EXERCISE 8-5: Travel Sales

NAME: _____   DATE: _____

Several sample clients need assistance in making travel plans. Act as their travel agent, and help them choose a destination and mode of transportation. In the space provided, indicate this information plus the various attractions the area offers that will sell the client on your choice.

SITUATION 1

Mr. and Mrs. Johnson recently retired and are hoping to spend one month during the summer traveling. They have saved their money for years and want to enjoy it now that they have the time. Although they are in their sixties, the Johnsons are very active and enjoy bicycling, hiking, swimming, and tennis. Because the summers in the Midwest are hot, they would like to visit a place that is a little cooler at that time of year. Where would you send them?

DESTINATION(S): _____

_____

TRANSPORTATION: _____

_____

ATTRACTIONS: _____

_____

_____

_____

SITUATION 2

Mary and George Holmes are planning to be married in February. They want an extravagant honeymoon but have only one week of vacation. Because it is very cold in February, they would like to go somewhere warm. They both enjoy swimming, scuba diving, and golf. Where would you send them?

DESTINATION(S): _____

_____

TRANSPORTATION: _____

_____

ATTRACTIONS: _____

_____

_____

_____

SITUATION 3

Greg and Sharon Williams want to take a family vacation in September. They will be traveling with their two children, ages eight and ten. They are hoping to find a place that will provide entertainment for the children but that they will enjoy also. The Williamses like to play golf, fish, swim, and go sight-seeing. Where would you send them?

DESTINATION(S): _____

_____

TRANSPORTATION: _____

_____

ATTRACTIONS: _____

_____

_____

_____

Chapter 9

Guest Service

EXERCISE 9-1: Sentence Completion

NAME: _____   DATE: _____

Test your knowledge of the material covered in Chapter 9 by completing the following sentences:

1. The product of the future is _____.
2. According to a 1985 Gallup poll on eating out, 83 percent of those surveyed said that they would stay away from a restaurant if it had poor _____.
3. If service is to improve, it must be constantly viewed as a _____.
4. The first step in developing a service management system is to come up with a _____.
5. When defining service in an organization, _____ _____ must be specified.
6. To communicate an effective service policy to employees, develop _____and _____.
7. Service training at Disney is called _____.
8. To be effective, incentive programs must reward the _____ _____.
9. Stew Leonard encourages his employees to become involved in customer service, through his _____ contest.
10. Managers who do not become involved with customers are service _____.

EXERCISE 9-2: Service Blunders

NAME: _____   DATE: _____

Review the five service blunders described in this chapter. First describe the problem and its cause, and then explain how it should have been handled.

BLUNDER 1:
Problem: _____
_____

Cause: _____
_____

Solution: _____
_____
_____

BLUNDER 2:
Problem: _____
_____

Cause: _____
_____

Solution: _____
_____
_____

BLUNDER 3:
Problem: _____
_____

Cause: _____
_____

Solution: _____
_____
_____

BLUNDER 4:

Problem: _____

_____

Cause: _____

_____

Solution: _____

_____

_____

BLUNDER 5:

Problem: _____

_____

Cause: _____

_____

Solution: _____

_____

_____

EXERCISE 9-3: More Service Blunders

NAME: _____ DATE: _____

Look back on service blunders you have experienced in restaurants, banks, grocery stores, or other places of business. Describe the poor service you received and its cause, and explain how the situation should have been handled.

BLUNDER 1:

Problem: _____

_____

Cause: _____

_____

Solution: _____

_____

_____

BLUNDER 2:

Problem: _____

_____

Cause: _____

_____

Solution: _____

_____

_____

BLUNDER 3:

Problem: _____

_____

Cause: _____

_____

Solution: _____

_____

_____

EXERCISE 9-4: Service Performance Appraisal

NAME: _____   DATE: _____

STEP 1: Create a service performance appraisal in the space provided below, listing the behavioral aspects of each service dimension (see example).

STEP 2: Visit a local restaurant and evaluate the service you receive, using your appraisal. Rate each of the behavioral aspects by assigning points as indicated.

Excellent   4
Average   3
Needs Improvement   2
Very Poor   1

WAITING TIME   POINTS

    Length of time until acknowledged   _____
    Length of time until seated   _____
    Comfort of waiting area   _____

APPROACH

_____   _____

_____   _____

_____   _____

ATTITUDE

_____   _____

_____   _____

_____   _____

PRODUCT KNOWLEDGE

_____   _____

_____   _____

_____   _____

SUGGESTIVE SELLING TECHNIQUES

_____   _____

_____   _____

_____   _____

FAREWELL

_____   _____

_____   _____

_____   _____

TOTAL POINTS ASSIGNED: _____

Chapter 10

Communication Skills

EXERCISE 10-1: Sentence Completion

NAME: _____   DATE: _____

Test your knowledge of the material covered in Chapter 10 by completing the following sentences:

1. Forty percent of our total interpersonal communication involves

    _____.

2. The _____ listener fails to respond to the speaker's needs.

3. The three components of active listening are _____

    _____, _____,

    and _____.

4. Body language is _____ communication.

5. Social scientists estimate that _____ of our communication is nonverbal.

6. Some employees try to hide their lack of experience by becoming

    _____.

7. When faced with an angry guest you might react _____

    _____, _____, or

    assertively.

8. _____ individuals look for ways to solve the problem.

9. _____ situations are more difficult to deal with than are day-to-day problems.

10. The best way to deal with an unreasonable guest is to react

    _____.

EXERCISE 10-2: Matching

NAME: _____ DATE: _____

Match the following terms with their definitions:

_____ 1. Aggressive reaction

_____ 2. Assertive reaction

_____ 3. Submissive reaction

_____ 4. Reflecting

_____ 5. Responding

_____ 6. Sorting

_____ 7. Passive listening

_____ 8. Active listening

_____ 9. Empathy

a. The ability to put yourself in someone else's shoes.
b. A sincere attempt to understand what is communicated.
c. The failure to hear what the other person is really saying.
d. An emphasis on important information.
e. A restatement of what was said.
f. The use of verbal and nonverbal cues to let the speaker know the listener is listening.
g. A lack of self-esteem and the avoidance of confrontation.
h. The pleasure of telling someone off.
i. The search for solutions to problems.

EXERCISE 10-3: Body Language

NAME: _____ DATE: _____

Review the situations described below, and indicate which of the nine nonverbal messages are being sent in each example.

NONVERBAL MESSAGES

a. Openness   d. Suspicion   g. Frustration
b. Defensiveness   e. Readiness   h. Confidence
c. Evaluation   f. Need for reassurance   i. Self-control

SITUATIONS

____ 1. A woman walks up to the front desk and, while waiting for the clerk to acknowledge her, stands with her arms crossed. When the clerk speaks to her, the customer turns slightly away and rubs her nose. During the interaction she maintains little eye contact.

____ 2. A man walks up to a guest service attendant in the lobby to ask for directions. His arms are relaxed; his hands are open; and his coat is unbuttoned.

____ 3. A woman reports for a job interview standing straight with her chin up.

____ 4. While speaking to her supervisor, a new employee brings her hands to her throat and chews on a pencil.

____ 5. While listening to a catering manager describe the banquet space available, the client leans forward with his face resting in his hands, and his eyes slightly squinting.

____ 6. When told that her room is not ready yet, the guest rubs the back of her neck while taking short breaths.

____ 7. A hostess grips her hands behind her back and locks her ankles together while listening to an angry guest complain about the wait.

____ 8. The new employee is sitting on the edge of his chair while listening to instructions from his supervisor.

____ 9. While being reprimanded by the supervisor, the employee leans back in his chair with his arms crossed on his chest.

93

EXERCISE 10-4: Submissive, Aggressive, and Assertive Situations

NAME: _____ DATE: _____

Review the following situations and indicate whether the corresponding response is submissive, aggressive, or assertive, by placing the correct letter in the space provided:

a. Submissive
b. Aggressive
c. Assertive

SITUATION	RESPONSE
1. A guest praises the out-standing service you provided.	____ Oh, it was nothing really. I didn't do that well.
2. A guest demands a room with a view, even though he failed to ask for it when making the reservation.	____ You should have asked for that when making your reservation. There's nothing I can do now.
3. A guest walks up and inter-rupts you while you are serving another customer.	____ I'll be with you as soon as I finish with Mr. Jones, sir.
4. The guest wants a separate room for her poodle, even though you have a no-pets policy.	____ You want what? We don't allow pets here!
5. You have just spilled hot coffee on a customer.	____ Oh my God! Look what you made me do. You shouldn't have had your arm out like that!
6. Your supervisor tells you that you will be required to work nights, even though you were hired for days.	____ I'd like to discuss this with you further. I just arranged my schedule at school so my days would be free, and this will cause some difficulties.

SITUATION	RESPONSE
7. Another employee asks you to work for her on Saturday, but you had planned to go to a friend's wedding that night.	____ Well, I guess I can do it. I had other plans, but they aren't important.

EXERCISE 10-5: Problems with Guests

NAME: _____ DATE: _____

Review the following guest situations, and answer the questions:

1. SERVER: Good afternoon. Are you ready to order?

2. CUSTOMER: Yes. I'll have the turkey club on whole wheat with a cup of the lentil soup.

3. SERVER: Would you like french fries with that?

4. CUSTOMER: No, but I will have coffee.

5. SERVER: I'll be right back with the coffee.

After bringing the coffee, the server returns to the table again. She brings her hand to her throat and says:

6. SERVER: I'm afraid that we're out of the turkey club today. Can I get you something else?

7. CUSTOMER: How are the hamburgers?

8. SERVER: Well, I guess they're pretty good.

The customer looks up at the server and rubs the back of her neck.

9. CUSTOMER: You mean you don't know?

10. SERVER: I haven't had any complaints about them, so I guess they're OK.

The customer leans back and crosses her arms on her chest.

11. CUSTOMER: Just bring me a medium-well-done hamburger.

12. SERVER: OK.

QUESTIONS

1. How was the server reacting—submissively, aggressively, or assertively? What did the server say or do that indicated that reaction?

_____

_____

_____

2. How was the customer reacting? What did the customer say or do that indicated that reaction?

_____

_____

_____

3. What did the server's body language indicate?

_____

_____

4. What did the customer's body language indicate?

_____

_____

5. In interaction 8, the server failed to respond to the customer's needs. What could the server have said to handle the situation better?

_____

_____

_____

Chapter 11

Supervision

EXERCISE 11-1: Sentence Completion

NAME: _____   DATE: _____

Test your knowledge of the material covered in Chapter 11 by completing the following sentences:

1. _____ is the driving force that makes us behave as we do.

2. If you want someone to work independently and creatively and to solve his or her own problems, hire a high _____ _____.

3. MBO uses _____ to motivate employees.

4. Research has shown that a (an) _____ leader is best when emergency situations arise.

5. If you are supervising a group of employees who have been on the job for several years, a (an) _____ style of management will be best.

6. Four components of an effective review session are _____, _____, _____, and _____.

7. Use a _____ disciplinary system based on the severity of the offense.

8. Disciplinary action provides _____ documentation only when the employee is aware of it.

9. When problems and solutions have been identified, the next step is to formulate the team-building _____.

10. _____ is defined as the process of establishing trust and opening communication channels in a group.

EXERCISE 11-2: Matching

NAME: _____   DATE: _____

Match the following management theories and leadership styles with the statements corresponding to them:

____ 1. Achievement motivation

____ 2. MBO

____ 3. Behavior modification

____ 4. Laissez-faire manager

____ 5. Participative leader

____ 6. Theory Y

____ 7. Bureaucratic leader

____ 8. Autocratic leader

a. A nondirective quality.

b. Decisions made by a work group.

c. Behavior shaped by reinforcement and punishment.

d. Goal setting.

e. Assumption that employees like work and seek responsibility.

f. Dependence on policy and rules when making decisions.

g. McClelland and Winter.

h. A belief in tight supervision.

EXERCISE 11-3: Performance Appraisal

NAME: _____   DATE: _____

Complete the behavioral rating scale for a dining room server by listing up to fifteen key job activities in the space provided below. Refer to the secretarial performance review depicted in Figure 11-3.

SERVER PERFORMANCE APPRAISAL

Name: _____   Position: _____

Supervisor: _____   Department: _____

Review Date: _____

Rating Factor: Always   5
              Frequently   4
              Occasionally 3
              Rarely   2
              Never   1

1. _____

2. _____

3. _____

4. _____

5. _____

6. _____

7. _____

8. _____

9. _____

10. _____

11. _____

12. _____

13. _____

14. _____

15. _____

Goals for Next Six-Month Period:

1. _____

2. _____

3. _____

Employee's Signature _____ Date: _____

Supervisor's Signature _____ Date: _____

EXERCISE 11-4: Motivation

NAME: _____   DATE: _____

The following case describes a motivational problem occurring in a restaurant. After reading it, describe the action to be taken using the different theories of motivation described in this chapter.

Over the past year, the food at the Excelsior Restaurant has been deteriorating. The current chef has been on board for several months, and although he is working hard himself, he is not getting the support that he needs from his staff. The cooks seem to take little pride in their work. They do not follow the recipes the chef has developed, maintain sanitation standards, or properly portion the food. They all are experienced and have been with the restaurant for several years. Good cooks are hard to find, and so he cannot just fire them all and start again.

Map out a course of action based on the four theories presented in this chapter to increase the cooks' motivation. Then indicate which theory you think is most appropriate, and why.

1. ACHIEVEMENT MOTIVATION

_____

_____

_____

_____

_____

2. GOAL SETTING

_____

_____

_____

_____

_____

3. BEHAVIOR MODIFICATION

_____

_____

_____

_____

_____

4. MOTIVATION–HYGIENE THEORY

_____

_____

_____

_____

_____

Which theory do you think would be most appropriate in this situation, and why?

_____

_____

_____

_____

_____

EXERCISE 11-5: Disciplinary Action

NAME: _____   DATE: _____

Review the following examples of disciplinary problems. In the space provided, indicate the course of action you would take in response to each if you were in charge.

SITUATION 1: The Tardy Desk Clerk

Mary Anne has been working at the front desk for six weeks. During that time she has been late for work five times. So far, no formal disciplinary action has been taken, although the supervisor has told Mary Anne that she must arrive at work on time. Mary Anne explained that she must take two buses to get to the hotel and that one of them always runs late. She now has come in late for the sixth time. What action would you take? Why?

_____

_____

_____

_____

SITUATION 2: The Intoxicated Banquet Captain

Joe has been a banquet captain for twenty-five years at the Green Palace Hotel. He has a fine work record and is currently acting as the union's shop steward. Today you received a complaint from a guest at a catering function at which he was working. The guest said that Joe appeared to be drunk and also that he could smell liquor on his breath. You suspected that Joe had a drinking problem, and so this is not a surprise. You have a security guard open Joe's locker, and he finds a bottle of liquor hidden there. Company policy states that drinking on the job is grounds for immediate termination. What would you do if you were Joe's supervisor? Why?

_____

_____

_____

_____

Chapter 12

Selecting the Right Employee

EXERCISE 12-1: Sentence Completion

NAME: _____   DATE: _____

Test your knowledge of the material covered in Chapter 12 by completing the following sentences:

1. To ensure that the interviewer is familiar with job standards, draw up a _____ for each position.

2. The Civil Rights Act, or _____, prohibits discrimination.

3. The Age Discrimination in Employment Act makes it unlawful to discriminate against people who are _____ to _____ years old.

4. The best way to avoid discrimination is to focus only on _____ when selecting employees.

5. _____ is testing applicants with situations simulating those found on the job.

6. As an interviewer, you should spend about _____ _____ percent of the interview listening and only _____ percent talking.

7. To encourage discussion, ask _____ questions.

8. To probe for specific information, ask _____ _____ questions.

9. Answer the applicant's questions about the job _____ _____ exploring his or her past work history.

10. Recent court rulings state that past employers who provide negative information about an employee's work history are guilty of _____.

EXERCISE 12-2: Bona Fide Occupational Qualifications

NAME: _____   DATE: _____

Indicate whether each of the following job criteria are bona fide occupational qualifications. In the space provided, explain the reasons for your answers.

Y = yes, it is a BFOQ.
N = No, it is not a BFOQ.
C = Could be a BFOQ in certain circumstances.

____ 1. Past Work History

_____

____ 2. Marital Status

_____

____ 3. Foreign Language

_____

____ 4. Height and Weight

_____

____ 5. Religion

_____

____ 6. Availability for Work

_____

____ 7. Age

_____

____ 8. Citizenship

_____

____ 9. Mode of Transportation

_____

EXERCISE 12-3: Job Description

NAME: _____   DATE: _____

In the space below, create a job description for a hospitality-related position other than dining room server. Refer to the sample in Figure 12-1.

JOB TITLE: _____

BASIC JOB FUNCTION: _____

REPORTS TO: _____

RESPONSIBILITIES: _____

1. _____
   _____

2. _____
   _____

3. _____
   _____

4. _____
   _____

5. _____
   _____

6. _____
   _____

7. _____
   _____

STANDARDS OF PERFORMANCE

1. _____
   _____

2. _____
   _____

3. _____
   _____

4. _____
   _____

5. _____
   _____

6. _____
   _____

7. _____
   _____

_____
_____
_____

EXERCISE 12-4: Advertising

Review the sample ads below, and in the space provided indicate whether the employer is risking discrimination. Explain your answers.

HOSTESS

A local restaurant chain is seeking a recent college graduate with strong communication skills. She should have a neat appearance and enjoy dealing with people. The successful candidate will take reservations, seat guests, and handle the dining room in the manager's absence. We offer a good starting salary and excellent benefits. Apply to Restaurant XYZ.

_____

_____

_____

DISHWASHER

A dishwasher is needed for a busy restaurant. Must be experienced and sober. Requires on-call and alternate Saturdays. Ability to speak English a must. Apply to Restaurant XYZ.

_____

_____

_____

SALES MANAGER

A prominent hotel chain is seeking a sales manager to deal with executive business clients. This person should be aggressive, energetic, and like dealing with people. Only experienced individuals with a college degree should apply. Send a résumé and salary history to Box XYZ.

_____

_____

_____

BARTENDERS

Must be over 21, high school grad, with own transportation. Must be able to work weekends and evenings. Prefer someone with past experience and a good appearance. Call 555–9999.

_____

_____

_____

FRONT DESK CLERK

Looking for a mature, attractive individual to work at the front desk in a large downtown convention hotel. Lots of people contact. The person we are looking for must have at least a high school degree, but a college degree is preferred, and must be fluent in English and Spanish. We offer a paid vacation, excellent benefits, and great working conditions. Call 666–7777.

_____

_____

_____

EXERCISE 12-5: Evaluation

NAME: _____   DATE: _____

You have just interviewed an applicant for a host/hostess position. Below are some of the person's responses to the questions you asked during the interview. Analyze each of them and indicate what the person has revealed about himself or herself. In the space provided, describe your interpretation of the response and how you would react to it when making a hiring decision.

Q-1. Why did you leave your last job before finding a new one?
A-1. I was working days and didn't have time to look for a new job, so I had to quit.
Interpretation:

_____

_____

_____

Q-2. What did you think of your last supervisor?
A-2. He was rather hard to deal with. He was very demanding, and everything had to always be his way.
Interpretation:

_____

_____

_____

Q-3. What do you like about your present job?
A-3. I like the people I work with, and the hours are great. I'm done every day by 3:30 P.M. and miss the rush-hour traffic.
Interpretation:

_____

_____

_____

Q-4. What did you dislike about your last job?
A-4. I never got to make decisions on my own. Everything was decided by the supervisor. The job was very routine, and that got boring after a while.

Interpretation:

_____

_____

_____

Q-5. What were your favorite courses in school?

A-5. Well, I liked them all about the same. I guess I did enjoy the lab experiences most. I liked working in the dining room and the kitchen. I didn't like some of the classes. There were too many projects to do.

Interpretation:

_____

_____

_____

Chapter 13

Training and Development

EXERCISE 13-1: Sentence Completion

NAME: _____   DATE: _____

Test your knowledge of the material covered in Chapter 13 by completing the following sentences:

1. The two basic types of training used are _____ and _____.

2. If uniforms are not required, discuss the _____ _____ with new employees before their first day.

3. _____ training is analyzing all elements of a job and teaching someone else how to perform them.

4. Take a more specific approach when developing training programs for _____ employees.

5. A more _____ approach is used when designing training programs for new employees.

6. Both _____ and _____ employee surveys are used in needs analysis.

7. In addition to employees, _____ also provide information about service-training needs.

8. Ideally, training sessions should be _____ to _____ hours in length.

9. Many training programs teach technical knowledge but overlook _____.

10. To enhance the lecture material, the detailed leader's guide should include _____ questions, _____, and _____.

EXERCISE 13-2: Matching

NAME: _____   DATE: _____

Match the following terms with their correct definitions:

____ 1. Role play

____ 2. Case study

____ 3. Canned programs

____ 4. Training plan

____ 5. Priority 1

____ 6. Management in Training

____ 7. Individual development

____ 8. Job Code Training

a. A list of all materials to be covered during each day of training.

b. Training program used by Marriott.

c. Training programs that can be bought.

d. Training program used by Hilton.

e. A situation acted out by participants.

f. Training program used by Domino's Pizza.

g. A simulated situation that is analyzed by trainees.

h. Training program used by Denny's.

EXERCISE 13-3: Case Study

NAME: _____   DATE: _____

Design a case study to be used to train servers. It should pertain to their job duties and facilitate problem solving. Include several discussion questions to encourage interaction.

CASE STUDY

_____

_____

_____

_____

_____

_____

_____

_____

_____

_____

_____

_____

_____

_____

_____

_____

_____

_____

_____

_____

_____

DISCUSSION QUESTIONS

1. _____

   _____

   _____

2. _____

_____

_____

3. _____

_____

_____

EXERCISE 13-3: Role Play

NAME: _____   DATE: _____

Review the following interaction between a waitress and a customer:

WAITRESS: Hi, What can I get you?

CUSTOMER: I'd like two eggs over easy, pancakes, hash browns. . . .

WAITRESS: The eggs don't come with hash browns.

CUSTOMER: Well, can I get them on the side?

WAITRESS: OK, but it will be $1.50 extra.

CUSTOMER: That's fine.

WAITRESS: Well, I'll put your order in. . . .

CUSTOMER: No, wait. I'd also like Canadian bacon and orange juice.

WAITRESS: OK.

(Fifteen minutes later the waitress brings the order.)

WAITRESS: Here you go.

CUSTOMER: Wait a minute, this is regular bacon; I wanted Canadian.

WAITRESS: Well, I don't know where this bacon is from; it might be from Canada.

CUSTOMER: Never mind, I'll just eat this.

WAITRESS: OK. Enjoy your meal.

Analyze this situation by answering the following questions:

1.   What mistakes did the waitress make in this situation?

_____

_____

_____

2. What might the customer be thinking about this waitress and the restaurant as a whole?

_____

_____

_____

3. If you observed this particular interaction in a restaurant you managed, what type of training program do you think might improve this waitress's skill?

_____

_____

_____

EXERCISE 13-4: Role Play Development

NAME: _____   DATE: _____

Create a role playing situation based on a problem interaction between a customer and server appropriate for use in a training program. Include questions at the end to facilitate problem solving and discussion.

SERVER: _____
_____

CUSTOMER: _____
_____

SERVER: _____
_____

CUSTOMER: _____
_____

SERVER: _____
_____

CUSTOMER: _____
_____

SERVER: _____
_____

CUSTOMER: _____
_____

SERVER: _____
_____

CUSTOMER: _____
_____

SERVER: _____

_____

CUSTOMER: _____

_____

DISCUSSION QUESTIONS

1. _____

_____

2. _____

_____

3. _____

_____

EXERCISE 13-5: Skills Training

NAME: _____   DATE: _____

Choose a task performed by a hotel or restaurant employee. Design a step-by-step guide that could be used to teach this skill to a new employee. In the space below, describe the particular task, the job position it pertains to, and the sequence of steps in its performance.

TASK: _____

POSITION: _____

STEP 1: _____

_____

STEP 2: _____

_____

STEP 3: _____

_____

STEP 4: _____

_____

STEP 5: _____

_____

STEP 6: _____

_____

STEP 7: _____

_____

Chapter 14

Trends in the Hospitality Industry

EXERCISE 14-1: Sentence Completion

NAME: _____   DATE: _____

Test your knowledge of the material covered in Chapter 14 by completing the following sentences:

1. As a result of a change in our society's demography, there will be more _____ in the future than ever before.

2. _____ restaurants are popular with women diners.

3. The _____ stated that there may be a link between diet and cancer.

4. Health-conscious Americans are eating more seafood because it is low in _____ and _____ and may prevent _____ buildup.

5. *Sous vide* cooking allows food to be chilled for up to _____ weeks with no loss of quality.

6. In *sous vide* cooking, food is heated in a _____ _____ to retard bacteria growth.

7. One of the first important third-party liability cases was the _____ case.

8. _____ outlaws sexual harassment.

9. Management must develop a strong _____ against sexual harassment in order to prevent it.

10. The next step in computer technology in the hospitality industry is _____ recognition.

EXERCISE 14-2: Matching

NAME: _____   DATE: _____

Match the following terms with the corresponding statements:

_____ 1. CHEF

_____ 2. *Sous vide*

_____ 3. Fish oil

_____ 4. Fat and cholesterol

_____ 5. VIEWTRON

_____ 6. Third-party liability

_____ 7. Electric shock

_____ 8. Cabbage family vegetables

a. Linked to heart disease.
b. May prevent cancer.
c. Linked to the prevention of cholesterol buildup.
d. Used to tenderize meat.
e. Computerized restaurant data bank.
f. Under vacuum.
g. Dramshop cases.
h. Recipe creation program.

EXERCISE 14-3: Trend Analysis

NAME: _____   DATE: _____

Listed below are trends pertaining to the foodservice industry. In the space provided, indicate whether you think each is a

a. Past trend
b. Current trend
c. Future trend

____ 1. Mexican food

____ 2. Chinese food

____ 3. Italian food

____ 4. *Sous vide* cooking

____ 5. Computerized inventory control

____ 6. Robotic kitchen equipment

____ 7. Seafood

____ 8. Fresh fruits and vegetables

____ 9. Pork

____10. Beef

____11. Desserts

____12. Grazing menus

____13. Low-calorie items

____14. Gourmet carryout

____15. Salad bars

EXERCISE 14-4: Policy Statements

NAME: _____   DATE: _____

Write policy statements pertaining to sexual harassment and guest intoxification. Include specific instructions telling employees what to do if they are sexually harassed and how to "cut off" a guest who has had too much to drink.

PART 1: SEXUAL HARASSMENT
General Policy Statement:

_____

_____

_____

Action to be taken by the employee when he or she is sexually harassed:

_____

_____

_____

Action to be taken by management when it receives a report from an employee who has been sexually harassed:

_____

_____

_____

_____

_____

PART 2: GUEST INTOXIFICATION
General Policy Statement:

_____

_____

_____

Steps to be taken by employees when "cutting off" a guest:

1. _____
   _____
   _____

2. _____
   _____
   _____

3. _____
   _____
   _____

4. _____
   _____
   _____